W9-BSQ-338

NEW WEBSTER'S
VEST POCKET
THESAURUS

NEW WEBSTER'S
VEST POCKET
THESAURUS

Delair Consolidated
A DELAIR PUBLISHING COMPANY
new york

Copyright © 1978 by
Delair Publishing Company, Inc.
420 Lexington Avenue,
New York, New York 10017

All rights reserved under the International and
Pan-American Copyright Conventions. Manu-
factured in the United States of America and
published simultaneously in Canada by George J.
McLeod Limited, Toronto, Ontario.

Library of Congress Catalog Card
Number: 78-52347
ISBN: 0-8326-0045-8

abandon, SYN.—abdicate, abjure, relinquish, renounce, resign, surrender, vacate, waive; desert, forsake, leave, quit. ANT.—defend, maintain, uphold; stay, support.

abate, SYN.—assuage, decrease, diminish, lessen, lower, moderate, reduce, suppress. ANT.—amplify, enlarge, increase, intensify, revive.

abbey, SYN.—cloister, convent, hermitage, monastery, nunnery, priory.

abbreviate, SYN.—abridge, condense, contract, curtail, diminish, lessen, limit, reduce, restrict, shorten. ANT.—elongate, extend, lengthen.

abbreviation, SYN.—abridgement, contraction, reduction, shortening. ANT.—amplification, enlargement, expansion, extension.

abdicate, SYN.—abjure, abolish, relinquish, renounce, resign, surrender, vacate, waive; desert, forsake, leave, quit. ANT.—defend, maintain, uphold; stay.

aberrant, SYN.—abnormal, capricious, devious, eccentric, irregular, unnatural, unusual, variable. ANT.—fixed, methodical, ordinary, regular, usual.

abet, SYN.—aid, assist, encourage, help, incite.

ANT.—discourage, hinder, oppose, resist.

abettor, SYN.—accessory, accomplice, ally, assistant, associate, confederate. ANT.—adversary, enemy, opponent, rival.

ability, SYN.—aptitude, aptness, capability, capacity, dexterity, efficiency, faculty, power, qualification, skill, talent. ANT.—disability, incapacity, incompetency, unreadiness.

abjure, SYN.—abandon, abdicate, relinquish, renounce, resign, surrender, vacate, waive; desert, forsake, leave, quit. ANT.—defend, maintain, uphold; stay.

abode, SYN.—domicile, dwelling, habitat, hearth, home, quarters, residence, seat.

abolish, SYN.—destroy, end, eradicate, obliterate, overthrow; abrogate, annul, cancel, invalidate, revoke. ANT.—continue, establish, promote, restore, sustain.

abominable, SYN.—detestable, execrable, foul, hateful, loathsome, odious, revolting, vile. ANT.—agreeable, commendable, delightful, pleasant.

abominate, SYN.—abhor, despise, detest, dislike, hate, loathe. ANT.—

admire, approve, cherish, like, love.

abroad, SYN.—away, departed; absent, absent-minded, abstracted, distracted, inattentive, pre-occupied. ANT.—attending, present; attentive, watchful.

abrupt, SYN.—hasty, precipitate, sudden, unannounced, unexpected; blunt, brusque, curt, rude; craggy, harsh, precipitous, rough, rugged, sharp, steep. ANT.—anticipated, expected; courteous, gradual, smooth.

absent, SYN.—abroad, away, departed; absent-minded, abstracted, distracted, inattentive, pre-occupied. ANT.—attending, present; attentive, watchful.

absolute, SYN.—actual, complete, entire, perfect, pure, ultimate, unconditional, unqualified, unrestricted; arbitrary, authoritative, despotic, tyrannous. ANT.—accountable, conditional, contingent, dependent, qualified.

absorb, SYN.—assimilate, consume, engulf, imbibe, swallow up; engage, engross, occupy. ANT.—discharge, dispense, emit, expel, exude.

abstinence, SYN.—abstention, continence, fasting, forbearance, moderation, self-denial, sobriety, temperance. ANT.—excess, gluttony, greed, intoxication, self-indulgence.

abstract, SYN.—draw from, part, remove, separate; appropriate, purloin, steal; abridge, summarize. ANT.—add, replace, restore, return, unite.

abstracted, SYN.—drawn from, parted, removed, separated; appropriated, purloined, stolen; abridged, summarized. ANT.—added, replaced, restored, returned, united.

abstraction, SYN.—concept, conception, fancy, idea, image, impression, notion, opinion, sentiment, thought. ANT.—entity, matter, object, substance, thing.

absurd, SYN.—foolish, inconsistent, irrational, nonsensical, preposterous, ridiculous, self-contradictory, silly, unreasonable. ANT.—consistent, rational, reasonable, sensible, sound.

abundant, SYN.—ample, bountiful, copious, over-flowing, plenteous, plentiful, profuse, rich, teeming. ANT.—deficient, insufficient, scant, scarce.

abuse, SYN.—aspersion, defamation, desecration, dishonor, disparagement, insult, invective, maltreatment, misuse, outrage, perversion, profanation, reproach, reviling, upbraiding. ANT.—approval, commendation, laudation, plaudit, respect.

abuse, SYN.—asperse, defame, disparage, ill-use, malign, revile, scandalize, traduce, vilify; misapply, misemploy, misuse. ANT.—cherish, honor, praise, protect, respect.

academic, SYN.—bookish, erudite, formal, learned, pedantic, scholarly, scholastic, theoretical. ANT. — common-sense, ignorant, practical, simple.

accelerate, SYN.—dispatch, expedite, facilitate, forward, hasten, hurry, push, quicken, rush, speed. ANT.—block, hinder, impede, retard, slow.

accident, SYN.—calamity, casualty, contingency, disaster, fortuity, misfortune, mishap. ANT.—calculation, design, intention, purpose.

accidental, SYN.—casual, chance, contingent, fortuitous, incidental, undesigned, unintended. ANT.—calculated, decreed, intended, planned, willed.

acclaim, SYN.—credit, distinction, eminence, fame, glory, honor, notoriety, renown, reputation. ANT.—disrepute, ignominy, infamy, obscurity.

accompany, SYN.—associate with, attend, chaperone, consort with, convoy, escort, go with. ANT.—abandon, avoid, desert, leave, quit.

accomplice, SYN.—abettor, accessory, ally, assistant, associate, confederate. ANT.—adversary, enemy, opponent, rival.

accomplish, SYN.—achieve, attain, complete, consummate, do, effect, execute, finish, fulfill, perfect, perform. ANT.—block, defeat, fail, frustrate, spoil.

accomplishment, SYN.—act, action, deed, doing, execution, feat, operation, performance, transaction; decree, edict, law, statute. ANT.—cessation, deliberation, inactivity, inhibition, intention.

accost, SYN.—address, approach, greet, hail, speak to. ANT.—avoid, pass by.

account, SYN.—chronicle, description, detail, history, narration, narrative, recital, relation; computation, reckoning, record. ANT.—caricature, confusion, distortion, misrepresentation.

account, SYN.—believe, consider, deem, esteem, estimate, hold, judge, rate, reckon, regard, think, view; elucidate, explain, expound.

accrue, SYN.—accumulate, amass, collect, gather, heap, hoard, increase, store. ANT.—diminish, disperse, dissipate, scatter, waste.

accumulate, SYN.—accrue, amass, collect, gather, heap, hoard, increase, store. ANT.—diminish, disperse, dissipate, scatter, waste.

accusation, SYN.—arraignment, charge, imputation, incrimination, indictment. ANT.—exculpation, exoneration, pardon.

accuse, SYN.—arraign, censure, charge, incriminate, indict. ANT.—absolve, acquit, exonerate, release, vindicate.

achieve, SYN.—accomplish, acquire, do, effect, execute, gain, obtain, realize, win. ANT.—fail, fall short, lose, miss.

achievement, SYN.—deed, exploit, feat; accomplishment, attainment, completion, performance, realization. ANT.—neglect, omission; defeat, failure.

acquaintance, SYN.—cognizance, companionship, familiarity, fellowship, friendship, intimacy, knowledge. ANT.—ignorance, inexperience, unfamiliarity.

acquire, SYN.—assimilate, attain, earn, get, obtain, procure, secure, win. ANT.—forego, forfeit, lose, miss, surrender.

act, SYN.—accomplishment, action, deed, doing, execution, feat, operation, performance, transaction; decree, edict, law, statute. ANT.—cessation, deliberation, inactivity, inhibition, intention.

action, SYN.—achievement, activity, deed,

exercise, exploit, feat, motion, movement, performance, play, procedure. ANT.—idleness, inactivity, inertia, repose, rest.

active, SYN.—operative, working; busy, industrious; agile, alert, brisk, lively, nimble, quick, sprightly, supple. ANT.—dormant, inactive; indolent, lazy, passive.

activity, SYN.—action, agility, briskness, energy, enterprise, exercise, intensity, liveliness, motion, movement, quickness, rapidity, vigor. ANT.—dullness, idleness, inactivity, inertia, sloth.

actuality, SYN.—certainty, fact, reality, truth; act, circumstance, deed, event, incident, occurrence. ANT.—fiction, supposition, theory; delusion, falsehood.

adapt, SYN.—accommodate, adjust, conform, fit, suit. ANT.—disturb, misapply, misfit.

add, SYN.—adjoin, affix, append, attach, augment, increase, sum, total. ANT.—deduct, detach, reduce, remove, subtract.

address, SYN.—accost, approach, greet, hail, speak to. ANT.—avoid, pass by.

adequate, SYN.—ample, capable, commensurate, enough, fitting, satisfactory, sufficient, suitable. ANT.—deficient, lacking, scant.

adhere, SYN.—clasp, clutch, grasp, grip; have, hold, keep, maintain, occupy, possess, retain, support; check, confine, curb, detain, restrain; accommodate, carry, contain, receive, stow. ANT.—abandon, relinquish, surrender, vacate.

adjoin, SYN.—add, affix, append, attach, augment, increase, sum, total. ANT.—deduct, detach, reduce, remove, subtract.

admire, SYN.—appreciate, approve, esteem, respect, venerate, wonder. ANT.—abhor, despise, dislike.

admissible, SYN.—allowable, fair, justifiable, permissible, probable, tolerable, warranted. ANT.—inadmissible, irrelevant, unsuitable.

admit, SYN.—accept, acknowledge, agree, allow, assent, concede, confess, grant, permit, welcome. ANT.—deny, dismiss, reject, shun.

adorn, SYN.—beautify, bedeck, decorate, embellish, garnish, gild, ornament, trim. ANT.—deface, deform, disfigure, mar, spoil.

advance, SYN.—aggrandize, elevate, forward, further, promote; adduce, allege, assign, bring forward, offer, propose, propound; improve, proceed, progress, rise, thrive; augment, enlarge, increase. ANT.—

hinder, oppose, retard, retreat, withhold.

advantage, SYN.—edge, mastery, superiority; benefit, good, profit, service, utility. ANT.—detriment, handicap, harm, impediment, obstruction.

adventurous, SYN.—bold, chivalrous, daring, enterprising, foolhardy, precipitate, rash. ANT.—cautious, hesitating, timid.

adverse, SYN.—antagonistic, contrary, hostile, opposed, opposite; counteractive, disastrous, unfavorable, unlucky. ANT.—benign, favorable, fortunate, lucky, propitious.

advice, SYN.—admonition, caution, counsel, exhortation, instruction, recommendation, suggestion, warning; information, intelligence, notification.

affect, SYN.—alter, change, influence, modify, transform; concern, interest, regard; impress, melt, move, soften, subdue, touch; adopt, assume, feign, pretend.

affection, SYN.—attachment, endearment, fondness, kindness, love, tenderness; disposition, emotion, feeling, inclination. ANT.—aversion, hatred, indifference, repugnance, repulsion.

affirm, SYN.—assert, aver, declare, maintain, protest, state, swear.

ANT.—contradict, demur, deny, dispute, oppose.

afraid, SYN.—apprehensive, fainthearted, fearful, frightened, scared, timid, timorous. ANT.—assured, bold, composed, courageous, sanguine.

age, SYN.—dotage, senescence, senility, seniority; antiquity, date, epoch, era, generation, period, time. ANT.—childhood, infancy, youth.

aggravate, SYN.—heighten, increase, intensify, magnify; annoy, chafe, embitter, exasperate, inflame, irritate, nettle, provoke, vex. ANT.—appease, mitigate, palliate, soften, soothe.

aggregate, SYN.—amount, collection, conglomeration, entirety, sum, total, whole. ANT.—element, ingredient, part, particular, unit.

agility, SYN.—action, activity, briskness, energy, enterprise, exercise, intensity, liveliness, motion, movement, quickness, rapidity, vigor. ANT.—dullness, idleness, inactivity, inertia, sloth.

agitate, SYN.—arouse, disconcert, disturb, excite, jar, perturb, rouse, ruffle, shake, trouble. ANT.—calm, ease, placate, quiet.

agony, SYN.—ache, anguish, distress, misery, pain, suffering, throe, torment, torture, woe.

ANT.—comfort, ease, mitigation, relief.

agree, SYN.—accede, acquiesce, assent, comply, consent; coincide, concur, conform, tally. ANT.—contradict, differ, disagree, dissent, protest.

agreeable, SYN.—acceptable, amiable, charming, gratifying, pleasant, pleasing, pleasurable, suitable, welcome. ANT.—disagreeable, obnoxious, offensive, unpleasant.

agreement, SYN.—accordance, coincidence, concord, concurrence, harmony, understanding, unison; bargain, compact, contract, covenant, pact, stipulation. ANT.—difference, disagreement, discord, dissension, variance.

agriculture, SYN.—agronomy, cultivation, farming, gardening, horticulture, husbandry, tillage.

alarm, SYN.—affright, apprehension, consternation, dismay, fright, signal, terror, warning. ANT.—calm, composure, quiet, security, tranquility.

alien, SYN.—adverse, contrasted, extraneous, foreign, irrelevant, remote, strange, unconnected. ANT.—akin, germane, kindred, relevant.

allege, SYN.—advance, affirm, assign, cite, claim, declare, maintain.

allegory, SYN.—chronicle, fable, fiction, legend, myth, parable, saga. ANT.—fact, history.

alleviate, SYN.—abate, allay, assuage, diminish, extenuate, mitigate, relieve, soften, solace, soothe. ANT.—aggravate, agitate, augment, increase, irritate.

alliance, SYN.—association, coalition, combination, confederacy, entente, federation, league, partnership, union; compact, covenant, marriage, treaty. ANT.—divorce, schism, separation.

allot, SYN.—apportion, deal, dispense, distribute, divide, mete; allocate, appropriate, assign, give, grant, measure. ANT.—confiscate, keep, refuse, retain, withhold.

allow, SYN.—let, permit, sanction, suffer, tolerate; authorize, give, grant, yield; acknowledge, admit, concede. ANT.—forbid, object, protest, refuse, resist.

allude, SYN.—advert, hint, imply, insinuate, intimate, refer, suggest. ANT.—declare, demonstrate, specify, state.

ally, SYN.—abettor, accessory, accomplice, assistant, associate, confederate. ANT.—adversary, enemy, opponent, rival.

alone, SYN.—deserted, desolate, isolated, lonely, secluded, unaided; lone, only, single, sole, solitary. ANT.—accompanied, attended, surrounded.

also, SYN.—besides, furthermore, in addition, likewise, moreover, similarly, too.

altruism, SYN.—beneficence, benevolence, charity, generosity, humanity, kindness, liberality, magnanimity, philanthropy, tenderness. ANT.—cruelty, inhumanity, malevolence, selfishness, unkindness.

always, SYN.—constantly, continually, eternally, ever, evermore, forever, incessantly, perpetually, unceasingly. ANT.—fitfully, never, occasionally, rarely, sometimes.

amalgamate, SYN.—blend, coalesce, combine, commingle, conjoin, consolidate, fuse, mingle, mix, merge, unify, unite. ANT.—analyze, decompose, disintegrate.

amateur, SYN.—apprentice, beginner, dabbler, dilettante, learner, neophyte, novice. ANT.—adept, authority, expert, master, professional.

ambiguous, SYN.—dubious, enigmatical, equivocal, obscure, uncertain, vague. ANT.—clear, explicit, obvious, plain, unequivocal.

ambition, SYN.—aspiration, eagerness,

emulation, goal, incentive, pretension. ANT.—contentment, indifference, indolence, resignation, satisfaction.

amiable, SYN.—agreeable, engaging, friendly, good-natured, gracious, pleasing. ANT.—churlish, disagreeable, hateful, ill-natured, surly.

among, SYN.—amid, amidst, between, betwixt, mingled, mixed. ANT.—apart, separate.

amount, SYN.—aggregate, number, quantity, sum, total, whole.

ample, SYN.—broad, extensive, great, large, spacious, wide; abundant, bountiful, copious, full, generous, liberal, plentiful, profuse, rich. ANT.—constricted, limited, small; insufficient, lacking, meager.

amplification, SYN.—accrual, augmentation, enhancement, enlargement, expansion, extension, growth, heightening, increase, intensification, magnification, multiplication, raising, waxing. ANT.—atrophication, contraction, decrease, diminishing, reduction.

analogous, SYN.—akin, alike, allied, comparable, correlative, correspondent, corresponding, like, parallel, similar. ANT.—different, dissimilar, divergent, incongruous, opposed.

anger, SYN.—animosity, choler, exasperation, fury, indignation, ire, irritation, passion, petulance, rage, resentment, temper, wrath. ANT.—conciliation, forbearance, patience, peace, self-control.

angry, SYN.—enraged, exasperated, furious, incensed, indignant, irate, maddened, provoked, wrathful, wroth. ANT.—calm, happy, pleased, satisfied.

anguish, SYN.—agony, distress, grief, misery, suffering, torment, torture. ANT.—comfort, joy, relief, solace.

animosity, SYN.—bitterness, enmity, grudge, hatred, hostility, malevolence, rancor, spite. ANT.—friendliness, goodwill, love.

announce, SYN.—advertise, declare, give out, herald, make known, notify, proclaim, promulgate, publish, report. ANT.—bury, conceal, stifle, suppress, withhold.

announcement, SYN.—advertisement, bulletin, declaration, notification, promulgation. ANT.—hush, muteness, silence, speechlessness.

annoy, SYN.—bother, chafe, disturb, inconvenience, irk, irritate, molest, pester, tease, trouble, vex. ANT.—accommodate, console, gratify, soothe.

answer, SYN.—rejoinder, reply, response, retort;

defense, rebuttal. ANT.—inquiry, questioning, summoning; argument.

anticipation, SYN.—contemplation, expectation, foresight, forethought, hope, preconception, prescience, presentiment. ANT.—doubt, dread, fear, worry.

anticipated, SYN.—contemplated, expected, foresought, forethought, hoped, preconceived. ANT.—doubted, dreaded, feared, worried.

anxiety, SYN.—apprehension, care, concern, disquiet, fear, solicitude, trouble, worry. ANT.—assurance, confidence, contentment, equanimity, nonchalance.

aperture, SYN.—abyss, cavity, chasm, gap, gulf, hole, opening, pore, void. ANT.—bridge, connection, link.

apology, SYN.—alibi, confession, defense, excuse, explanation, justification. ANT.—accusation, complaint, denial, dissimulation.

apostate, SYN.—dissenter, heretic, nonconformist, schismatic, sectarian, sectary, unbeliever. ANT.—believer, conformist, saint.

appalling, SYN.—awful, dire, dreadful, fearful, frightful, ghastly, hideous, horrible, horrid, repulsive, terrible. ANT.—beautiful, enchanting, enjoyable, fascinating.

apparent, SYN.—clear, evident, manifest, obvious, palpable, plain, self-evident, transparent, unambiguous, unmistakable, visible; illusory, ostensible, seeming. ANT.—ambiguous, dubious, indistinct, real, uncertain.

appear, SYN.—look, seem; arise, arrive, emanate, emerge, issue. ANT.—be, exist; disappear, vanish, withdraw.

appearance, SYN.—advent, apparition, arrival; air, aspect, demeanor, look, manner, mien; fashion, guise, pretense, semblance. ANT.—departure, disappearance; reality.

appease, SYN.—allay, alleviate, assuage, calm, compose, lull, pacify, placate, quell, quiet, relieve, satisfy, soothe, still, tranquilize. ANT.—arouse, excite, incense, inflame.

appetite, SYN.—hunger, relish, stomach, thirst, zest; craving, desire, inclination, liking, longing, passion. ANT.—disgust, distaste, renunciation, repugnance, satiety.

apply, SYN.—administer, affix, allot, appropriate, assign, attach, avail, devote, direct, employ, use; bear, pertain, refer, relate; appeal, petition, request. ANT.—detach, give away; demand.

appreciate, SYN.—admire, cherish, enjoy, esteem, prize, regard, value; appraise, estimate, evaluate, rate; apprehend, comprehend, understand; go up, improve, rise. ANT.—belittle, degrade, depreciate; misapprehend, misunderstand.

approach, SYN.—accost, address, greet, hail, speak to. ANT.—avoid, pass by.

appropriate, SYN.—applicable, apt, becoming, fitting, particular, proper, suitable. ANT.—contrary, improper, inappropriate.

appropriate, SYN.—burglarize, embezzle, loot, pilfer, pillage, plagiarize, plunder, purloin, rob, snitch, steal, swipe. ANT.—buy, refund, repay, restore, return.

approval, SYN.—approbation, assent, commendation, consent, endorsement, praise, sanction, support. ANT.—censure, reprimand, reproach, stricture.

approve, SYN.—appreciate, commend, like, praise; authorize, confirm, endorse, ratify, sanction. ANT.—criticize, disparage; condemn, nullify.

aptness, SYN.—ability, aptitude, capability, capacity, dexterity, efficiency, faculty, power, qualification, skill, talent. ANT.—disability, incapacity, incompetency, unreadiness.

arbitrary, SYN.—

unconditional, unqualified, unrestricted; absolute, authoritative, despotic, tyrannous. ANT.—accountable, conditional, contingent, dependent, qualified.

ardent, SYN.—eager, enthusiastic, fervent, fervid, fiery, glowing, hot, impassioned, intense, keen, passionate, vehement, zealous. ANT.—apathetic, cool, indifferent, nonchalant.

ardor, SYN.—devotion, eagerness, enthusiasm, fervor, fire, passion, rapture, spirit, zeal. ANT.—apathy, disinterest, indifference, unconcern.

argue, SYN.—debate, discuss, dispute, plead, reason, wrangle; denote, imply, indicate, prove, show. ANT.—ignore, overlook, reject, spurn.

arise, SYN.—begin, commence, enter, inaugurate, initiate, institute, open, originate, start. ANT.—close, complete, end, finish, terminate.

arraign, SYN.—accuse, censure, charge, incriminate, indict. ANT.—absolve, acquit, exonerate, release, vindicate.

arraignment, SYN.—accusation, charge, imputation, incrimination, indictment. ANT.—exculpation, exoneration, pardon.

arrange, SYN.—adjust, assort, classify, dispose, organize, place, regulate; devise, organize, plan, prepare. ANT.—confuse, disorder, disturb, jumble, scatter.

arrest, SYN.—apprehend, check, detain, hinder, interrupt, obstruct, restrain, seize, stop, withhold. ANT.—activate, discharge, free, liberate, release.

arrive, SYN.—appear, attain, come, emerge, land, reach, visit. ANT.—depart, exit, leave.

art, SYN.—adroitness, aptitude, cunning, knack, skill, tact; artifice, duplicity, guile, shrewdness, subtlety. ANT.—clumsiness, unskillfulness; forthrightness, honesty, innocence.

artificial, SYN.—affected, assumed, bogus, counterfeit, ersatz, fake, feigned, fictitious, phony, sham, spurious, synthetic, unreal. ANT.—genuine, natural, real, true.

ascend, SYN.—climb, mount, rise, scale, soar, tower. ANT.—descend, fall, sink.

ask, SYN.—beg, claim, demand, entreat, invite, request, solicit; inquire, interrogate, query, question. ANT.—command, dictate, insist, order, reply.

aspersion, SYN.—abuse, defamation, desecration, dishonor, disparagement, insult, invective, maltreatment, misuse, outrage, perversion, reproach,

reviling, upbraiding. ANT.—approval, commendation, laudation, plaudit, respect.

aspiration, SYN.—aim, ambition, craving, desire, goal, hope, longing, objective, passion.

assault, SYN.—assail, attack, bombard, charge, invade, pound, storm, strike. ANT.—defend, oppose, protect.

assert, SYN.—affirm, allege, aver, claim, declare, express, maintain, state; defend, support, uphold, vindicate. ANT.—contradict, deny, refute.

assess, SYN.—appraise, assign, calculate, compute, estimate, evaluate, fix, levy, reckon, tax.

assign, SYN.—allot, apportion, appropriate, ascribe, attribute, cast, designate, distribute, specify. ANT.—discharge, release, relieve, unburden.

assist, SYN.—abet, aid, back, further, help, promote, serve, support, sustain. ANT.—hamper, hinder, impede, prevent.

assistance, SYN.—aid, alms, backing, furtherance, help, patronage, relief, succor, support. ANT.—antagonism, counteraction, defiance, hostility, resistance.

assistant, SYN.—abettor, accessory, accomplice, ally, associate, confederate. ANT.—adversary, enemy, opponent, rival.

associate, SYN.—affiliate,

ally, combine, conjoin, connect, join, link, mingle, mix. ANT.—disrupt, divide, estrange, separate.

assume, SYN.—appropriate, arrogate, take, usurp; adopt, affect, pretend, simulate, wear; postulate, presume, suppose. ANT.—concede, grant, surrender; doff; demonstrate, prove.

assurance, SYN.—assuredness, certainty, confidence, conviction, courage, firmness, security, self-reliance, surety; pledge, promise, word; assertion, declaration, statement. ANT.—bashfulness, humility, modesty, shyness, suspicion.

attach, SYN.—adjoin, affix, annex, append, connect, join, stick, unite; assign, associate, attribute. ANT.—detach, disengage, separate, unfasten, untie.

attachment, SYN.—adherence, affection, affinity, devotion, friendship, liking, regard. ANT.—alienation, aversion, estrangement, opposition, separation.

attack, SYN.—aggression, assault, criticism, denunciation, invasion, offense, onslaught; convulsion, fit, paroxysm. ANT.—defense, opposition, resistance, surrender, vindication.

attack, SYN.—assail, assault, besiege, charge, encounter, invade; abuse, censure, impugn. ANT.—aid, defend, protect, repel, resist.

attain, SYN.—accomplish, achieve, acquire, arrive, effect, gain, get, obtain, procure, reach, secure, win. ANT.—abandon, desert, discard, relinquish.

attainment, SYN.—achievement, deed, exploit, feat; accomplishment, completion, performance, realization. ANT.—neglect, omission; defeat, failure.

attempt, SYN.—effort, endeavor, essay, experiment, trial, undertaking. ANT.—inaction, laziness, neglect.

attend, SYN.—accompany, escort, follow, guard, lackey, protect, serve, tend, watch; be present, frequent. ANT.—abandon, avoid, desert.

attention, SYN.—alertness, care, circumspection, consideration, heed, mindfulness, notice, observance, watchfulness; application, contemplation, reflection, study. ANT.—disregard, indifference, negligence, omission, oversight.

attentive, SYN.—alert, alive, awake, aware, careful, considerate, heedful, mindful, observant, thoughtful, wary, watchful; assiduous, diligent, studious. ANT.—apathetic, indifferent, oblivious, unaware.

attitude, SYN.—disposition,

standpoint, viewpoint; aspect, pose, position, posture, stand.

attract, SYN.—allure, captivate, charm, enchant, entice, fascinate, lure. ANT.—alienate, deter, repel, repulse.

attractive, SYN.—alluring, charming, enchanting, engaging, inviting, magnetic, pleasant, pleasing, seductive, winning. ANT.—forbidding, obnoxious, repellent, repulsive.

audacity, SYN.—boldness, effrontery, fearlessness, hardihood, temerity. ANT. — circumspection, fearfulness, humility, meekness.

authentic, SYN.—genuine, pure, real, true, verifiable; accurate, authoritative, correct, reliable, trustworthy. ANT.—counterfeit, erroneous, false, spurious.

author, SYN.—composer, creator, father, inventor, maker, originator, writer.

authoritative, SYN.—certain, dependable, safe, secure, sure, tried, trustworthy, trusty. ANT.—dubious, fallible, questionable, uncertain, unreliable.

authority, SYN.—control, domination, dominion, force, justification, power, supremacy; authorization, license, permission, sanction; ground, importance, influence, prestige, weight. ANT.—impotence, incapacity,

weakness; denial, prohibition.

auxiliary, SYN.—ancillary, assisting, conducive, furthering, helping, instrumental, subsidiary. ANT.—cumbersome, obstructive, opposing, retarding.

available, SYN.—accessible, handy, obtainable, prepared, ready, usable. ANT.—inaccessible, unavailable.

average, SYN.—fair, intermediate, mean, median, mediocre, medium, middling, moderate, ordinary. ANT.—exceptional, extraordinary, outstanding.

aversion, SYN.—abhorrence, antipathy, disgust, disinclination, dislike, distaste, dread, hatred, loathing, repugnance, repulsion, reluctance. ANT.—affection, attachment, devotion, enthusiasm.

avoid, SYN.—avert, dodge, escape, eschew, elude, forbear, forestall, free, shun, ward. ANT.—confront, encounter, meet, oppose.

aware, SYN.—apprised, cognizant, conscious, informed, mindful, observant, perceptive, sensible. ANT.—ignorant, insensible, oblivious, unaware.

away, SYN.—abroad, absent, departed; absentminded, abstracted, distracted, inattentive, preoccupied. ANT.—

attending, present, attentive, watchful.

awful, SYN.—appalling, dire, dreadful, frightful, horrible, terrible; awe-inspiring, imposing, majestic, solemn. ANT.—commonplace, humble, lowly, vulgar.

awkward, SYN.—clumsy, gauche, inept, rough, unpolished, untoward. ANT.—adroit, graceful, neat, polished, skillful.

axiom, SYN.—adage, aphorism, apothegm, byword, fundamental, maxim, principle, proverb, saw, saying, theorem, truism.

B

backward, SYN.—regressive, retrograde, revisionary; dull, sluggish, stupid; disinclined, hesitating, indisposed, loath, reluctant, unwilling, wavering. ANT.—advanced, civilized, progressive.

bad, SYN.—baleful, base, deleterious, evil, immoral, iniquitous, noxious, pernicious, sinful, unsound, unwholesome, villainous, wicked. ANT.—excellent, good, honorable, moral, reputable.

balance, SYN.—composure, equilibrium, poise, stability, steadiness, proportion, symmetry; excess, remainder, remains, residue, rest. ANT.—fall, imbalance, instability, unsteadiness.

baleful, SYN.—bad, base,

deleterious, evil, immoral, iniquitous, noxious, pernicious, sinful, unsound, unwholesome, villainous, wicked. ANT.—excellent, good, honorable, moral, reputable.

banal, SYN.—commonplace, hackneyed, inane, insipid, trite, vapid. ANT.—fresh, novel, original, stimulating, striking.

banish, SYN.—deport, dismiss, dispel, eject, exclude, exile, expatriate, expel, ostracize, oust. ANT.—accept, admit, harbor, receive, shelter.

banquet, SYN.—celebration, dinner, entertainment, feast, festival, regalement.

barbarous, SYN.—barbarian, barbaric, brutal, crude, cruel, inhuman, merciless, remorseless, rude, ruthless, savage, uncivilized, uncultured, unrelenting. ANT.—civilized, humane, kind, polite, refined.

base, SYN.—abject, contemptible, despicable, dishonorable, groveling, ignoble, ignominious, low, lowly, mean, menial, servile, sordid, vile, vulgar. ANT.—esteemed, exalted, honored, lofty, noble, righteous.

bashful, SYN.—abashed, coy, diffident, embarrassed, humble, modest, recoiling, shamefaced, sheepish, shy, timid, timorous. ANT.—adventurous, daring, fearless, gregarious, outgoing.

basis, SYN.—base, bottom, foundation, ground, groundwork, support, underpinning, assumption, postulate, premise, presumption, presupposition, principle. ANT.—derivative, implication, superstructure, trimming.

battle, SYN.—combat, conflict, contest, fight, fray, skirmish, strife, struggle. ANT.—agreement, concord, peace, truce.

bear, SYN.—support, sustain, uphold; allow, brook, endure, permit, stand, suffer, tolerate, undergo; carry, convey, take, transport; produce, spawn, yield. ANT.—avoid, dodge, evade, refuse, shun.

beat, SYN.—belabor, buffet, dash, hit, knock, pound, pummel, punch, smite, strike, thrash, thump; conquer, defeat, overpower, overthrow, rout, subdue, vanquish; palpitate, pulsate, pulse, throb. ANT.—defend, shield, stroke; fail, surrender.

beautiful, SYN.—beauteous, charming, comely, elegant, fair, fine, handsome, lovely, pretty. ANT.—foul, hideous, homely, repulsive, unsightly.

beauty, SYN.—attractiveness, charm, comeliness, elegance, fairness, grace, hand-

someness, loveliness, pulchritude. ANT.—deformity, disfigurement, eyesore, homeliness, ugliness.

because, SYN.—as, for, inasmuch as, since.

bed, SYN.—berth, bunk, cot, couch, cradle; accumulation, deposit, layer, stratum, vein.

beg, SYN.—adjure, ask, beseech, crave, entreat, implore, importune, petition, pray, request, solicit, supplicate. ANT.—bestow, cede, favor, give, grant.

beget, SYN.—breed, create, engender, father, generate, originate, procreate, produce, propagate, sire. ANT.—abort, destroy, extinguish, kill, murder.

beggar, SYN.—mendicant, pauper, ragamuffin, scrub, starveling, tatterdemalion, vagabond, wretch.

begin, SYN.—arise, commence, enter, inaugurate, initiate, institute, open, originate, start. ANT.—close, complete, end, finish, terminate.

beginning, SYN.—commencement, inception, opening, origin, outset, source, start. ANT.—close, completion, consummation, end, termination.

behave, SYN.—act, bear, carry, comport, conduct, demean, deport, interact, manage, operate.

behavior, SYN.—action, bearing, carriage, conduct, deed, demeanor, deportment, disposition, manner.

belief, SYN.—certitude, confidence, conviction, credence, faith, feeling, opinion, persuasion, reliance, trust. ANT.—denial, doubt, heresy, incredulity.

believe, SYN.—accept, apprehend, conceive, credit, fancy, hold, imagine, support, suppose. ANT.—distrust, doubt, question, reject.

belittle, SYN.—decry, depreciate, disparage, minimize, underrate. ANT.—admire, appreciate, esteem.

belongings, SYN.—commodities, effects, estate, goods, merchandise, possessions, property, stock, wares, wealth; attribute, characteristic, peculiarity, quality.

beloved, SYN.—dear, esteemed, precious, valued; costly, expensive, valuable. ANT.—despised, unwanted; cheap.

below, SYN.—beneath, lower, under, underneath. ANT.—above, aloft, over, overhead.

bend, SYN.—bow, crook, curve, deflect, incline, lean, stoop, turn, twist; influence, mold; submit, yield. ANT.—break, resist, stiffen, straighten.

beneath, SYN.—below, under, underneath. ANT.—above, over.

beneficial, SYN.—advantageous, good, helpful, profitable, salutary, serviceable, useful, wholesome. ANT.—deleterious, destructive, detrimental, harmful, injurious.

benefit, SYN.—account, advantage, avail, behalf, favor, gain, good, interest, profit, service. ANT.—calamity, distress, handicap, trouble.

benevolence, SYN.—altruism, beneficence, charity, generosity, humanity, kindness, liberality, magnanimity, philanthropy, tenderness. ANT.—cruelty, inhumanity, malevolence, selfishness, unkindness.

benevolent, SYN.—altruistic, benign, charitable, friendly, generous, humane, kind, liberal, merciful, obliging, philanthropic, tender, unselfish. ANT.—greedy, harsh, malevolent, wicked.

benign, SYN.—altruistic, benevolent, charitable, friendly, generous, humane, kind, liberal, merciful, obliging, philanthropic, tender, unselfish. ANT.—greedy, harsh, malevolent, wicked.

bias, SYN.—bent, disposition, inclination, leaning, partiality, penchant, predilection, predisposition, prejudice, proclivity, proneness, propensity, slant, tendency, turn.

big, SYN.—august, bulky, colossal, enormous, grand, great, huge, hulking, immense, large, majestic, massive, monstrous. ANT.—little, petite, small, tiny.

bigoted, SYN.—dogmatic, fanatical, illiberal, intolerant, narrow-minded, prejudiced. ANT.—liberal, progressive, radical, tolerant.

bind, SYN.—attach, connect, engage, fasten, fetter, join, link, oblige, restrain, restrict, tie. ANT.—free, loose, unfasten, untie.

bite, SYN.—champ, chew, crunch, gnash, gnaw, nibble, nip, pierce, rend, tear.

bitter, SYN.—acrid, biting, distasteful, pungent, sour, tart; galling, grievous, painful, poignant; cruel, fierce, relentless, ruthless; acrimonious, caustic, harsh, sardonic, severe. ANT.—delicious, mellow, pleasant, sweet.

blame, SYN.—accuse, censure, condemn, implicate, rebuke, reproach, upbraid. ANT.—absolve, acquit, exonerate.

blemish, SYN.—blot, speck, stain; defect, disgrace, fault, flaw, imperfection. ANT.—adornment, embellishment, perfection, purity.

blend, SYN.—amalgamate, coalesce, combine, commingle, conjoin, consolidate, fuse, mingle, mix, merge, unify, unite. ANT.—analyze, decompose, disintegrate, separate.

bless, SYN.—adore, celebrate, delight, exalt, extol, gladden, glorify. ANT.—blaspheme, curse, denounce, slander.

blind, SYN.—ignorant, oblivious, sightless, undiscerning, unmindful, unseeing; headlong, heedless, rash. ANT.—aware, calculated, discerning, perceiving, sensible.

bliss, SYN.—blessedness, blissfulness, ecstasy, felicity, happiness, joy, rapture. ANT.—grief, misery, sorrow, woe, wretchedness.

block, SYN.—bar, barricade, clog, close, stop; impede; hinder, obstruct. ANT.—clear, open; aid, further, promote.

blunt, SYN.—dull, edgeless, obtuse, pointless, stolid, thick-witted, unsharpened; abrupt, bluff, brusque, impolite, outspoken, plain, rough, rude, unceremonious. ANT.—polished, polite, suave, subtle, tactful.

boast, SYN.—brag, crow, flaunt, glory, vaunt. ANT.—apologize, deprecate, humble, minimize.

body, SYN.—carcass, corpse, remains; form, frame, torso; bulk, corpus, mass; aggregate, association, company, society. ANT.—intellect, mind, soul, spirit.

bold, SYN.—adventurous, audacious, brave, courageous, daring, dauntless, fearless, intrepid; brazen, forward, impudent, insolent, pushy, rude; abrupt, conspicuous, prominent, striking. ANT.—cowardly, flinching, timid; bashful, retiring.

bondage, SYN.—captivity, confinement, imprisonment, serfdom, servitude, slavery, thralldom, vassalage. ANT.—freedom, liberation.

book, SYN.—booklet, brochure, compendium, handbook, manual, monograph, pamphlet, textbook, tract, treatise, volume, work.

bookish, SYN.—academic, erudite, formal, learned, pedantic, scholarly, scholastic, theoretical. ANT. — common-sense, ignorant, practical, simple.

border, SYN.—boundary, brim, brink, edge, fringe, frontier, limit, margin, outskirts, rim, termination, verge. ANT.—center, core, interior, mainland.

boredom, SYN.—doldrums, dullness, ennui, tedium, weariness. ANT.—activity, excitement, motive, stimulus.

bother, SYN.—annoy, disturb, harass, haunt, inconvenience, molest, perplex, pester, plague, tease, trouble, upset, worry. ANT.—gratify, please, relieve, soothe.

bottom, SYN.—base, basis, foot, foundation, fundament, groundwork. ANT.—apex, peak, summit, top.

bound, SYN.—hop, jerk, jump, leap, skip; spring, start, vault. ANT.—crawl, walk.

bountiful, SYN.—abundant, ample, copious, overflowing, plenteous, plentiful, profuse, rich, teeming. ANT.—deficient, insufficient, scant, scarce.

brag, SYN.—bluster, boast, crow, flaunt, flourish, vaunt. ANT.—debase, degrade, demean, denigrate.

brave, SYN.—adventurous, audacious, bold, chivalrous, courageous, daring, dauntless, fearless, gallant, heroic, intrepid, magnanimous, valiant, valorous. ANT.—cowardly, cringing, fearful, timid, weak.

break, SYN.—burst, crack, crush, demolish, destroy, fracture, infringe, pound, rack, rend, rupture, shatter, smash, squeeze; disobey, transgress, violate. ANT.—join, mend, renovate, repair, restore.

breed, SYN.—bear, beget, conceive, engender, generate, procreate, propagate; foster, nurture, raise, rear, train. ANT.—abort, kill, murder.

brief, SYN.—compendious, concise, curt, laconic, pithy, short, succinct, terse; fleeting, momentary, passing, transient. ANT.—extended, lengthy, long, prolonged, protracted.

bright, SYN.—brilliant, clear, gleaming, lucid, luminous, lustrous, radiant, shining, translucent, transparent; clever, intelligent, witty. ANT.—dark, dull, gloomy, murky, sullen.

brisk, SYN.—cool, fresh, refreshing. ANT.—decayed, faded, hackneyed, musty, stagnant.

briskness, SYN.—action, activity, agility, energy, enterprise, exercise, intensity, liveliness, motion, movement, quickness, rapidity, vigor. ANT.—dullness, idleness, inactivity, inertia, sloth.

brittle, SYN.—breakable, crisp, crumbling, delicate, fragile, frail, splintery. ANT.—enduring, thick, tough, unbreakable.

broad, SYN.—expanded, extensive, large, sweeping, vast, wide; liberal, tolerant. ANT.—confined, narrow, restricted.

broken, SYN.—crushed, destroyed, flattened, fractured, interrupted, reduced, rent, ruptured, separated, shattered, smashed, wrecked. ANT.—integral, repaired, united, whole.

brook, SYN.—bear, endure, permit, stand, suffer, tolerate, undergo. ANT.—avoid, dodge, evade, refuse, shun.

brotherhood, SYN.—brotherliness, fellowship, kindness, solidarity; association, clan, fraternity, society. ANT.—acrimony, discord, opposition, strife.

brusque, SYN.—hasty, precipitate, sudden, unannounced, unexpected; abrupt, blunt, curt, rude; craggy, harsh, precipitous, rough, rugged, sharp, steep. ANT.—anticipated, expected; courteous, gradual, smooth.

brutal, SYN.—barbarous, bestial, brute, brutish, carnal, coarse, cruel, ferocious, gross, inhuman, merciless, remorseless, rough, rude, ruthless, savage, sensual. ANT.—civilized, courteous, gentle, humane, kind.

build, SYN.—construct, erect, establish, found, raise, rear. ANT.—demolish, destroy, overthrow, raze, undermine.

bulky, SYN.—big, enormous, great, huge, hulking, immense, large, massive, monstrous. ANT.—little, petite, small, tiny.

bunk, SYN.—bed, berth, cot, couch.

buoyant, SYN.—effervescent, light, resilient; animated, blithe, cheerful, elated, hopeful, jocund, lively, spirited, sprightly, vivacious. ANT.—dejected, depressed, despondent, hopeless, sullen.

burden, SYN.—afflict, encumber, load, oppress, overload, tax, trouble, weigh. ANT.—alleviate, console, ease, lighten, mitigate.

burn, SYN.—blaze, char, consume, incinerate, scald, scorch, sear, singe. ANT.—extinguish, put out, quench.

bury, SYN.—conceal, cover, entomb, hide, immure, inhume, inter. ANT.—display, exhume, expose, open, reveal.

business, SYN.—art, commerce, employment, engagement, enterprise, job, occupation, profession, trade, trading, vocation, work. ANT.—avocation, hobby, pastime.

busy, SYN.—active, assiduous, careful, diligent, hard-working, industrious, patient, perseverant. ANT.—apathetic, careless, indifferent, lethargic, unconcerned.

butcher, SYN.—assassinate, execute, kill, massacre, murder, put to death, slaughter, slay. ANT.—animate, protect, resuscitate, save, vivify.

buy, SYN.—acquire, get, obtain, procure, purchase. ANT.—dispose of, sell, vend.

by, SYN.—beside, near, next to; by means of, through, with; according to; from.

C

cabal, SYN.—collusion, combination, conspiracy, intrigue, machination, plot, treachery, treason.

calamity, SYN.—adversity, casualty, catastrophe, disaster, mishap, ruin. ANT.—advantage, fortune, welfare.

calculate, SYN.—compute, consider, count, estimate, figure, reckon. ANT.—conjecture, guess, miscalculate.

calculation, SYN.—computation, consideration, count, estimation, figure, reckoning. ANT.—conjecture, guess, miscalculation.

caliber, SYN.—attribute, characteristic, distinction, feature, peculiarity, property, quality, trait; grade, value. ANT.—being, essence, nature, substance.

callous, SYN.—hard, impenitent, indurate, insensible, insensitive, obdurate, tough, unfeeling. ANT.—compassionate, sensitive, soft, tender.

calm, SYN.—alloy, alleviate, appease, assuage, compose, lull, pacify, placate, quell, quiet, relieve, satisfy, soothe, still, tranquilize. ANT.—arouse, incite, incense, inflame.

calm, SYN.—composed, dispassionate, imperturbable, pacific, peaceful, placid, quiet, serene, still, tranquil, undisturbed, unruffled. ANT.—excited, frantic, stormy, turbulent, wild.

calumny, SYN.—aspersion, backbiting, defamation, libel, scandal, slander, vilification. ANT.—applause, commendation, defense, flattery, praise.

cancel, SYN.—cross out, delete, eliminate, erase, expunge, obliterate; abolish, abrogate, annul, invalidate, nullify, quash, repeal, rescind, revoke. ANT.—confirm, enact, enforce, perpetuate.

candid, SYN.—frank, free, honest, ingenuous, open, plain, sincere, straightforward, truthful; fair, impartial, just, unbiased. ANT.—contrived, scheming, sly, wily.

candor, SYN.—fairness, frankness, honesty, integrity, justice, openness, rectitude, responsibility, sincerity, trustworthiness, uprightness. ANT.—cheating, deceit, dishonesty, fraud, trickery.

cant, SYN.—deceit, dissimulation, hypocrisy, pretense, sanctimony. ANT.—candor, frankness, honesty, openness, truth.

capability, SYN.—ability, aptitude, aptness, capacity, dexterity, efficiency, faculty, power, qualification, skill, talent. ANT.—disability, inca-

pacity, incompetency, unreadiness.

capable, SYN.—able, clever, competent, efficient, fitted, qualified, skillful. ANT.—inadequate, incapable, incompetent, unfitted.

capacity, SYN.—ability, capability, faculty, power, skill, talent; magnitude, size, volume. ANT.—impotence, inability, incapacity, stupidity.

capitulate, SYN.—abandon, acquiesce, capitulate, cede, relinquish, renounce, resign, sacrifice, submit, surrender, yield. ANT.—conquer, overcome, resist, rout.

caprice, SYN.—face, humor, inclination, notion, quick, vagary, whim, whimsy.

capricious, SYN.—changeable, fickle, fitful, inconstant, restless, unstable, variable. ANT.—constant, reliable, stable, steady, trustworthy.

captivity, SYN.—bondage, confinement, imprisonment, serfdom, servitude, slavery, thralldom, vassalage. ANT.—freedom, liberation.

capture, SYN.—apprehend, arrest, catch, clutch, grasp, grip, lay hold of, seize, snare, trap. ANT.—liberate, lose, release, throw.

carcass, SYN.—corpse, remains; form, frame, torso; bulk, corpus, mass; aggregate, association, company, society.

ANT.—intellect, mind, soul, spirit.

care, SYN.—anxiety, concern, solicitude, worry; attention, caution, regard, vigilance, wariness; charge, custody, guardianship, ward. ANT.—disregard, indifference, neglect, negligence.

careful, SYN.—attentive, heedful, prudent, scrupulous, thoughtful; cautious, circumspect, discreet, guarded, vigilant, wary. ANT.—forgetful, improvident, indifferent, lax.

careless, SYN.—heedless, imprudent, inattentive, inconsiderate, indiscreet, reckless, thoughtless, unconcerned; desultory, inaccurate, lax, neglectful, negligent, remiss. ANT.—accurate, careful, meticulous, nice.

carelessness, SYN.—default, disregard, failure, heedlessness, neglect, negligence, oversight, slight. ANT.—attention, care, diligence, thoughtfulness, watchfulness.

caress, SYN.—coddle, cuddle, embrace, fondle, hug, kiss, pet. ANT.—annoy, buffet, spurn, tease, vex.

carnal, SYN.—animal, base, bodily, corporeal, fleshly, gross, lustful, sensual, voluptuous, worldly. ANT.—exalted, intellectual, refined, spiritual, temperate.

carping, SYN.—accurate, discerning, discriminating, exact, fastidious, particular; captious, caviling, censorious, faultfinding, hypercritical; acute, crucial, decisive, hazardous, important, momentous. ANT.—cursory, shallow, superficial, uncritical; appreciative, approving, commendatory, encouraging, insignificant; unimportant.

carriage, SYN.—action, bearing, behavior, conduct, deed, demeanor, deportment, disposition, manner.

carry, SYN.—bring, convey, transmit, transport; bear, support, sustain. ANT.—abandon, drop.

caste, SYN.—category, class, denomination, genre, kind; grade, order, rank, set; elegance, excellence.

casual, SYN.—accidental, chance, fortuitous, unexpected; incidental, informal, nonchalant, offhand, relaxed, unconcerned, unpremeditated. ANT.—expected, intended; formal, planned, pretentious.

casualty, SYN.—accident, calamity, contingency, disaster, fortuity, misfortune, mishap. ANT.—calculation, design, intention, purpose.

catastrophe, SYN.—adversity, calamity, casualty, disaster, mishap, ruin. ANT.—advantage, fortune, welfare.

catch, SYN.—apprehend, arrest, capture, clutch, grasp, grip. lay hold of, seize, snare, trap. ANT.—liberate, lose, release, throw.

catching, SYN.—communicable, contagious, infectious, pestilential, virulent. ANT.—healthful, hygienic, noncommunicable.

category, SYN.—caste, class, denomination, genre, kind; grade, order, rank, set; elegance, excellence.

cause, SYN.—agent, determinant, incentive, inducement, motive, origin, principle, reason, source. ANT.—consequence, effect, end, result.

cause, SYN.—create, effect, evoke, incite, induce, make, occasion, originate, prompt.

caustic, SYN.—acrid, bitter, biting, distasteful, pungent, sour, tart; galling, grievous, painful, poignant; cruel, fierce, relentless, ruthless; acrimonious, harsh, sardonic, severe. ANT.—delicious, mellow, pleasant, sweet.

caution, SYN.—care, heed, prudence, vigilance, wariness, watchfulness; admonition, counsel, injunction, warning. ANT.—abandon, carelessness, recklessness.

cautious, SYN.—attentive, heedful, prudent, scru-pulous, thoughtful; careful, circumspect, discreet, guarded, vigilant, wary. ANT.—forgetful, improvident, indifferent.

cease, SYN.—abandon, desist, discontinue, stop; give up, relinquish, resign, surrender; abandon, depart, leave, withdraw. ANT.—continue, endure, occupy, persist, stay.

celebrate, SYN.—commemorate, honor, keep, observe, solemnize; commend, extol, glorify, honor, laud, praise. ANT.—disregard, overlook; decry, disgrace, dishonor, profane.

celebrated, SYN.—distinguished, eminent, famous, glorious, illustrious, noted, renowned, well known. ANT.—hidden, ignominious, infamous, obscure, unknown.

celestial, SYN.—divine, godlike, heavenly, holy, superhuman, supernatural, transcendant. ANT.—blasphemous, diabolical, mundane, profane, wicked.

censure, SYN.—blame, condemn, denounce, reprehend, reproach, reprobate, reprove, upbraid; convict, sentence. ANT.—approve, commend, condone, forgive, praise; absolve, acquit, exonerate, pardon.

center, SYN.—core, heart, middle, midpoint, midst, nucleus. ANT.—border, boundary, outskirts, periphery, rim.

ceremonious, SYN.—affected, correct, decorous, exact, formal, methodical, precise, proper, regular, solemn, stiff; external, outward, perfunctory. ANT.—easy, material, unconstrained, unconventional; heartfelt.

ceremony, SYN.—formality, observance, parade, pomp, protocol, rite, ritual, solemnity. ANT.—casualness, informality.

certain, SYN.—assured, definite, fixed, indubitable, inevitable, positive, secure, sure, undeniable, unquestionable. ANT.—doubtful, probable, questionable, uncertain.

certainty, SYN.—assuredness, confidence, conviction, courage, firmness, security, self-reliance, surety; pledge, promise, word; assertion, declaration, statement. ANT.—bashfulness, humility, modest, shyness, suspicion.

certitude, SYN.—belief, confidence, conviction, credence, faith, feeling, opinion, persuasion, reliance, trust. ANT.—denial, doubt, heresy, incredulity.

challenge, SYN.—object to, question; brave, dare, defy; call, invite, summon; demand, require.

chance, SYN.—accident, bechance, befall, betide, calamity, casualty, contingency, disaster, fortuity, happen, misfortune, mishap, occur, take place, transpire. ANT.—calculation, design, intention, purpose.

change, SYN.—alteration, alternation, modification, mutation, substitution, variation, variety, vicissitude. ANT.—monotony, stability, uniformity.

change, SYN.—exchange, substitute; alter, convert, modify, shift, transfigure, transform, vary, veer. ANT.—retain; continue, establish, preserve, settle, stabilize.

changeable, SYN.—fickle, fitful, inconstant, shifting, unstable, vacillating, variable, wavering. ANT.—constant, stable, steady, unchanging, uniform.

chaos, SYN.—anarchy, confusion, disorder, disorganization, jumble, muddle. ANT.—order, organization, system.

chaperone, SYN.—accompany, associate with, attend, consort with, convoy, escort, go with. ANT.—abandon, avoid, desert, leave, quit.

character, SYN.—class, description, disposition, individuality, kind, nature, reputation, repute, sort, standing, mark, sign, symbol.

characteristic, SYN.—attribute, feature, mark, peculiarity, property, quality, trait.

charge, SYN.—accusation,

arraignment, imputation, incrimination, indictment. ANT.—exculpation, exoneration, pardon.

charge, SYN.—accuse, arraign, censure, incriminate, indict. ANT.—absolve, acquit, exonerate, release, vindicate.

charitable, SYN.—altruistic, benevolent, benign, friendly, generous, humane, kind, liberal, merciful, obliging, philanthropic, tender, unselfish. ANT.—greedy, harsh, malevolent, wicked.

charity, SYN.—altruism, beneficence, benevolence, generosity, humanity, kindness, liberality, magnanimity, philanthropy, tenderness. ANT.—cruelty, inhumanity, malevolence, selfishness, unkindness.

charming, SYN.—alluring, attractive, bewitching, captivating, enchanting, engaging, fascinating, winning. ANT.—repugnant, repulsive, revolting.

chart, SYN.—cabal, conspiracy, design, intrigue, machination, plan, plot, scheme, stratagem; diagram, graph, sketch.

chase, SYN.—follow, hunt, persist, pursue, track, trail. ANT.—abandon, elude, escape, evade, flee.

chaste, SYN.—clean, clear, genuine, immaculate, spotless, unadulterated; guiltless, innocent, modest, sincere, undefiled, virgin; absolute, bare, sheer. ANT.—foul, polluted, sullied, tainted; corrupt, defiled.

chastise, SYN.—castigate, correct, discipline, pummel, punish, strike. ANT.—acquit, exonerate, free, pardon, release.

chat, SYN.—colloquy, conference, conversation, dialogue, interview, parley, talk.

chat, SYN.—blab, converse, gossip, jabber, mutter, prattle, speak, talk, tattle; argue, comment, claim, discourse, harangue, lecture, plead, preach, rant, spout; confer, consult, deliberate, discuss.

chatter, SYN.—conference, conversation, dialogue, discourse, discussion, gossip, lecture, report, rumor, speech, talk. ANT.— correspondence, meditation, silence, writing.

cheap, SYN.—inexpensive, low-priced, poor; beggarly, common, inferior, mean, shabby. ANT.—costly, dear, expensive; dignified, honorable, noble.

cheat, SYN.—bilk, circumvent, deceive, defraud, dupe, fool, gull, hoax, hoodwink, outwit, swindle, trick, victimize.

check, SYN.—analyze, assess, audit, contemplate, dissect, examine, inquire, interrogate, notice, question, quiz, review, scan, scrutinize, survey, view, watch. ANT.—disregard, neglect, omit, overlook.

cheer, SYN.—comfort, console, encourage, gladden, solace, soothe, sympathize. ANT.—antagonize, aggravate, depress, dishearten.

cheerful, SYN.—gay, glad, happy, jolly, joyful, lighthearted, merry, sprightly. ANT.—depressed, glum, mournful, sad, sullen.

cherish, SYN.—appreciate, hold dear, prize, treasure, value; foster, nurture, sustain. ANT.—dislike, disregard, neglect; abandon, reject.

chief, SYN.—captain, chieftain, commander, head, leader, master, principal, ruler. ANT.—attendant, follower, servant, subordinate.

chilly, SYN.—arctic, cold, cool, freezing, frigid, frozen, icy, wintry; passionless, phlegmatic, stoical, unfeeling. ANT.—burning, fiery, heated, hot, torrid; ardent, passionate.

choice, SYN.—alternative, election, option, preference, selection.

choice, SYN.—dainty, delicate, elegant, exquisite, fine, nice, pure, refined, splendid, subtle; beautiful, handsome, pretty; minute, powdered, pulverized, sharp, slender, small, thin. ANT.—blunt, coarse, large, rough, thick.

choose, SYN.—cull, elect, opt, pick, select. ANT.—refuse, reject.

chronicle, SYN.—account, description, detail, history, narration, narrative, recital, relation; computation, reckoning, record. ANT.—caricature, confusion, distortion, misrepresentation.

cinema, SYN.—appearance, drawing, effigy, engraving, etching, film, illustration, image, likeness, painting, panorama, photograph, picture, portrait, portrayal, print, representation, resemblance, scene, sketch, view.

circuitous, SYN.—crooked, devious, distorted, erratic, indirect, roundabout, swerving, tortuous, wandering, winding; crooked, cunning, tricky. ANT.—direct, straight; honest, straightforward.

circular, SYN.—bulbous, chubby, complete, curved, cylindrical, entire, globular, plump, rotund, round, spherical.

circumspection, SYN.—anxiety, care, concern, solicitude, worry; attention, caution, regard, vigilance, wariness; charge, custody, guardianship, ward. ANT.—disregard, indifference, neglect, negligence.

circumstance, SYN.—condition, event, fact, happening, incident, occurrence, position, situation.

cite, SYN.—advance, affirm, allege, assign, claim, declare, maintain. ANT.—contradict, deny, disprove, gainsay, refute.

civil, SYN.—accomplished, considerate, courteous, cultivated, genteel, polite, refined, urbane, well-bred, well-mannered. ANT.—boorish, impertinent, rude, uncivil, uncouth.

civilization, SYN.—breeding, cultivation, culture, education, enlightenment, refinement. ANT.—boorishness, ignorance, illiteracy, vulgarity.

claim, SYN.—affirm, allege, assert, aver, declare, express, maintain, state; defend, support, uphold, vindicate. ANT.—contradict, deny, refute.

clamor, SYN.—babel, cry, din, noise, outcry, racket, row, sound, tumult, uproar. ANT.—hush, quiet, silence, stillness.

clan, SYN.—brotherliness, fellowship, kindness, solidarity; association, brotherhood, fraternity. society. ANT.—acrimony, discord, opposition, strife.

clandestine, SYN.—concealed, covert, hidden, latent, private, secret, surreptitious, unknown. ANT.—conspicuous, disclosed, exposed, known, obvious.

clarify, SYN.—decipher, educate, explain, expound, illustrate, interpret, resolve, unfold, unravel. ANT.—baffle, confuse, darken, obscure.

clasp, SYN.—adhere, clutch, grasp, grip, hold, have, keep, maintain, occupy, possess, retain, support; check confine, curb, detain, restrain; accommodate, carry, contain, receive, stow. ANT.—abandon, relinquish, surrender, vacate.

class, SYN.—caste, category, denomination, genre, kind; grade, order, rank, set; elegance, excellence.

clean, SYN.—cleanse, mop, purify, scrub, sweep, wash. ANT.—dirty, pollute, soil, stain, sully.

cleanse, SYN.—clean, mop, purify, scrub, sweep, wash. ANT.—dirty, pollute, soil, stain, sully.

clear, SYN.—cloudless, fair, sunny; limpid, transparent; apparent, distinct, evident, intelligible, lucid, manifest, obvious, plain, unmistakable, visible; open, unobstructed. ANT.—cloudy, foul, overcast, ambiguous, obscure, unclear, vague.

clemency, SYN.—charity, compassion, forgiveness, grace, leniency, mercy, mildness, pity. ANT.—cruelty, punishment, retribution, vengeance.

clever, SYN.—adroit, apt, dexterous, quick, quick-witted, skillful, talented, witty; bright, ingenious, sharp, smart. ANT.—awkward, bungling, clumsy, slow, unskilled; dull, foolish, stupid.

cleverness, SYN.—comprehension, intellect, intelligence, mind, perspicacity, reason, sagacity, sense, understanding; banter, fun, humor, irony, pleasantry, raillery, sarcasm, satire, wit, witticism. ANT.— commonplace, platitude, sobriety, solemnity, stupidity.

climax, SYN.—acme, apex, consummation, culmination, height, peak, summit, zenith. ANT.—anticlimax, base, depth, floor.

climb, SYN.—ascend, mount, rise, scale, soar, tower. ANT.—descend, fall, sink.

cloak, SYN.—clothe, conceal, cover, curtain, disguise, envelop, guard, hide, mask, protect, screen, shield, shroud, veil. ANT.—bare, divulge, expose, reveal, unveil.

cloister, SYN.—abbey, convent, hermitage, monastery, nunnery, priory.

close, SYN.—abutting, adjacent, adjoining, immediate, impending, near, nearby, neighboring; confidential, dear, devoted, intimate. ANT.—afar, distant, faraway, re-

moved.

close, SYN.—occlude, seal, shut; clog, obstruct, stop; cease, complete, conclude, end, finish, terminate. ANT.—open, unbar, unlock; begin, commence, inaugurate, start.

clothes, SYN.—apparel, array, attire, clothing, drapery, dress, garb, garments, raiment, vestments, vesture. ANT.—nakedness, nudity.

clothing, SYN.—apparel, array, attire, clothes, drapery, dress, garb, garments, raiment, vestments, vesture. ANT.—nakedness, nudity.

cloudy, SYN.—dark, dim, indistinct, murky, mysterious obscure, overcast, shadowy. ANT.—bright, clear, distinct, limpid, sunny.

clumsy, SYN.—awkward, gauche, inept, rough, unpolished, untoward. ANT.—adroit, graceful, neat, polished, skillful.

coalition, SYN.—alliance, association, combination, confederacy, entente, federation, league, partnership, union; compact, covenant, marriage, treaty. ANT.—divorce, schism, separation.

coarse, SYN.—crude, impure, rough, rugged, unrefined; gross, gruff, immodest, indelicate, rude, unpolished, vulgar. ANT.—fine, polished, refined, smooth; cultivated, cultured, delicate.

coerce, SYN.—compel, constrain, drive, enforce, force, impel, oblige. ANT.—allure, convince, induce, persuade, prevent.

coercion, SYN.—dint, emphasis, energy, intensity, might, potency, power, strength, vigor; compulsion, constraint, force, violence. ANT.—feebleness, frailty, impotence, weakness; persuasion.

cognizance, SYN.—acquaintance, apprehension, erudition, information, knowledge, learning, lore, scholarship, science, understanding, wisdom. ANT.—ignorance, illiteracy, misunderstanding, stupidity.

cognizant, SYN.—apprised, aware, conscious, informed, mindful, observant, perceptive, sensible. ANT.—ignorant, insensible, oblivious, unaware.

coincide, SYN.—accede, acquiesce, agree, assent, comply, consent; concur, conform, tally. ANT.—contradict, differ, disagree, dissent, protest.

coincident, SYN.—equal, equivalent, identical, indistinguishable, like, same. ANT.—contrary, disparate, dissimilar, distinct, opposed.

cold, SYN.—arctic, chilly, cool, freezing, frigid, frozen, icy, wintry; passionless, phlegmatic, stoical, unfeeling. ANT.—burning, fiery, heated, hot, torrid; ardent, passionate.

collapse, SYN.—decline, decrease, descend, diminish, drop, fall, sink, subside; stumble, topple, tumble; droop, extend downward, hang. ANT.—arise, ascend, climb, mount, soar; steady.

colleague, SYN.—associate, attendant, companion, comrade, consort, crony, friend, mate, partner. ANT.—adversary, enemy, stranger.

collect, ANT.—accumulate, amass, assemble, concentrate, congregate, consolidate, gather, heap, hoard, mass, pile. ANT.—assort, disperse, distribute, divide, dole.

collected, SYN.—calm, composed, cool, imperturbable, peaceful; placid, quiet, sedate, tranquil, unmoved. ANT.—agitated, aroused, excited, perturbed, violent.

collection, SYN.—aggregate, amount, conglomeration, entirety, sum, total, whole. ANT.—element, ingredient, part, particular, unit.

collision, SYN.—battle, combat, conflict, duel, encounter, fight, struggle; contention, controversy, discord, inconsistency, interference, opposition, variance. ANT.—amity, concord, consonance, harmony.

collusion, SYN.—cabal, combination, conspiracy, intrigue, machination, plot, treachery, treason.

color, SYN.—complexion, dye, hue, paint, pigment, shade, stain, tincture, tinge, tint. ANT.—achromatism, paleness, transparency.

colossal, SYN.—elephantine, enormous, gargantuan, gigantic, huge, immense, large, prodigious, vast. ANT.—diminutive, little, minute, small, tiny.

combat, SYN.—battle, collision, conflict, duel, encounter, fight, struggle; contention, controversy; discord, inconsistency, interference, opposition, variance. ANT.—amity, concord, consonance, harmony.

combat, SYN.—battle, brawl, conflict, contend, dispute, encounter, fight, quarrel, scuffle, skirmish, squabble, struggle, wrangle.

combination, SYN.—alliance, association, coalition; confederacy, entente, federation, league; partnership, union; compact, covenant, marriage, treaty. ANT.—divorce, schism, separation.

combine, SYN.—accompany, adjoin, associate, attach, conjoin, connect, couple, go with, join, link, unite. ANT.—detach, disconnect, dis-

join, separate.

comely, SYN.—beauteous, beautiful, charming, elegant, fair, fine, handsome, lovely, pretty. ANT.—foul, hideous, homely, repulsive, unsightly.

comfort, SYN.—consolation, contentment, ease, enjoyment, relief, solace, succor. ANT.—affliction, discomfort, misery, suffering, torment, torture.

comfort, SYN.—cheer, console, encourage, gladden, solace, soothe, sympathize. ANT.—antagonize, aggravate, depress, dishearten.

comfortable, SYN.—acceptable, agreeable, convenient, cozy, gratifying, pleasing, pleasurable, relaxed, restful, welcome. ANT.—distressing, miserable, troubling, uncomfortable, wretched.

comical, SYN.—amusing, droll, farcical, funny, humorous, laughable, ludicrous, ridiculous, witty; curious, odd, queer. ANT.—melancholy, sad, serious, sober, solemn.

command, SYN.—arrangement, class, method, plan, rank, regularity, sequence, series, succession, system; bidding, decree, dictate, injunction, instruction, mandate, order, requirement. ANT.—confusion, disarray, disorder, irregularity; consent, license, permission.

command, SYN.—aim, level, point, train; conduct, govern, guide, manage, regulate, rule; bid, direct, instruct, order. ANT.—deceive, distract, misdirect, misguide.

commensurate, SYN.—celebrate, honor, keep, observe, solemnize; commend, extol, glorify, honor, laud, praise. ANT.—disregard, overlook; decry, disgrace, dishonor, profane.

commence, SYN.—arise, begin, enter, inaugurate, initiate, institute, open, originate, start. ANT.—close, complete, end, finish, terminate.

commencement, SYN.—beginning, inception, opening, origin, outset, source, start. ANT.—close, completion, consummation, end, termination.

commend, SYN.—appreciate, approve, like, praise; authorize, confirm, endorse, ratify, sanction. ANT.—criticize, disparage; condemn, nullify.

commendable, SYN.—acceptable, agreeable, amiable, charming, gratifying, pleasant, pleasing, pleasurable, suitable, welcome. ANT.—disagreeable, obnoxious, offensive, unpleasant.

commendation, SYN.—acclaim, adulation, applause, approval, compliment, eulogy, flattery, laudation, praise.

ANT.—abuse, censure, condemnation, disapproval.

comment, SYN.—annotation, assertion, declaration, observation, remark, statement, utterance.

commerce, SYN.—art, business, employment, engagement, enterprise, job, occupation, profession, trade, trading, vocation, work. ANT.—avocation, hobby, pastime.

commit, SYN.—do, perform, perpetrate; commend, consign, entrust, relegate, trust; bind, obligate, pledge. ANT.—fail, miscarry, neglect, mistrust, release, renounce; free, loose.

commodious, SYN.—accessible, adapted, advantageous, appropriate, favorable, fitting, handy, suitable, timely. ANT.—awkward, inconvenient, inopportune, troublesome.

common, SYN.—familiar, frequent, general, ordinary, popular, prevalent, universal, usual; low, mean, vulgar. ANT.—exceptional, extraordinary, odd, scarce; noble, refined.

common-sense, SYN.—appreciable, apprehensible, perceptible; alive, awake, aware, cognizant, comprehending, conscious, perceiving, sentient; discreet, intelligent, judicious, practical, prudent, reasonable, sagacious, sage, sensible, sober, sound, wise. ANT.—absurd, impalpable, imperceptible, stupid, unaware.

commotion, SYN.—agitation, chaos, confusion, disarrangement, disarray, disorder, ferment, jumble, stir, tumult, turmoil. ANT.—certainty, order, peace, tranquility.

communicable, SYN.—catching, contagious, infectious, pestilential, virulent. ANT.—healthful, hygienic, noncommunicable.

communicate, SYN.—confer, convey, disclose, divulge, impart, inform, notify, relate, reveal, tell, transmit. ANT.—conceal, hide, withhold.

communion, SYN.—association, fellowship, intercourse, participation, sacrament, union. ANT.—alienation, nonparticipation.

compact, SYN.—close, constricted, contracted, firm, narrow, snug, stretched, taught, tense, tight; closefisted, niggardly, parsimonious, penny-pinching, stingy. ANT.—lax, loose, open, relaxed, slack.

compact, SYN.—accordance, coincidence, concord, concurrence, harmony, understanding, unison; agreement, bargain, contract, covenant, pact, stipulation. ANT.—difference, disagreement, discord, dissension, variance.

companion, SYN.—associate, attendant, colleague, comrade, consort, crony, friend, mate, partner. ANT.—adversary, enemy, stranger.

companionship, SYN.—acquaintance, cognizance, familiarity, fellowship, friendship, intimacy, knowledge. ANT.—ignorance, inexperience, unfamiliarity.

company, SYN.—assemblage, band, crew, group, horde, party, throng, troop; association, fellowship, society, corporation, firm. ANT.—dispersion, individual, seclusion, solitude.

comparable, SYN.—akin, alike, allied, analogous, correlative, correspondent, corresponding, like, parallel, similar. ANT.—different, dissimilar, divergent, incongruous, opposed.

compare, SYN.—contrast, differentiate, discriminate, distinguish, oppose.

compassion, SYN.—commiseration, condolence, mercy, pity, sympathy. ANT.—brutality, cruelty, hardness, inhumanity, ruthlessness.

compassionate, SYN.—affable, benevolent, benign, forbearing, gentle, good, humane, indulgent, kind, kindly, merciful, sympathetic, tender, thoughtful. ANT.—cruel, inhuman, merciless, severe, unkind.

compatible, SYN.—accordant, agreeing, consistent, conforming, congruous, consonant, constant, correspondent. ANT.— contradictory, discrepant, incongruous, inconsistent, paradoxical.

compel, SYN.—coerce, constrain, drive, enforce, impel, oblige. ANT.—allure, convince, induce, persuade, prevent.

compensation, SYN.—allowance, earnings, fee, pay, payment, recompense, salary, stipend, wages. ANT.—gift, gratuity, present.

competent, SYN.—able, capable, clever, efficient, fitted, qualified, skillful. ANT.—inadequate, incapable, incompetent, unfitted.

complain, SYN.—grouch, grumble, drive, lament, murmur, protest, regret, remonstrate, repine, whine. ANT.—applaud, approve, praise, rejoice.

complete, SYN.—concluded, consummate, ended, entire, finished, full, perfect, thorough, total, unbroken, undivided. ANT.—imperfect, lacking, unfinished.

complete, SYN.—accomplish, achieve, close, conclude, consummate, do, end, execute, finish, fulfill, get done, perfect, perform, terminate.

completion, SYN.—accomplishment, achievement, attainment, realization, ANT.—neglect, omission; defeat, failure.

complex, SYN.—complicated, compound, intricate, involved, perplexing. ANT.—plain, simple, uncompounded.

complexion, SYN.—color, dye, hue, paint, pigment, shade, stain, tincture, tinge, tint. ANT.—achromatism, paleness, transparency.

compliant, SYN.—humble, lowly, meek, modest, plain, simple, submissive, unassuming, unostentatious, unpretentious. ANT.—arrogant, boastful, haughty, proud, vain.

complicated, SYN.—complex, compound, intricate, involved, perplexing. ANT.—plain, simple, uncompounded.

compliment, SYN.—adulation, commendation, eulogy, flattery, praise, tribute. ANT.—affront, criticism, insult, taunt.

comply, SYN.—accede, acquiesce, agree, assent, consent; coincide, concur, conform, tally. ANT.—contradict, differ, disagree, dissent, protest.

component, SYN.—allotment, apportionment, division, fragment, moiety, piece, portion, scrap, section, segment, share; element, ingredient, member, organ; concern, faction, interest, party, side; character, lines, role. ANT.—entirety, whole.

comport, SYN.—act, bear, behave, carry, conduct, demean, deport, interact, manage, operate.

compose, SYN.—construct, create, fashion, forge, make, mold, produce, shape; constitute, form, make up; arrange, combine, organize; devise, frame, invent. ANT.—destroy, disfigure, dismantle, misshape, wreck.

composed, SYN.—calm, collected, cool, imperturbable, peaceful, placid, quiet, sedate, tranquil, unmoved. ANT.—agitated, aroused, excited, perturbed, violent.

composer, SYN.—author, creator, father, inventor, maker, originator, writer.

composure, SYN.—balance, calmness, carriage, equanimity, equilibrium, poise, self-possession. ANT.—agitation, anger, excitement, rage, turbulence.

compound, SYN.—alloy, amalgamate, blend, combine, commingle, concoct, confound, fuse, jumble, mingle, mix; associate consort, fraternize, join. ANT.—dissociate, divide, segregate, separate, sort.

comprehend, SYN.—appreciate, apprehend, conceive, discern, grasp, know, learn, perceive, realize, see, understand. ANT.—ignore, misapprehend, mistake, misunderstand.

comprehension, SYN.—apprehension, cognizance, conception, discernment, insight, perception, understanding. ANT.—ignorance, insensibility, misapprehension, misconception.

comprise, SYN.—accommodate, contain, embody, embrace, hold, include; repress, restrain. ANT.—discharge, emit, exclude, encourage, yield.

compulsion, SYN.—dint, emphasis, energy, intensity, might, potency, power, strength, vigor; coercion, constraint, force, violence. ANT.—feebleness, frailty, impotence, weakness; persuasion.

computation, SYN.—account, reckoning, record. ANT.—misrepresentation.

compute, SYN.—calculate, consider, count, estimate, figure, reckon. ANT.—conjecture, guess, miscalculate.

comrade, SYN.—associate, attendant, colleague, companion, consort, crony, friend, mate, partner. ANT.—adversary, enemy, stranger.

conceal, SYN.—cloak, cover, disguise, hide, mask, screen, secrete, suppress, veil, withhold. ANT.—disclose, divulge, expose, reveal, show, uncover.

concede, SYN.—let, permit, sanction, suffer, tolerate; authorize, give, grant, yield; acknowledge, admit, allow. ANT.—forbid, object, protest, refuse, resist.

conceit, SYN.—complacency, egotism, pride, self-esteem, vanity; caprice, conception, fancy, idea, imagination, notion, whim. ANT.—diffidence, humility, meekness, modesty.

conceited, SYN.—abortive, bootless, empty, fruitless, futile, idle, ineffectual, pointless, unavailing, useless, valueless, vapid, worthless; proud, vain, vainglorious. ANT.—effective, potent, profitable; meek, modest.

conceive, SYN.—concoct, contrive, design, devise, fabricate, frame, invent. ANT.—copy, imitate, reproduce.

concentrated, SYN.—close, compact, compressed, crowded, dense, thick; dull, obtuse, slow, stupid. ANT.—dispersed, dissipated, sparse; clever, quick.

concept, SYN.—abstraction, conception, fancy, idea, image, impression, notion, opinion, sentiment, thought. ANT.—entity, matter, object, substance, thing.

conception, SYN.—cogitation, consideration, contemplation, deliberation, fancy, idea, imagination, impression, judgment, meditation, memory, notion, opinion, recollection, reflection, regard, retrospection, sentiment, thought, view.

concern, SYN.—affair, business, matter, transaction; anxiety, care, solicitude, worry. ANT.—apathy, indifference, negligence, unconcern.

concise, SYN.—brief, compact, condensed, incisive, neat, pithy, succinct, summary, terse. ANT.—lengthy, prolix, verbose, wordy.

conclude, SYN.—accomplish, achieve, close, complete, consummate, do, end, execute, finish, fulfill, get done, perfect, perform, terminate.

concluding, SYN.—extreme, final, hindmost, last, latest, terminal, ultimate, utmost. ANT.—beginning, first, foremost, initial, opening.

conclusion, SYN.—close, completion, end, finale, issue, settlement, termination; decision, deduction, inference, judgment. ANT.—beginning, commencement, inception, prelude, start.

conclusive, SYN.—concluding, decisive, ending, eventual, final, last, latest, terminal, ultimate. ANT.—first, inaugural, incipient, original, rudimentary.

concord, SYN.—accordance, agreement, coincidence, concord, concurrence, harmony, understanding, unison; bargain, compact, contract, covenant, pact, stipulation. ANT.—difference, disagreement, discord, dissension, variance.

concur, SYN.—accede, acquiesce, agree, assent, comply, consent; coincide, conform, tally. ANT.—contradict, differ, disagree, dissent, protest.

condemn, SYN.—blame, censure, denounce, reprehend, reproach, reprobate, reprove, upbraid; convict, sentence. ANT.—approve, commend, condone, forgive, praise; absolve, acquit, exonerate, pardon.

condition, SYN.—case, circumstance, plight, predicament, situation, state; provision, requirement, stipulation, term.

condition, SYN.—concoct, contrive, equip, fit, furnish, get ready, make ready, predispose, prepare, provide, qualify, ready.

conditional, SYN.—contingent, dependent, depending, relying, subject, subordinate. ANT.—absolute, autonomous, casual, independent, original.

condolence, SYN.—affinity, agreement, commiseration, compassion, concord, congeniality, empathy, harmony, pity, sympathy, tenderness, warmth. ANT.—antipathy, harshness, indifference, malevolence, unconcern.

conduct, SYN.—action, bearing, behavior, carriage, deed, demeanor, deportment, disposition, manner.

conduct, SYN.—direct, escort, guide, lead, steer; control, manage, regulate, supervise.

confederate, SYN.—abettor, accessory, accomplice, ally, assistant, associate. ANT.—adversary, enemy, opponent; rival.

confederation, SYN.—alliance, association, coalition, combination, confederacy, entente, federation, league, partnership, union; compact, covenant, marriage, treaty. ANT.—divorce, schism, separation.

confer, SYN.—blab, chat, converse, gossip, jabber, mutter, prattle, speak, tattle; argue, comment, declaim, discourse, harangue, lecture, plead, preach, rant, spout; consult, deliberate, discuss, reason, talk.

confess, SYN.—acknowledge, admit, allow, avow, concede, divulge, grant, own, reveal. ANT.—conceal, deny, disclaim, disown, renounce.

confession, SYN.—alibi,

apology, defense, excuse, explanation, justification. ANT.—accusation, complaint, denial, dissimulation.

confidence, SYN.—assurance, assuredness, certainty, conviction, courage, firmness, security, self-reliance, surety; pledge, promise, word; assertion, declaration, statement. ANT.—bashfulness, humility, modesty, shyness, suspicion.

confine, SYN.—bound, circumscribe, enclose, encompass, envelop, fence, limit, surround. ANT.—develop, distend, enlarge, expand, expose, open.

confirm, SYN.—corroborate, substantiate, verify; acknowledge, assure, establish, settle; approve, fix, ratify, sanction; strengthen.

confirmation, SYN.—corroboration, demonstration, evidence, experiment, proof, test, testimony, trial, verification. ANT.—failure, fallacy, invalidity.

conflict, SYN.—battle, collision, combat, duel, encounter, fight, struggle; contention, controversy, discord, inconsistency, interference, opposition, variance. ANT.—amity, concord, consonance, harmony.

confiscate, SYN.—appropriate, capture, catch, ensnare, gain, purloin, remove, steal, take; clasp, clutch, grasp, grip, seize; accept, get, obtain, receive; bear, endure, stand, tolerate; bring, carry, convey, escort; attract, captivate, charm, delight, interest; claim, demand, necessitate, require; adopt, assume, choose, espouse, select.

conflagration, SYN.—blaze, burning, combustion, fire, flame, glow, heat, warmth; ardor, fervor, intensity, passion, vigor. ANT.—cold; apathy, quiescence.

conform, SYN.—accommodate, adapt, adjust, fit, suit. ANT.—disturb, misapply, misfit.

confront, SYN.—bar, combat, confront, contradict, counteract, defy, hinder, osbtruct, resist, thwart, withstand. ANT.—agree, cooperate, submit, succumb, support.

confuse, SYN.—bewilder, confound, confuse, dumbfound, mystify, nonplus, perlex, puzzle. ANT.—clarify, explain, illumine, instruct, solve.

confused, SYN.—bewildered, deranged, disconcerted, disordered, disorganized, indistinct, mixed, muddled, perplexed. ANT.—clear, lucid, obvious, organized, plain.

confusion, SYN.—agitation, chaos, commotion, disarrangement, disarray, disorder, ferment, jumble, stir, tumult, turmoil.

ANT.—certainty, order, peace, tranquility.

congruous, SYN.—accordant, agreeing, compatible, conforming, consonant, consistent, constant, correspondent. ANT.— contradictory, discrepant, incongruous, inconsistent, paradoxical.

conjecture, SYN.—hypothesis, law, supposition, theory. ANT.—certainty, fact, proof.

conjecture, SYN.—chance, dare, endanger, hazard, imperil, jeopardize, peril, risk, venture. ANT.—determine, guard, insure, know.

connect, SYN.—adjoin, affix, annex, append, attach, join, stick, unite; assign, associate, attribute. ANT.—detach, disengage, separate, unfasten, untie.

connection. SYN.—affinity, alliance, association, bond, conjunction, link, relationship, tie, union. ANT.—disunion, isolation, separation.

conquer, SYN.—beat, crush, defeat, humble, master, overcome, quell, rout, subdue, subjugate, surmount, vanquish. ANT.—capitulate, cede, lose, retreat, surrender.

conquest, SYN.— achievement, jubilation, ovation, triumph, victory. ANT.—defeat, failure.

conscious, SYN.—apprised, aware, cognizant, in-

formed, mindful, observant, perceptive, sensible. ANT.—ignorant, insensible, oblivious, unaware.

consecrate, SYN.—adore, dignify, enshrine, enthrone, exalt, extol, glorify, hallow, honor, revere, venerate. ANT.—abuse, debase, degrade, dishonor, mock.

consecrated, SYN.— blessed, devout, divine, hallowed, holy, pious, religious, sacred, saintly, spiritual. ANT.—evil, profane, sacrilegious, secular, worldly.

consent, SYN.—authority, authorization, leave, liberty, license, permission, permit. ANT.—denial, opposition, prohibition, refusal.

consent, SYN.—accede, acquiesce, agree, assent, comply, coincide, concur, conform, tally. ANT.—contradict, differ, disagree, dissent, protest.

consequently, SYN.— accordingly, hence, so, then, thence, therefore.

conserve, SYN.—maintain, preserve, save; confine, hold, reserve, retain; keep, guard, protect; support, sustain. ANT.—discard, reject; dismiss, relinquish; neglect.

consider, SYN.—contemplate, deliberate, examine, heed, meditate, ponder, reflect, study, weigh; esteem, regard, respect. ANT.—ignore, neglect, overlook.

considerate, SYN.—attentive, careful, cautious, concerned, considerate, heedful, provident, prudent; contemplative, dreamy, introspective, meditative, pensive, reflective. ANT.—heedless, inconsiderate, precipitous, rash, thoughtless.

consideration, SYN.—attention, care, circumspection, consideration, heed, mindfulness, notice, observance, watchfulness; application, contemplation, reflection, study. ANT.—disregard, indifference, negligence, omission, oversight.

consistent, SYN.—accordant, agreeing, compatible, conforming, congruous, consonant, constant, correspondent. ANT.—contradictory, discrepant, incongruous, inconsistent, paradoxical.

consolation, SYN.—comfort, contentment, ease, enjoyment, relief, solace, succor. ANT.—affliction, discomfort, misery, suffering, torment, torture.

console, SYN.—allay, assuage, comfort, solace, soothe. ANT.—annoy, distress, worry.

consolidate, SYN.—amalgamate, blend, coalesce, combine, commingle, conjoin, fuse, mingle, mix, merge, unify, unite. ANT.—analyze, decompose, disintegrate, separate.

consort, SYN.—associate, attendant, colleague, companion, comrade, crony, friend, mate, partner. ANT.—adversary, enemy, stranger.

conspicuous, SYN.—clear, distinguished, manifest, noticeable, obvious, prominent, salient, striking, visible. ANT.—common, hidden, inconspicuous, obscure.

conspiracy, SYN.—cabal, collusion, combination, intrigue, machination, plot, treachery, treason.

constancy, SYN.—allegiance, devotion, faithfulness, fealty, fidelity, loyalty; accuracy, exactness, precision. ANT.—disloyalty, faithlessness, perfidy, treachery.

constant, SYN.—abiding, ceaseless, continual, enduring, faithful, fixed, immutable, invariant, permanent, perpetual, persistent, unalterable, unchanging, unwavering. ANT.—fickle, mutable, vacillating, wavering.

constantly, SYN.—always, continually, eternally, ever, evermore, forever, incessantly, perpetually, unceasingly. ANT.—fitfully, never, occasionally, rarely, sometimes.

consternation, SYN.—alarm, apprehension, cowardice, dismay, dread, fear, fright, horror, panic, scare, terror, timidity, trepidation. ANT.—assurance, boldness, bravery, courage, fearlessness.

constrain, SYN.—destiny, fate, necessity, requirement, requisite; exigency, indigence, need, poverty, want. ANT.—choice, freedom, luxury, option, uncertainty.

construct, SYN.—build, erect, fabricate, form, frame, make, raise. ANT.—demolish, destroy, raze.

construe, SYN.—decipher, decode, elucidate, explain, explicate, interpret, render, solve, translate, unravel. ANT.—confuse, distort, falsify, misconstrue, misinterpret.

consult, SYN.—chatter, conference, conversation, dialogue, discourse, discussion, gossip, lecture, report, rumor, speech, talk. ANT.—correspondence, meditation, silence, writing.

consume, SYN.—absorb, assimilate, engulf, imbibe, swallow up; engage, engross, occupy. ANT.—discharge, dispense, emit, expel, exude.

consummate, SYN.—accomplish, achieve, close, complete, conclude, do, end, execute, finish, fulfill, get done, perfect, perform, terminate.

consummation, SYN.—acme, apex, climax, culmination, height, peak, summit, zenith. ANT.—anticlimax, base, depth, floor.

contagious, SYN.—catching, communicable, infectious, pestilential, virulent. ANT.—healthful, hygienic, noncommunicable.

contain, SYN.—accommodate, comprise, embody, embrace, hold, include; repress, restrain. ANT.—discharge, emit, exclude; encourage, yield.

contaminate, SYN.—befoul, corrupt, defile, infect, poison, pollute, sully, taint. ANT.—disinfect, purify.

contaminated, SYN.—corrupt, corrupted, crooked, debased, depraved, dishonest, impure, profligate; putrid, spoiled, tainted, unsound, venal, vitiated.

contamination, SYN.—contagion, germ, pest, virus; ailment, disease, infection, poison, pollution, taint.

contemplate, SYN.—conceive, imagine, picture, recall, recollect, remember; cogitate, deliberate, meditate, muse, ponder, reason, reflect, speculate, think; apprehend, believe, consider, deem, esteem, judge, opine, reckon, regard, suppose; devise, intend, mean, plan, purpose. ANT.—conjecture, forget, guess.

contemplative, SYN.— attentive, careful, cautious, concerned, considerate, heedful, provident, prudent; dreamy, introspective, meditative, pensive. reflective, thoughtful. ANT.— heedless, inconsiderate, precipitous, rash, thoughtless.

contemporary, SYN.— current, modern, new, novel, present, recent. ANT.—ancient, antiquated, bygone, old, past.

contempt, SYN.—contumely, derision, detestation, disdain, hatred, scorn. ANT.—awe, esteem, regard, respect, reverence.

contemptible, SYN.— average, medium, middle; base, despicable, low, mean, sordid, vile, vulgar, malicious, nasty, offensive, selfish. ANT.—admirable, dignified, exalted, generous, noble.

contented, SYN.—blessed, cheerful, delighted, fortunate, gay, glad, happy, joyful, joyous, lucky, merry, opportune, propitious. ANT.—blue, depressed, gloomy, morose.

contention, SYN.—battle, collision, combat, conflict, duel, encounter, fight, struggle; controversy, discord, inconsistency, interference, opposition, variance. ANT.—amity, concord, consonance, harmony.

contentment, SYN.— beatitude, blessedness, bliss, delight, felicity, gladness, happiness, pleasure, satisfaction, well-being. ANT.— despair, grief, misery, sadness, sorrow.

contest, SYN.—altercate, argue, bicker, contend, debate, discuss, dispute, quarrel, squabble, wrangle. ANT.—agree, allow, assent, concede.

continence, SYN.— abstention, abstinence, fasting, forbearance, moderation, self-denial, sobriety, temperance. ANT.—excess, gluttony, greed, intoxication, self-indulgence.

contingent, SYN.—conditional, dependent, depending, relying, subject, subordinate. ANT.— absolute, autonomous, casual, independent, original.

contingency, SYN.—conditionality, dependency, reliance on, subject to, subordination. ANT.— absoluteness, autonomousness, casuality, independence, originality.

continual, SYN.—ceaseless, constant, continuous, endless, everlasting, incessant, perennial, perpetual, unceasing, uninterrupted, unremitting. ANT.—interrupted, occasional, periodic, rare.

continue, SYN.—advance, extend, proceed; endure, last, remain; persevere, persist, prolong, pursue.

ANT.—arrest, check, interrupt; cease, defer, halt, stop, suspend.

contract, SYN.—abbreviate, abridge, condense, curtail, diminish, lessen, limit, reduce, restrict, shorten. ANT.—elongate, extend, lengthen.

contract, SYN.—agreement, bargain, compact, covenant, pact, promise, stipulation, treaty.

contraction, SYN.—abbreviation, abridgment, reduction, shortening. ANT.—amplification, enlargement, expansion, extension.

contradict, SYN.—confute, controvert, counter, dispute, gainsay, oppose. ANT.—agree, confirm, support, verify.

contradictory, SYN.—contrary, discrepant, illogical, incompatible, incongruous, inconsistent, irreconcilable, paradoxical, unsteady, vacillating, wavering. ANT.—compatible, congruous, consistent, correspondent.

contrary, SYN.—adverse, antagonistic, hostile, opposed, opposite; counteractive, disastrous, unfavorable, unlucky. ANT.—benign, favorable, fortunate, lucky, propitious.

contrast, SYN.—compare, differentiate, discriminate, distinguish, oppose.

contrite, SYN.—penitent, regretful, remorseful, repentant, sorrowful, sorry. ANT.—obdurate, remorseless.

contrition, SYN.—compunction, grief, penitence, qualm, regret, remorse, repentance, self-reproach, sorrow. ANT.—complacency, impenitence, obduracy, self-satisfaction.

contrive, SYN.—delineate, design, devise, intend, outline, plan, plot, prepare, project, scheme, sketch.

control, SYN.—command, direct, dominate, govern, manage, regulate, rule, superintend; bridle, check, curb, repress, restrain. ANT.—abandon, follow, forsake, ignore, submit.

controversy, SYN.—argument, contention, debate, disagreement, dispute, quarrel, squabble. ANT.—agreement, concord, decision, harmony.

convenient, SYN.—accessible, adapted, advantageous, appropriate, commodious, favorable, fitting, handy, suitable, timely. ANT.—awkward, inconvenient, inopportune, troublesome.

conversant, SYN.—acquainted, aware, cognizant, familiar, intimate, knowing, versed; affable, amicable, close, courteous, friendly, informal, sociable, unreserved. ANT.—affected, cold, distant, reserved, unfamiliar.

conversation, SYN.—chat, colloquy, conference, dialogue, interview, parley, talk.

converse, SYN.—blab, chat, gossip, jabber, mutter, prattle, speak, talk, tattle; argue, comment, declaim, discourse, harangue, lecture, plead, preach, rant, spout; confer, consult, deliberate, discuss, reason.

convert, SYN.—exchange, substitute; alter, change, modify, shift, transfigure, transform, vary, veer. ANT.—retain; continue, establish, preserve, settle, stabilize.

convey, SYN.—bring, carry, transmit, transport; bear, support, sustain. ANT.—abandon, drop.

convict, SYN.—criminal, culprit, delinquent, felon, malefactor, offender, transgressor.

convict, SYN.—blame, censure, denounce, reprehend, reproach, reprobate, reprove, upbraid; condemn, sentence. ANT.—approve, commend, condone, forgive, praise; absolve, acquit, exonerate, pardon.

conviction, SYN.—belief, certitude, confidence, credence, faith, feeling, opinion, persuasion, reliance, trust. ANT.—denial, doubt, heresy, incredulity.

convince, SYN.—allure, coax, entice, exhort, incite, induce, influence, persuade, prevail upon, urge, win over. ANT.—coerce, compel, deter, dissuade, restrain.

convoy, SYN.—accompany, associate with, attend, chaperone, consort with, escort, go with. ANT.—abandon, avoid, desert, leave, quit.

copious, SYN.—abundant, ample, bountiful, overflowing, plenteous, plentiful, profuse, rich, teeming. ANT.—deficient, insufficient, scant, scarce.

copy, SYN.—duplicate, exemplar, facsimile, imitation, replica, reproduction, transcript. ANT.—original, prototype.

cordial, SYN.—ardent, earnest, gracious, hearty, sincere, sociable, warm. ANT.—aloof, cool, reserved, taciturn.

core, SYN.—center, heart, middle, midpoint, midst, nucleus. ANT.—border, boundary, outskirts, periphery, rim.

corporal, SYN.—bodily, carnal, corporeal, physical, somatic; material, natural. ANT.—mental, spiritual.

corporation, SYN.—assemblage, band, crew, group, horde, party, throng, troop; association, fellowship, society; company, firm. ANT.—dispersion, individual, seclusion, solitude.

corpse, SYN.—body, carcass, remains; form, frame, torso; bulk, corpus, mass; aggregate, association, company, society. ANT.—intellect, mind, soul, spirit.

corpulent, SYN.—chubby, fat, obese, paunchy, plump, portly, pudgy, rotund, stocky, stout, thickset. ANT.—gaunt, lean, slender, slim, thin.

correct, SYN.—accurate, exact, faultless, impeccable, precise, proper, right, strict. ANT.—erroneous, false, faulty, untrue, wrong.

correct, SYN.—amend, mend, rectify, reform, right; admonish, discipline, punish. ANT.—aggravate, ignore, spoil; condone, indulge.

correction, SYN.—control, order, regulation, restraint, self-control; exercise, instruction, practice, training; discipline, punishment. ANT.—chaos, confusion, turbulence.

correlative, SYN.—akin, alike, allied, analogous, comparable, correspondent, corresponding, like, parallel, similar. ANT.—different, dissimilar, divergent, incongruous, opposed.

correspondent, SYN.—akin, alike, allied, analogous, comparable, corresponding, like, parallel, similar. ANT.—different, dissimilar, divergent, incongruous, opposed.

corrupt, SYN.—contaminated, corrupted, crooked, debased, depraved, dishonest, impure, profligate, putrid, spoiled, tainted, unsound, venal, vitiated.

corrupted, SYN.—contaminated, crooked, debased, depraved, dishonest, impure, profligate, putrid, spoiled, tainted, unsound, venal, vitiated.

cost, SYN.—charge, expense, price, value, worth.

council, SYN.—admonition, advice, caution, counsel, exhortation, instruction, recommendation, suggestion, warning; information, intelligence, notification.

counsel, SYN.—advise, allude, hint, imply, insinuate, intimate, offer, propose, recommend, refer, suggest. ANT.—declare, demand, dictate, insist.

count, SYN.—calculate, compute, consider, estimate, figure, reckon. ANT.—conjecture, guess, miscalculate.

countenance, SYN.—face, mug, visage; assurance, audacity, cover, exterior, front, surface. ANT.—timidity; back, interior, rear.

counterfeit, SYN.—affected, artificial, assumed, bogus, ersatz, fake, feigned, fictitious, phony, sham, spurious, synthetic, unreal. ANT.—genuine, natural, real, true.

couple, SYN.—accompany, adjoin, associate, attach, combine, conjoin, connect, go with, join, link, unite. ANT.—detach, disconnect, disjoin, separate.

courage, SYN.—boldness, bravery, chivalry, fearlessness, fortitude, intrepidity, mettle, prowess, resolution. ANT.—cowardice, fear, pusillanimity, timidity.

courageous, SYN.—adventurous, audacious, bold, brave, chivalrous, daring, dauntless, fearless, gallant, heroic, intrepid, magnanimous, valiant, valorous. ANT.—cowardly, cringing, fearful, timid, weak.

course, SYN.—avenue, channel, passage, path, road, route, street, thoroughfare, track, trail, walk, way.

courteous, SYN.—accomplished, civil, considerate, cultivated, genteel, polite, refined, urbane, wellbred, well-mannered. ANT.—boorish, impertinent, rude, uncivil, uncouth.

covenant, SYN.—accordance, agreement, coincidence, concord, concurrence, harmony, understanding, unison; bargain, compact, contract, pact, stipulation. ANT.—difference, disagreement, discord, dissension, variance.

cover, SYN.—cloak, clothe, conceal, curtain, disguise, envelop, guard, hide, mask, protect, screen, shield, shroud,

veil. ANT.—bare, divulge, expose, reveal, unveil.

covert, SYN.—concealed, dormant, hidden, inactive, potential, quiescent, secret, undeveloped, unseen. ANT.—conspicuous, evident, explicit, manifest, visible.

covetousness, SYN.—envy, jealousy, spitefulness. ANT.—generosity, geniality, indifference.

cowardice, SYN.—alarm, apprehension, consternation, dismay, dread, fear, fright, horror, panic, scare, terror, timidity, trepidation. ANT.—assurance, boldness, bravery, courage, fearlessness.

coy, SYN.—abashed, bashful, diffident, embarrassed, humble, modest, recoiling, shamefaced, sheepish, shy, timid, timorous. ANT.—adventurous, daring, fearless, gregarious, outgoing.

crafty, SYN.—artful, astute, clandestine, covert, cunning, foxy, furtive, guileful, insidious, shrewd, stealthy, subtle, surreptitious, sly, tricky, underhand, wily. ANT.—candid, frank, ingenuous, open, sincere.

craggy, SYN.—irregular, jagged, rough, rugged, scratchy, uneven; unpolished; harsh, severe. ANT.—even, level, sleek, slippery, smooth; fine, finished, polished, refined; gentle, mild.

crass, SYN.—coarse, green, harsh, ill-prepared, raw, rough, unfinished, unpolished, unrefined; crude, uncouth, unrefined. ANT.—finished, well-prepared; cultivated, refined.

craving, SYN.—appetite, hunger, relish, stomach, thirst, zest; desire, inclination, liking, longing, passion. ANT.—disgust, distaste, renunciation, repugnance, satiety.

crazy, SYN.—delirious, demented, deranged, foolish, idiotic, imbecilic, insane, mad, maniacal. ANT.—rational, reasonable, sane, sensible, sound.

create, SYN.—cause, engender, fashion, form, formulate, generate, invent, make, originate, produce; appoint, constitute, ordain. ANT.—annihilate, demolish, destroy; disband, terminate.

creative, SYN.—clever, fanciful, imaginative, inventive, mystical, poetical, visionary. ANT.—dull, literal, prosaic, unromantic.

credence, SYN.—belief, certitude, confidence, conviction, faith, feeling, opinion, persuasion, reliance, trust. ANT.—denial, doubt, heresy, incredulity.

credit, SYN.—accept, apprehend, believe, conceive, fancy, hold, imagine, support, suppose.

ANT.—distrust, doubt, question, reject.

creed, SYN.—belief, doctrine, dogma, precept, teaching, tenet. ANT.—conduct, deed, performance, practice.

crest, SYN.—acme, head, pinnacle, summit, top. ANT.—base, bottom, foot.

crime, SYN.—affront, atrocity, indignity, insult, outrage; aggression, injustice, misdeed, offense, sin, transgression, trespass, vice, wrong. ANT.—gentleness, innocence, morality, right.

criminal, SYN.—convict, culprit, delinquent, felon, malefactor, offender, transgressor.

crippled, SYN.—defective, deformed, disabled, feeble, halt, hobbling, lame, limping, maimed, unconvincing, unsatisfactory, weak. ANT.—agile, athletic, robust, sound, vigorous.

crisis, SYN.—acme, conjuncture, contingency, emergency, exigency, juncture, pass, pinch, strait. ANT.—calm, equilibrium, normality, stability.

crisp, SYN.—breakable, brittle, crumbling, delicate, fragile, frail, splintery. ANT.—enduring, thick, tough, unbreakable.

criterion, SYN.—gauge, law, measure, principle, proof, rule, standard, test, touchstone. ANT.—

chance, fancy, guess, supposition.

critical, SYN.—accurate, discerning, discriminating, exact, fastidious, particular; captious, carping, caviling, censorious, faultfinding, hypercritical; acute, crucial, decisive, hazardous, important, momentous. ANT.—cursory, shallow, superficial, uncritical; appreciative, approving, commendatory, encouraging, insignificant, unimportant.

criticize, SYN.—analyze, appraise, evaluate, examine, inspect, scrutinize; blame, censure, reprehend. ANT.—approve, neglect, overlook.

critique, SYN.—commentary, criticism, examination, inspection, reconsideration, retrospect, retrospection, review, revision, survey, synopsis.

crony, SYN.—associate, attendant, colleague, companion, comrade, consort, friend, mate, partner. ANT.—adversary, enemy, stranger.

crooked, SYN.—abased, adulterated, corrupt, defiled, degraded, depraved, impaired, lowered, perverted, vitiated. ANT.—enhanced, improved, raised, restored, vitalized.

crop, SYN.—fruit, harvest, proceeds, produce, product, reaping, result,

store, yield.

crowd, SYN.—bevy, crush, horde, host, masses, mob, multitude, populace, press, rabble, swarm, throng.

crown, SYN.—apex, chief, crest, head, pinnacle, summit, top, zenith. ANT.—base, bottom, foot, foundation.

crude, SYN.—coarse, green, harsh, ill-prepared, raw, rough, unfinished, unpolished, unrefined; crass, uncouth, unrefined. ANT.—finished, well-prepared; cultivated, refined.

crucial, SYN.—acute, critical, decisive, hazardous, important, momentous. ANT.—cursory, shallow, superficial, uncritical; insignificant, unimportant.

cruel, SYN.—barbarous, brutal, ferocious, inhuman, malignant, merciless, ruthless, savage. ANT.—benevolent, compassionate, forbearing, gentle, humane, kind, merciful.

crumb, SYN.—bit, grain, iota, jot, mite, particle, scrap, shred, smidgen, speck. ANT.—aggregate, bulk, mass, quantity.

crunch, SYN.—bite, champ, chew, gnash, gnaw, nibble, nip, pierce, rend, tear.

cuddle, SYN.—caress, coddle, embrace, fondle, hug, kiss, pet. ANT.—annoy, buffet, spurn, tease, vex.

cull, SYN.—choose, elect,

opt, pick, select. ANT.—
refuse, reject.

culmination, SYN.—acme,
apex, climax, consummation, height, peak,
summit, zenith. ANT.—
anticlimax, base, depth,
floor.

culprit, SYN.—convict,
criminal, delinquent, felon, malefactor, offender,
transgressor.

cultivation, SYN.—agriculture, agronomy, farming,
gardening, horticulture,
husbandry, tillage.

culture, SYN.—breeding,
civilization, cultivation,
education, enlightenment, refinement.
ANT.—boorishness, ignorance, illiteracy, vulgarity.

cultivated, SYN.—blasé, cultivated, sophisticated,
worldly, worldly-wise.
ANT.—crude, ingenuous,
naive, simple, uncouth.

cunning, SYN.—crooked,
devious, tricky. ANT.—
direct, straight; honest,
straightforward.

cunning, SYN.—aptitude,
cleverness, faculty, ingeniousness, ingenuity,
inventiveness, resourcefulness, skill. ANT.—
clumsiness, dullness, ineptitude, stupidity.

curb, SYN.—bridle, check,
constrain, hinder, hold
back, inhibit, limit, repress, restrain, stop, suppress. ANT.—aid, encourage, incite, loosen.

cure, SYN.—antidote, help,
medicant, restorative;
redress, relief, remedy,

reparation.

curiosity, SYN.—marvel,
miracle, phenomenon,
prodigy, rarity, spectacle; admiration, amazement, astonishment,
awe, bewilderment, surprise, wonder, wonderment. ANT.—familiarity,
triviality; apathy, expectation, indifference.

curious, SYN.—inquiring,
inquisitive, interrogative,
meddling, nosy, peeping,
peering, prying, searching, snoopy; odd, peculiar, queer; strange, unusual. ANT.—incurious,
indifferent, unconcerned, uninterested;
common, ordinary.

current, SYN.—contemporary, modern, new,
novel, present, recent.
ANT.—ancient, antiquated, bygone, old,
past.

cursory, SYN.—exterior,
flimsy, frivolous, imperfect, shallow, slight, superficial. ANT.—
abstruse, complete,
deep, profound, thorough.

curt, SYN.—abrupt, hasty,
precipitate, sudden;
blunt, brusque, rude;
harsh, rough, sharp.
ANT.—courteous, gradual, smooth.

curtail, SYN.—abbreviate,
abridge, condense, contract, diminish, lessen,
limit, reduce, restrict,
shorten. ANT.—elongate,
extend, lengthen.

curve, SYN.—bend, bow,
crook, deflect, incline,

lean, stoop, turn, twist. ANT.—break, resist, stiffen, straighten.

custody, SYN.—care, charge, guardianship, ward. ANT.—disregard, indifference, neglect, negligence.

custom, SYN.—fashion, habit, practice, routine, usage, use, wont.

customary, SYN.—accustomed, common, everyday, familiar, general, habitual, normal, ordinary, usual. ANT.—abnormal, exceptional, extraordinary, irregular, rare.

cylindrical, SYN.—bulbous, chubby, circular, complete, curved, entire, globular, plump, rotund, round, spherical.

D

dainty, SYN.—delicate, elegant, exquisite, fastidious, frail, slender, slight, pleasant, pleasing. ANT.—brutal, coarse, rude, tough, vulgar

damage, SYN.—deface, harm, hurt, impair, injure, mar, spoil. ANT.—ameliorate, benefit, enhance, mend, repair.

damaging, SYN.—deleterious, detrimental, harmful, hurtful, injurious, mischievous. ANT.—advantageous, beneficial, helpful, profitable, salutary.

danger, SYN.—hazard, jeopardy, peril, risk. ANT.—defense, immunity, protection, safety.

dangerous, SYN.—critical, hazardous, insecure, menacing, perilous, precarious, risky, threatening, unsafe. ANT.—firm, protected, safe, secure.

dare, SYN.—object to, question, brave, challenge, defy, call, invoke, summon.

daring, SYN.—adventurous, bold, chivalrous, enterprising, foolhardy, precipitate, rash. ANT.—cautious, hesitating, timid.

dark, SYN.—black, dim, gloomy, murky, obscure, shadowy, unilluminated; dusky, opaque, sable, swarthy; dismal, gloomy, mournful, somber, sorrowful; evil, sinister, sullen, wicked; hidden, mystic, occult, secret. ANT.—light; bright, clear; pleasant, lucid.

dash, SYN.—beat, buffet, hit, knock, pound, pummel, punch, smite, strike, thrash, thump. ANT.—defend, shield, stroke.

dead, SYN.—deceased, defunct, departed, dull, gone, inanimate, insensible, lifeless, spiritless, unconscious. ANT.—alive, animate, living, stirring.

deafening, SYN.—clamorous, loud, noisy, resounding, sonorous, stentorian, vociferous. ANT.—dulcet, inaudible, quiet, soft, subdued.

dear, SYN.—beloved, esteemed, precious, valued; costly, expensive, valuable. ANT.—despised, unwanted; cheap.

debase, SYN.—abase, adulterate, alloy, corrupt, defile, degrade, deprave, depress, humiliate, impair, lower, pervert, vitiate. ANT.—enhance, improve, raise, restore, vitalize.

debate, SYN.—argue, discuss, dispute, plead, reason, wrangle. ANT.—ignore, overlook, reject, spurn.

decay, SYN.—decline, decompose, crease, disintegrate, dwindle, ebb, putrefy, rot, spoil, wane, waste. ANT.—flourish, grow, increase, luxuriate, rise.

deceased, SYN.—dead, defunct, departed, dull, gone, inanimate, insensible, lifeless, spiritless, unconscious. ANT.—alive, animate, living, stirring.

deceit, SYN.—beguilement, cheat, chicanery, cunning, deceitfulness, deception, duplicity, fraud, guile, sham, trick, wiliness. ANT.—candor, honesty, openness, sincerity, truthfulness.

deceitful, SYN.—deceptive, delusive, delusory, fallacious, false, illusive, misleading, specious. ANT.—authentic, genuine, honest, real, truthful.

decent, SYN.—adequate, becoming, befitting, comely, decorous, fit, proper, respectable, seemly, suitable, tolerable. ANT.—coarse, gross, indecent, reprehensible, vulgar.

deception, SYN.—beguilement, cheat, chicanery, cunning, deceit, deceitfulness, duplicity, fraud, guile, sham, trick, wiliness. ANT.—candor, honesty, openness, sincerity, truthfulness.

deceptive, SYN.—deceitful, delusive, delusory, fallacious, false, illusive, misleading, specious. ANT.—authentic, genuine, honest, real, truthful.

decide, SYN.—adjudicate, close, conclude, determine, end, resolve, settle, terminate. ANT.—doubt, hesitate, suspend, vacillate, waver.

decipher, SYN.—construe, decode, elucidate, explain, explicate, interpret, render, solve, translate, unravel. ANT.—confuse, distort, falsify, misconstrue, misinterpret.

declare, SYN.—affirm, announce, assert, aver, broadcast, express, make known, proclaim, profess, promulgate, protest, state, tell. ANT.—conceal, repress, suppress, withhold.

declaration, SYN.—allegation, announcement, mention, report, assertion, proposition, statement, thesis.

decline, SYN.—incline, slant, slope; descend,

sink, wane; decay, decrease, degenerate, depreciate, deteriorate, diminish, dwindle, weaken; refuse, reject. ANT.—ameliorate, appreciate, ascend, increase; accept.

decorate, SYN.—adorn, beautify, deck, embellish, enrich, garnish, ornament, trim. ANT.—debase, defame, expose, strip, uncover.

decoration, SYN.—adornment, embellishment, garnish, ornament, ornamentation.

decrease, SYN.—abate, curtail, decline, deduct, diminish, dwindle, lessen, reduce, remove, shorten, subtract, wane. ANT.—amplify, enlarge, expand, grow, increase.

decree, SYN.—act, edict, law, statute. ANT.—inactivity.

decree, SYN.—decide, determine; adjudicate, arbitrate, condemn, judge.

decrepit, SYN.—delicate, enervated, exhausted, faint, feeble, forceless, impaired, infirm, languid, powerless, puny, weak. ANT.—forceful, lusty, stout, strong, vigorous.

decry, SYN.—belittle, depreciate, derogate, discredit, lower, minimize, undervalue. ANT.—aggrandize, commend, exalt, magnify, praise.

dedicated, SYN.—affectionate, ardent, attached, devoted, disposed, earnest, faithful, fond, given

up to, inclined, loyal, prone, true, wedded. ANT.—detached, disinclined, indisposed, untrammeled.

deduct, SYN.—abate, curtail, decrease, diminish, dwindle, lessen, reduce, remove, shorten, subtract. ANT.—amplify, enlarge, expand, grow, increase.

deed, SYN.—accomplishment, act, action, doing, execution, feat, operation, performance, transaction. ANT.—cessation, deliberation, inactivity, inhibition, intention.

deem, SYN.—account, believe, consider, esteem, estimate, hold, judge, rate, reckon, regard, think, view; elucidate, explain, expound.

deface, SYN.—damage, harm, hurt, impair, injure, mar, spoil. ANT.—ameliorate, benefit, enhance, mend, repair.

defamation, SYN.—abuse, aspersion, desecration, dishonor, disparagement, insult, invective, maltreatment, misuse, outrage, perversion, profanation, reproach, reviling, upbraiding. ANT.—approval, commendation, laudation, plaudit, respect.

default, SYN.—dereliction, failure, omission, deficiency, lack, loss, want. ANT.—achievement, success, victory, sufficiency.

defeat, SYN.—beat, conquer, crush, humble, master, overcome, quell, rout, subdue, subjugate, surmount, vanquish. ANT.—capitulate, cede, lose, retreat, surrender.

defect, SYN.—blemish, error, failure, fault, flaw, imperfection, mistake, omission, shortcoming, vice. ANT.—completeness, correctness, perfection.

defend, SYN.—fortify, guard, protect, safeguard, screen, shield; assert, espouse, justify, maintain, uphold, vindicate. ANT.—assault, attack, deny, oppose, submit.

deference, SYN.—admiration, adoration, dignity, esteem, fame, glory, homage, honor, praise, renown, respect, reverence, worship. ANT.—contempt, derision, disgrace, dishonor, reproach.

defense, SYN.—bulwark, fence, refuge, safeguard, shelter, shield; guard, protection, security.

deficient, SYN.—defective, inadequate, incomplete, insufficient, lacking, scanty, short. ANT.—adequate, ample, enough, satisfactory, sufficient.

definite, SYN.—certain, correct, determined, exact, explicit, fixed, precise, prescribed, specific. ANT.—ambiguous, confused, dubious, equivocal, indefinite.

defunct, SYN.—dead, deceased, departed, dull, gone, inanimate, insensible, lifeless, spiritless, unconscious. ANT.—alive, animate, living, stirring.

defy, SYN.—attack, confront, hinder, impede, obstruct, oppose, resist, thwart, withstand. ANT.—accede, allow, cooperate, relent, yield.

degenerate, SYN.—decay, decrease, decline, depreciate, deteriorate, diminish, dwindle, weaken. ANT.—ameliorate, appreciate, ascend, increase.

degrade, SYN.—abase, abash, break, crush, debase, humble, humiliate, mortify, shame, subdue. ANT.—elevate, exalt, honor, praise.

delay, SYN.—defer, postpone, procrastinate; arrest, detain, hinder, impede, retard, stay; dawdle, linger, loiter, tarry. ANT.—expedite, hasten, precipitate, quicken.

delectable, SYN.—delightful, delicious, luscious, palatable, savory, sweet, tasty. ANT.—acrid, distasteful, nauseous, unpalatable, unsavory.

deleterious, SYN.—bad, baleful, base, evil, immoral, iniquitous, noxious, pernicious, sinful, unsound, unwholesome, villainous, wicked. ANT.—excellent, good, honorable, moral, reputable.

deliberate, SYN.—contemplated, designed, intended, intentional, premeditated, studied, voluntary, wilful. ANT.—accidental, fortuitous.

deliberate, SYN.—consider, contemplate, examine, heed, meditate, ponder, reflect, study, weigh. ANT.—ignore, neglect, overlook.

delicate, SYN.—dainty, elegant, exquisite, fastidious, feeble, frail, sensitive, slender, slight, weak; pleasant, pleasing, savory. ANT.—brutal, coarse, rude, tough, vulgar.

delicious, SYN.—delectable, delightful, luscious, palatable, savory, sweet, tasty. ANT.—acrid, distasteful, nauseous, unpalatable, unsavory.

delight, SYN.—bliss, ecstasy, enjoyment, gladness, happiness, joy, pleasure, rapture, transport. ANT.—annoyance, dejection, melancholy, misery, sorrow.

delighted, SYN.—blessed, cheerful, contented, fortunate, gay, glad, happy, joyful, lucky, merry, opportune, propitious. ANT.—blue, depressed, gloomy, morose.

delightful, SYN.—acceptable, amiable, agreeable, charming, gratifying, pleasant, pleasing, pleasurable, suitable, welcome. ANT.—

disagreeable, obnoxious, offensive, unpleasant.

deliver, SYN.—commit, give, impart, transfer, yield; announce, communicate, impart, proclaim, publish; emancipate, free, liberate, release, rescue, save. ANT.—confine, withhold; capture, imprison, restrict.

delusion, SYN.—dream, fantasy, hallucination, illusion, mirage, phantom, vision. ANT.—actuality, reality, substance.

demand, SYN.—ask, ask for, challenge, claim, exact, require; inquire, necessitate. ANT.—give, offer, present, tender.

demean, SYN.—act, bear, behave, carry, comport, conduct, deport, interact, manage, operate.

demolish, SYN.—annihilate, destroy, devastate, eradicate, exterminate, extinguish, obliterate, ravage, raze, ruin, wreck. ANT.—construct, establish, make, preserve, save.

demonstrate, SYN.—display, exhibit, show; establish, evince, manifest, prove. ANT.—conceal, hide.

demur, SYN.—delay, doubt, falter, hesitate, pause, scruple, stammer, stutter, vacillate, waver. ANT.—continue, decide, persevere, proceed, resolve.

denounce, SYN.—blame, censure, condemn, reprehend, reproach, reprobate, reprove, upbraid. ANT.—approve, commend, condone, forgive, praise.

dense, SYN.—close, compact, compressed, concentrated, crowded, thick; dull, obtuse, slow, stupid. ANT.—dispersed, dissipated, sparse; clever, quick.

deny, SYN.—contradict, contravene, gainsay, refute; abjure, disavow, disown, forbid; refuse, repudiate, withhold. ANT.—affirm, assert, concede, confirm.

depart, SYN.—abandon, desert, forsake, give up, go, leave, quit, relinquish, renounce, withdraw. ANT.—abide, remain, stay, tarry.

departure, SYN.—farewell, good-by, leave-taking, valediction. ANT.—greeting, salutation, welcome.

dependable, SYN.—certain, reliable, safe, secure, sure, tried, trustworthy, trusty. ANT.—dubious, fallible, questionable, uncertain, unreliable.

dependent, SYN.—conditional, contingent, depending, relying, subject, subordinate. ANT.—absolute, autonomous, casual, independent, original.

depict, SYN.—characterize, describe, explain, narrate, portray, recount, relate.

deplore, SYN.—bemoan, bewail, grieve, lament, mourn, repine, wail, weep.

deport, SYN.—banish, dismiss, dispel, eject, exclude, exile, expatriate, expel, ostracize, oust. ANT.—accept, admit, harbor, receive, shelter.

deportment, SYN.—action, bearing, behavior, carriage, conduct, deed, demeanor, disposition, manner.

depreciate, SYN.—descend, sink, wane; decay, decline, decrease, degenerate, deteriorate, diminish, dwindle, weaken. ANT.—ameliorate, appreciate, ascend, increase.

depression, SYN.—despair, desperation, despondency, discouragement, gloom, hopelessness, pessimism. ANT.—confidence, elation, hope, optimism.

dereliction, SYN.—failure, fiasco, miscarriage; default, omission; decay, decline; deficiency, lack, loss, want. ANT.—achievement, success, victory; sufficiency.

derision, SYN.—banter, gibe, irony, jeering, mockery, raillery, ridicule, sarcasm, satire, sneering.

derivation, SYN.—beginning, birth, commencement, cradle, foundation, inception, origin, source, spring, start. ANT.—end, harvest, issue, outcome, product.

descend, SYN.—incline, slant, slope; decline, sink, wane. ANT.—ameliorate, appreciate, ascend, increase.

description, SYN.—account, chronicle, detail, history, narration, narrative, recital, relation; computation, reckoning, record. ANT.—caricature, confusion, distortion, misrepresentation.

desecration, SYN.—abuse, aspersion, defamation, dishonor, disparagement, insult, maltreatment, misuse, outrage, perversion, profanation, reviling. ANT.—approval, commendation, laudation, respect.

desert, SYN.—abandon, abdicate, abjure, relinquish, renounce, resign, surrender, vacate, waive; forsake, leave, quit. ANT.—defend, maintain, uphold; stay, support.

design, SYN.—delineation, draft, drawing, outline, plan, sketch; artfulness, contrivance, cunning, objective, purpose. ANT.—result, candor, sincerity; accident, chance.

design, SYN.—contrive, create, devise, invent, plan, scheme; intend, mean, purpose; draw, sketch.

designate, SYN.—denote, disclose, imply, indicate, intimate, manifest, reveal, show, signify, specify. ANT.—conceal, distract, divert, falsify, mislead.

desire, SYN.—appetite, aspiration, craving, hungering, longing, lust, urge, wish, yearning. ANT.— abomination, aversion, distaste, hate, loathing.

desist, SYN.—abstain, arrest, bar, cease, check, close, cork, discontinue, end, halt, hinder, impede, interrupt, obstruct, plug, seal, stop, terminate. ANT.—begin, proceed, promote, speed, start.

desolate, SYN.—abandoned, bare, bleak, deserted, forlorn, forsaken, lonely, solitary, uninhabited, waste, wild. ANT.—attended, cultivated, fertile.

despair, SYN.—depression, desperation, despondency, discouragement, gloom, hopelessness, pessimism. ANT.—confidence, elation, hope, optimism.

desperate, SYN.—audacious, daring, despairing, despondent, determined, hopeless, reckless, wild. ANT.—assured, composed, confident, hopeful, optimistic.

desperation, SYN.—depression, despair, despondency, discouragement, gloom, hopelessness, pessimism. ANT.—confidence, elation, hope, optimism.

despicable, SYN.—base, contemptible, low, mean, sordid, vile, vulgar; malicious, nasty, offensive, selfish. ANT.—admirable, dignified, exalted, generous, noble.

despise, SYN.—abhor, abominate, detest, dislike, hate, loathe. ANT.—admire, approve, cherish, like, love.

despondent, SYN.—dejected, depressed, disconsolate, dismal, dispirited, doleful, gloomy, glum, melancholy, moody, sad, somber, sorrowful. ANT.—cheerful, happy, joyous, merry.

despotic, SYN.—absolute, complete, entire, ultimate, unconditional, unqualified, unrestricted; arbitrary, authoritative, tyrannous. ANT.—accountable, conditional, contingent, dependent, qualified.

destiny, SYN.—consequence, doom, fate, fortune, lot, portion; issue, necessity, outcome, result.

destitute, SYN.—impecunious, indigent, needy, penniless, poor, poverty-stricken. ANT.—affluent, opulent, rich, wealthy.

destroy, SYN.—annihilate, demolish, devastate, eradicate, exterminate, extinguish, obliterate, ravage, raze, ruin, wreck. ANT.—construct, establish, make, preserve, save.

destroyed, SYN.—broken, crushed, flattened, fractured, interrupted, reduced, rent, ruptured, separated, shattered, smashed, wrecked. ANT.—integral, repaired, united, whole.

destructive, SYN.—baneful, deadly, deleterious, detrimental, devastating, fatal, injurious, noxious, pernicious, ruinous. ANT.—beneficial, constructive, creative, profitable, salutary.

detach, SYN.—curtail, decrease, deduct, diminish, lessen, reduce, remove, shorten, subtract. ANT.—amplify, enlarge, expand, grow, increase.

detain, SYN.—arrest, delay, hinder, impede, retard, stay. ANT.—expedite, hasten, precipitate, quicken.

detail, SYN.—circumstance, item, minutia, part, particular; detachment, party, squad. ANT.—generality.

detect, SYN.—ascertain, devise, discover, expose, find, find out, invent, learn, originate, reveal. ANT.—cover, hide, lose, mask, screen.

determinant, SYN.—agent, cause, incentive, inducement, motive, origin, principle, reason, source. ANT.—consequence, effect, end, result.

determination, SYN.—courage, decision, firmness, fortitude, persistence, resolution, resolve, steadfastness. ANT.—inconstancy, indecision, vacillation.

determine, SYN.—conclude, decide, end, fix, resolve, settle; ascertain, verify; incline, induce, influence; condition, define, limit; compel, necessitate.

detest, SYN.—abhor, abominate, despise, dislike, hate, loathe. ANT.—admire, approve, cherish, like, love.

detestable, SYN.—abominable, execrable, foul, hateful, loathsome, odious, revolting, vile. ANT.—agreeable, commendable, delightful, pleasant.

detriment, SYN.—damage, evil, harm, hurt, ill, infliction, injury, mischief, misfortune, mishap, wrong. ANT.—benefit, boon, favor, kindness.

detrimental, SYN.—damaging, deleterious, harmful, hurtful, injurious, mischievous. ANT.—advantageous, beneficial, helpful, profitable, salutary.

develop, SYN.—amplify, create, elaborate, enlarge, evolve, expand, mature, unfold. ANT.—compress, contract, restrict, stunt, wither.

development, SYN.—elaboration, expansion, unfolding, unraveling; evolution, growth, maturing, progress. ANT.—abbreviation, compres-

sion, curtailment.

deviate, SYN.—bend, crook, deflect, digress, diverge, divert, sidetrack, stray, wander. ANT.—continue, follow, persist, preserve, remain.

device, SYN.—agent, apparatus, channel, instrument, means, medium, tool, utensil, vehicle. ANT.—hindrance, impediment, obstruction, preventive.

devious, SYN.—circuitous, crooked, distorted, erratic, indirect, roundabout, swerving, tortuous, wandering, winding; crooked, cunning, tricky. ANT.—direct, straight, honest, straightforward.

devoted, SYN.—addicted, affectionate, ardent, attached, dedicated, disposed, earnest, faithful, fond, given up to, inclined, loyal, prone, true, wedded. ANT.—detached, disinclined, indisposed, untrammeled.

devotion, SYN.—affection, ardor, attachment, consecration, dedication, devoutness, fidelity, love, loyalty, piety, religiousness, zeal. ANT.—alienation, apathy, aversion, indifference, unfaithfulness.

devout, SYN.—holy, pietistic, pious, religious, reverent, sacred, sanctimonious, spiritual, theological. ANT.—atheistic, impious, profane, secular, skeptical.

dexterity, SYN.—ability, aptitude, aptness, capability, efficiency, faculty, power, qualification, skill, talent. ANT.—disability, incapacity, incompetency, unreadiness.

dialect, SYN.—cant, diction, idiom, jargon, language, lingo, phraseology, slang, speech, tongue, vernacular. ANT.—babble, drivel, gibberish, nonsense.

dialogue, SYN.—chat, colloquy, conference, conversation, interview, parley, talk.

dictator, SYN.—autocrat, despot, oppressor, persecutor, tyrant.

die, SYN.—cease, decay, decease, decline, depart, expire, fade, languish, perish, sink, wane, wither. ANT.—begin, flourish, grow, live, survive.

difference, SYN.—disparity, dissimilarity, distinction, separation, variety; disagreement, discord, dissension. ANT.—identity, resemblance, similarity; agreement, harmony.

different, SYN.—contrary, dissimilar, distinct, diverse, incongruous, opposite, unlike, variant; divers, miscellaneous, sundry, various. ANT.—alike, congruous, identical, same, similar.

differentiate, SYN.—detect, discern, discriminate, distinguish, perceive, recognize, separate. ANT.—confound, confuse, mingle, omit, overlook.

difficult, SYN.—arduous, complicated, demanding, hard, intricate, involved, laborious, obscure, perplexing, toilsome, trying. ANT.—easy, effortless, facile, simple.

digress, SYN.—bend, crook, deflect, deviate, diverge, divert, sidetrack, stray, wander. ANT.—continue, follow, persist, preserve, remain.

dilate, SYN.—amplify, augment, distend, enlarge, expand, increase, magnify, widen. ANT.—abridge, contract, diminish, restrict, shrink.

dilemma, SYN.—condition, difficulty, fix, plight, predicament, scrape, situation, strait. ANT.—calmness, comfort, ease, satisfaction.

diligent, SYN.—active, assiduous, busy, careful, hard-working, industrious, patient, perseverant. ANT.—apathetic, careless, indifferent, lethargic, unconcerned.

dim, SYN.—faded, faint, indistinct, pale. ANT.—conspicuous, glaring.

diminish, SYN.—abate, assuage, decrease, lessen, lower, moderate, reduce, suppress. ANT.—amplify, enlarge, increase, intensify, revive.

din, SYN.—babble, clamor, noise, outcry, racket, row, sound, tumult, uproar. ANT.—hush, quiet, silence, stillness.

diplomacy, SYN.—address, adroitness, dexterity, finesse, knack, poise, savoir fair, skill, tact. ANT.— awkwardness, blunder, incompetence, rudeness, vulgarity.

diplomatic, SYN.—adroit, discreet, discriminating, judicious, politic, tactful. ANT.—boorish, churlish, coarse, gruff, rude.

dire, SYN.—appalling, awful, dreadful, fearful, frightful, ghastly, hideous, horrible, horrid, repulsive, terrible. ANT.—beautiful, enchanting, enjoyable, fascinating, lovely.

direct, SYN.—aim, level, point, train; conduct, govern, guide, manage, regulate, rule; bid, command, instruct, order. ANT.—deceive, distract, misdirect, misguide.

direction, SYN.—course, inclination, tendency, trend, way; administration, management, superintendence; guidance, instruction, order.

dirty, SYN.—filthy, foul, grimy, muddy, soiled, squalid; indecent, nasty, obscene; base, contemptible, despicable, low, mean, pitiful, shabby. ANT.—clean, neat, presentable; pure, wholesome.

disability, SYN.—handicap, impotence, inability, incapacity, incompetence, weakness. ANT.—ability, capability, power, strength.

disabled, SYN.—crippled, defective, deformed, feeble, halt, hobbling, lame, limping, maimed, unconvincing, unsatisfactory, weak. ANT.—agile, athletic, robust, sound, vigorous.

disagreement, SYN.—challenge, difference, dissent, dissentience, noncompliance, nonconformity, objection, protest, recusancy, rejection, remonstrance, variance. ANT.—acceptance, agreement, assent, compliance.

disaster, SYN.—adversity, calamity, casualty, catastrophe, mishap, ruin. ANT.—advantage, fortune, welfare.

disavow, SYN.—disclaim, disown, reject, renounce, retract, revoke. ANT.—acknowledge, assert, recognize.

discern, SYN.—descry, detect, differentiate, discriminate, distinguish, observe, perceive, recognize, see, separate. ANT.—confound, confuse, mingle, omit, overlook.

discerning, SYN.—accurate, critical, discriminating, exact, fastidious, particular. ANT.—cursory, shallow, superficial, uncritical.

discernment, SYN.—acumen, insight, intuition, penetration, perspicuity. ANT.—obtuseness.

discharge, SYN.—banish,

discard, dismiss, eject, exile, oust, remove, send off. ANT.—accept, detain, recall, retain.

disciple, SYN.—adherent, devotee, follower, supporter, votary; learner, pupil, scholar, student.

discipline, SYN.—control, order, regulation, restraint, self-control; exercise, instruction, practice, training; correction, punishment. ANT.—chaos, confusion, turbulence.

disclaim, SYN.—deny, disavow, disown, reject, renounce, retract, revoke. ANT.—acknowledge, assent, recognize.

disclose, SYN.—betray, discover, divulge, expose, impart, reveal, show, uncover. ANT.—cloak, conceal, cover, hide, obscure.

disconsolate, SYN.—cheerless, dejected, depressed, despondent, dismal, doleful, downcast, gloomy, lugubrious, melancholy, mournful, sad, somber, sorrowful. ANT.—cheerful, glad, happy, joyous, merry.

discontinue, SYN.—adjourn, defer, delay, interrupt, postpone, stay, suspend. ANT.—continue, maintain, persist, proceed, prolong.

discourage, SYN.—block, check, hamper, hinder, impede, obstruct, prevent, resist, restrain, retard, stop, thwart. ANT.—assist, expedite,

facilitate, further, promote.

discourteous, SYN.—blunt, boorish, gruff, impolite, impudent, insolent, rough, rude, saucy, surly, uncivil, vulgar. ANT.—civil, genteel, polished, courtly, dignified, noble, stately.

discover, SYN.—ascertain, detect, devise, expose, find, find out, invent, learn, originate, reveal. ANT.—cover, hide, lose, mask, screen.

discreet, SYN.—adroit, diplomatic, discriminating, judicious, politic, tactful. ANT.—boorish, churlish, coarse, gruff, rude.

discrepant, SYN.—contradictory, contrary, illogical, incompatible, incongruous, inconsistent, irreconcilable, paradoxical, unsteady, vacillating, wavering. ANT.—compatible, congruous, consistent, correspondent.

discriminate, SYN.—descry, detect, differentiate, discern, distinguish, perceive, recognize, separate. ANT.—confound, confuse, mingle, omit, overlook.

discriminating, SYN.—accurate, critical, discerning, exact, fastidious, particular. ANT.—cursory, shallow, superficial, uncritical, insignificant, unimportant.

discrimination, SYN.—discernment, intelligence, judgment, perspicacity, sagacity, understanding, wisdom. ANT.—arbitrariness, senselessness, stupidity, thoughtlessness.

discuss, SYN.—blab, chat, converse, gossip, jabber, mutter, prattle, speak, tattle; argue, comment, declaim, discourse, harangue, lecture, plead, preach, rant, spout; confer, consult, deliberate, reason, talk.

discussion, SYN.—chatter, conference, conversation, dialogue, discourse, gossip, lecture, report, rumor, speech, talk. ANT.— correspondence, meditation, silence, writing.

disdain, SYN.—contempt, contumely, derision, detestation, hatred, scorn. ANT.—awe, esteem, regard, respect, reverence.

disease, SYN.—ailment, complaint, disorder, illness, infirmity, malady, sickness. ANT.—health, healthiness, soundness, vigor.

disgrace, SYN.—abashment, chagrin, humiliation, mortification, dishonor, disrepute, ignominy, odium, opprobrium, scandal, shame. ANT.—dignity, glory, honor, praise, renown.

disgraceful, SYN.—discreditable, dishonorable, disreputable, ignominious, scandalous, shameful. ANT.—esteemed, honorable, renowned, respectable.

disguise, SYN.—affectation, cloak, excuse, garb, mask, pretense, pretension, pretext, semblance, show, simulation, subterfuge. ANT.—actuality, fact, reality, sincerity, truth.

disguise, SYN.—cloak, conceal, cover, hidden, mask, screen, secrete, suppress, veil, withhold. ANT.—disclose, divulge, expose, reveal, show, uncover.

dishonest, SYN.—contaminated, corrupt, corrupted, crooked, debased, depraved, impure, profligate, putrid, spoiled, tainted, unsound, venal, vitiated.

dishonor, SYN.—abashment, chagrin, humiliation, mortification; disgrace, disrepute, ignominy, odium, opprobrium, scandal, shame. ANT.—dignity, glory, honor, praise, renown.

disintegrate, SYN.—decay, decline, decompose, decrease, dwindle, ebb, putrefy, rot spoil, wane, waste. ANT.—flourish, grow, increase, luxuriate, rise.

dislike, SYN.—abhorrence, antipathy, aversion, disgust, disinclination, distaste, dread, hatred, loathing, repugnance, repulsion, reluctance. ANT.—affection, attachment, devotion, enthusiasm.

dislike, SYN.—abhor, abominate, despise, detest, dislike, hate, loathe. ANT.—admire, approve, cherish, like, love.

disloyal, SYN.—apostate, faithless, false, perfidious, recreant, traitorous, treacherous, treasonable. ANT.—constant, devoted, loyal, true.

dismal, SYN.—bleak, cheerless, dark, doleful, dreary, dull, funereal, gloomy, lonesome, melancholy, sad, somber. ANT.—cheerful, gay, joyous, lively.

dismiss, SYN.—banish, discard, discharge, eject, exile, oust, remove, send off. ANT.—accept, detain, recall, retain.

disobedient, SYN.—defiant, forward, insubordinate, rebellious, refractory, undutiful, unruly. ANT.—compliant, dutiful, obedient, submissive.

disobey, SYN.—break, infringe, invade, transgress, violate, defile.

disorder, SYN.—anarchy, chaos, confusion, disorganization, jumble, muddle. ANT.—order, organization, system.

disorganization, SYN.—anarchy, chaos, confusion, disorder, jumble, muddle. ANT.—order, organization, system.

disorganized, SYN.—bewildered, confused, deranged, disconcerted, disordered, indistinct, mixed, muddled, perplexed. ANT.—clear, lucid, obvious, organized, plain.

disparage, SYN.—belittle, decry, depreciate, derogate, discredit, lower, minimize, undervalue. ANT.—aggrandize, commend, exalt, magnify, praise.

disparagement, SYN.—belittling, decrying, depreciation, derogation, discredit, lowering, minimizing, undervaluing. ANT. — aggrandizement, commendation, exalting, magnification, praise.

dispatch, SYN.—cast, discharge, emit, impel, propel, send, throw, transmit. ANT.—bring, get, hold, receive, retain.

dispel, SYN.—diffuse, disperse, disseminate, dissipate, scatter, separate. ANT.—accumulate, amass, assemble, collect, gather.

dispense, SYN.—allot, apportion, deal, distribute, divide, mete; allocate, appropriate, assign, give, grant, measure. ANT.—confiscate, keep, refuse, retain, withhold.

disperse, SYN.—diffuse, dispel, disseminate, dissipate, scatter, separate. ANT.—accumulate, amass, assemble, collect, gather.

displace, SYN.—dislodge, move, remove, shift, transfer, transport. ANT.—leave, remain, stay, retain.

display, SYN.—exhibit, expose, flaunt, parade, reveal, show, spread out.

ANT.—conceal, cover, disguise, hide.

disposition, SYN.—action, bearing, behavior, carriage, conduct, deed, demeanor, deportment, manner.

dispute, SYN.—argument, contention, controversy, debate, disagreement, quarrel, squabble. ANT.—agreement, concord, decision, harmony.

dispute, SYN.—altercate, argue, bicker, contend, contest, debate, discuss, quarrel, squabble, wrangle. ANT.—agree, allow, assent, concede.

disregard, SYN.—ignore, neglect, omit, overlook, skip, slight. ANT.—include, notice, regard.

dissent, SYN.—challenge, difference, disagreement, dissentience, noncompliance, nonconformity, objection, protest, recusancy, rejection, remonstrance, variance. ANT.—acceptance, agreement, assent, compliance.

dissimilar, SYN.—contrary, different, distinct, divergent, diverse, incongruous, opposite, unlike, variant; divers, miscellaneous, sundry, various. ANT.—alike, congruous, identical, same, similar.

dissimulation, SYN.—cant, deceit, hypocrisy, pretense, sanctimony. ANT.—candor, frankness, honesty, openness, truth.

dissipate, SYN.—consume,

lavish, misuse, scatter, spend, squander, waste, wear out; diminish, dwindle. ANT.—accumulate, conserve, economize, preserve, save.

distant, SYN.—far, faraway, remote, removed; aloof, cold, reserved, stiff, unfriendly. ANT.—close, near, nigh, cordial, friendly.

distinct, SYN.—apparent, clear, evident, intelligible, lucid, manifest, obvious, plain, unmistakable, visible. ANT.—ambiguous, obscure, unclear, vague.

distinction, SYN.—attribute, characteristic, feature, peculiarity, property, quality, trait. ANT.—being, essence, nature, substance.

distinctive, SYN.—eccentric, exceptional, odd, rare, singular, strange, striking, unusual; characteristic, individual, particular, peculiar, special. ANT.—common, general, normal, ordinary.

distinguish, SYN.—descry, detect, differentiate, discern, discriminate, perceive, recognize, separate. ANT.—confound, confuse, mingle, omit, overlook.

distinguished, SYN.—conspicuous, elevated, eminent, famous, glorious, illustrious, noted, prominent, renowned. ANT.—common, obscure, ordinary, unimportant, unknown.

distracted, SYN.—absent, absent-minded, abstracted, inattentive, preoccupied. ANT.—attending, present; attentive, watchful.

distress, SYN.—agony, anguish, grief, misery, suffering, torment, torture. ANT.—comfort, joy, relief, solace.

distribute, SYN.—allot, apportion, deal, dispense, divide, dole, mete, scatter, spread; classify, group, sort.

district, SYN.—country, division, domain, dominion, land, place, province, quarter, region, section, territory.

distrust, SYN.—ambiguity, doubt, hesitation, incredulity, scruple, skepticism, suspense, suspicion, unbelief, uncertainty. ANT.—belief, certainty, conviction, determination, faith.

disturb, SYN.—agitate, annoy, confuse, derange, discompose, interrupt, perplex, perturb, rouse, trouble, unsettle, vex, worry. ANT.—order, pacify, quiet, settle, soothe.

divide, SYN.—part, separate, sever, sunder; allot, deal out, dispense, distribute, share. ANT.—combine, convene, gather, join, unite.

divine, SYN.—celestial, godlike, heavenly, holy, superhuman, supernatural, transcendent.

ANT.—blasphemous, diabolical, mundane, profane, wicked.

diverse, SYN.—contrary, different, dissimilar, distinct, divergent, incongruous, opposite, unlike, variant; divers, miscellaneous, sundry, various. ANT.—alike, congruous, identical, same, similar.

diversity, SYN.—assortment, change, difference, dissimilarity, heterogeneity, medley, miscellany, mixture, multifariousness, variety, variousness. ANT.—homogeneity, likeness, monotony, sameness, uniformity.

divert, SYN.—avert, deflect, deviate, swerve, turn; alter, change, transmute. ANT.—arrest, fix, stand, stop; continue, proceed; endure, perpetuate.

divulge, SYN.—betray, disclose, discover, expose, impart, reveal, show, uncover. ANT.—cloak, conceal, cover, hide, obscure.

do, SYN.—accomplish, complete, conclude, consummate, effect, execute, finish, fulfill, perform, settle, terminate; carry on, conduct, discharge, transact; observe, perform, practice; make, produce, work; answer, serve, suffice.

docile, SYN.—compliant, obedient, pliant, submissive, tame, teachable, tractable, yielding.

doctrine, SYN.—belief, creed, dogma, precept, teaching, tenet. ANT.—conduct, deed, performance, practice.

doctrinaire, SYN.—arrogant, authoritarian, dictatorial, dogmatic, domineering, magisterial, opinionated, overbearing, positive; authoritative, doctrinal, formal. ANT.—fluctuating, indecisive, open-minded, questioning, skeptical.

document, SYN.—account, archive, chronicle, memorandum, minute, note, record, report, register; mark, memorial, trace, vestige.

dogma, SYN.—belief, creed, doctrine, precept, teaching, tenet. ANT.—conduct, deed, performance, practice.

dogmatic, SYN.—arrogant, authoritarian, dictatorial, doctrinaire, domineering, magisterial, opinionated, overbearing, positive; authoritative, doctrinal, formal. ANT.—fluctuating, indecisive, open-minded, questioning, skeptical.

doing, SYN.—accomplishment, act, action, deed, execution, feat, operation, performance, transaction. ANT.—cessation, deliberation, inactivity, inhibition, intention.

dole, SYN.—allot, apportion, deal, dispense, distribute, divide, mete, scatter, spread.

doleful, SYN.—bleak, cheerless, dark, dismal, dreary, dull, funereal, gloomy, lonesome, melancholy, sad, somber. ANT.—cheerful, gay, joyous, lively.

domain, SYN.—country, district, division, dominion, land, place, province, quarter, region, section, territory.

dominate, SYN.—command, control, direct, govern, manage, regulate, rule, superintend. ANT.—abandon, follow, forsake, ignore, submit.

domination, SYN.—ascendancy, mastery, predominance, sovereignty, supremacy, sway, transcendence. ANT.—inferiority.

donation, SYN.—benefaction, bequest, boon, charity, endowment, favor, gift, grant, gratuity, largess, present. ANT.—deprivation, earnings, loss, purchase.

doom, SYN.—consequence, fate, fortune, lot, portion; destiny, issue, necessity, outcome, result.

dormant, SYN.—idle, inactive, indolent, inert, lazy, slothful, unemployed, unoccupied. ANT.—active, employed, industrious, occupied, working.

doubt, SYN.—ambiguity, distrust, hesitation, incredulity, scruple, skepticism, suspense, suspicion, unbelief, uncertainty. ANT.—belief, certainty, conviction, determination, faith.

doubt, SYN.—hesitate, question, waver; distrust, mistrust, suspect. ANT.—believe, confide, decide, rely on, trust.

dour, SYN.—crabbed, fretful, gloomy, glum, moody, morose, sulky, surly. ANT.—amiable, gay, joyous, merry, pleasant.

draw, SYN.—drag, haul, pull, tow, tug; extract, remove, take out, unsheathe; allure, attract, entice, induce, lure, persuade; delineate, depict, sketch, trace; compose, draft, formulate, write; deduce, derive, get, infer, obtain; extend, lengthen, prolong, protract, stretch. ANT.—alienate, contract, drive, propel, shorten.

draw from, SYN.—extract, remove, withdraw. ANT.—leave, remain, stay; retain.

drawing, SYN.—engraving, etching, illustration, image, likeness, panorama, picture, portrait, portrayal, print, representation, resemblance, scene, sketch, view.

dread, SYN.—alarm, apprehension, awe, fear, foreboding, horror, reverence, terror. ANT.—assurance, boldness, confidence, courage.

dreadful, SYN.—appalling, awful, dire, fearful, frightful, ghastly, hideous, horrible, horrid, repulsive, terrible. ANT.—beautiful, enchanting, enjoyable, fascinating, lovely.

dreary, SYN.—bleak, cheerless, dark, dismal, doleful, dull, funereal, gloomy, lonesome, melancholy, sad, somber. ANT.—cheerful, gay, joyous, lively.

dress, SYN.—apparel, array, attire, clothing, drapery, garb, garments, raiment, vestments, vesture. ANT.—nakedness, nudity.

drill, SYN.—activity, application, employment, exercise, exertion, lesson, operation, performance, practice, task, training, use. ANT.—idleness, indolence, relaxation, repose, rest.

drive, SYN.—coerce, compel, constrain, enforce, force, impel, oblige. ANT.—allure, convince, induce, persuade, prevent.

droll, SYN.—amusing, comical, farcical, funny, humorous, laughable, ludicrous, ridiculous, witty. ANT.—melancholy, sad, serious, sober, solemn.

drop, SYN.—collapse, decline, decrease, descend, diminish, fall, sink, subside; stumble, topple, tumble, droop, extend downward, hang. ANT.—arise, ascend, climb, mount, soar, steady.

drudgery, SYN.—effort, endeavor, exertion, labor, striving, task, toil, travail, work. ANT.—idleness, indolence, leisure, recreation.

drunk, SYN.—drunken, high, inebriated, intoxicated, tight, tipsy. ANT.—clear-headed, sober, temperate.

dry, SYN.—arid, dehydrated, desiccated, drained, parched, thirsty; barren, dull, insipid, plain, tedious, tiresome, uninteresting, vapid. ANT.—damp, moist; fresh, interesting, lively.

dull, SYN.—dense, slow, stupid; blunt, obtuse; boring, commonplace, dismal, dreary, monotonous, sad, tedious. ANT.—animated, lively, sharp; clear, interesting.

dumb, SYN.—brainless, crass, dense, dull, foolish, obtuse, senseless, stupid, witless. ANT.—alert, bright, clever, discerning, intelligent.

dunk, SYN.—dip, douse, immerse, plunge, sink, submerge. ANT.—elevate, recover, uplift.

duplicate, SYN.—copy, exemplar, facsimile, imitation, replica, reproduction, transcript. ANT.—original, prototype.

durability, SYN.—force, fortitude, intensity, lustiness, might, potency, power, stamina, stout-ness, strength, sturdiness, toughness, vigor. ANT.—feebleness, frailty, infirmity, weakness.

durable, SYN.—abiding, changeless, constant, enduring, fixed, indestructible, lasting, permanent, unchangeable. ANT.—ephemeral, temporary, transient, transitory, unstable.

duration, SYN.—boundary, limit, period, term, time.

dusky, SYN.—dark, dim, gloomy, murky, obscure, shadowy, unilluminated; opaque, sable, swarthy; dismal, gloomy, mournful, somber. ANT.—light; bright, clear, pleasant; lucid.

duty, SYN.—accountability, bond, compulsion, contract, engagement, obligation, responsibility. ANT.—choice, exemption, freedom.

dwelling, SYN.—abode, domicile, habitat, hearth, home, quarters, residence, seat.

E

eager, SYN.—anxious, ardent, avid, enthusiastic, fervent, hot, impassioned, impatient, keen, yearning. ANT.—apathetic, indifferent, unconcerned, uninterested.

early, SYN.—beforehand, betimes, shortly, soon. ANT.—belated, late, overdue, tardy.

earn, SYN.—achieve, acquire, attain, deserve, gain, get, merit, obtain, win. ANT.—consume, forfeit, lose, spend, waste.

earned, SYN.—adequate, condign, deserved, merited, proper, suitable. ANT.—improper, undeserved, unmerited.

earnest, SYN.—candid, frank, genuine, heartfelt, honest, open, sincere, straightforward, true, truthful, unfeigned, upright. ANT.—affected, dishonest, hypocritical, insincere, untruthful.

earth, SYN.—continent, country, field, ground, island, land, plain, region, soil, tract.

ease, SYN.—allay, alleviate, assuage, calm, comfort, facilitate, lighten, mitigate, pacify, relieve, soothe. ANT.—confound, distress, disturb, trouble, worry.

easy, SYN.—facile, light, pleasant, relaxed, simple, uncomplicated. ANT.—arduous, demanding, difficult, hard.

eccentric, SYN.—bizarre, curious, odd, peculiar, quaint, queer, singular, strange, unique, unusual. ANT.—common, familiar, normal, regular, typical.

economical, SYN.—frugal, niggardly, provident, saving, sparing, thrifty. ANT.—extravagant, improvident, lavish, prodigal, wasteful.

ecstasy, SYN.—delight, ex-

altation, gladness, rapture, transport; frenzy, madness, trance. ANT.—depression, melancholy.

edge, SYN.—border, boundary, brim, brink, extremity, hem, margin, periphery, rim, verge; intensity, keenness, sharpness, sting. ANT.—center, interior; bluntness, dullness.

edict, SYN.—act, decree, law, statute. ANT.—deliberation, inactivity, intention.

educate, SYN.—inculcate, inform, instill, instruct, school, teach, train, tutor. ANT.—misguide, misinform.

education, SYN.—cultivation, development, instruction, knowledge, learning, schooling, study, training, tutoring.

effect, SYN.—achieve, accomplish, attain, complete, consummate, do, execute, finish, fulfill, perfect, perform. ANT.—block, defeat, fail, frustrate, spoil.

effective, SYN.—adept, capable, competent, effectual, efficacious, efficient, proficient, skillful. ANT.—incompetent, ineffectual, inefficient, unskilled.

efficacy, SYN.—ability, capability, competency, effectiveness, efficiency, potency, skillfulness. ANT.—inability, ineptitude, wastefulness.

efficiency, SYN.—clarify,

decipher, explain, expound, illustrate, interpret, resolve, unfold, unravel. ANT.—baffle, confuse, darken, obscure.

efficient, SYN.—adept, capable, competent, effective, effectual, efficacious, proficient, skillful. ANT.—incompetent, ineffectual, inefficient, unskilled.

effort, SYN.—attempt, endeavor, essay, exertion, trial; labor, pains, strain, strife, struggle, toil, trouble.

effrontery, SYN.—assurance, audacity, boldness, impertinence, impudence, insolence, presumption, rudeness, sauciness. ANT.—diffidence, politeness, subserviency, truckling.

egotism, SYN.—conceit, pride, self-esteem, vanity. ANT.—diffidence, humility, meekness, modesty.

elastic, SYN.—compliant, ductile, flexible, lithe, pliable, pliant, resilient, supple, tractable. ANT.—brittle, hard, rigid, stiff, unbending.

elect, SYN.—choose, cull, opt, pick, select. ANT.—refuse, reject.

elegance, SYN.—attractiveness, beauty, charm, comeliness, fairness, grace, handsomeness, loveliness, pulchritude. ANT.—deformity, disfigurement, eyesore, homeliness, ugliness.

elegant, SYN.—beauteous, beautiful, charming, comely, fair, fine, handsome, lovely, pretty. ANT.—foul, hideous, homely, repulsive, unsightly.

elementary, SYN.—basic, fundamental, primary, rudimentary, simple. ANT.—abstract, abstruse, complex, elaborate, intricate.

elevate, SYN.—erect, exalt, heave, heighten, hoist, lift, uplift; breed, cultivate, grow, produce, raise. ANT.—abase, depreciate, depress, destroy.

elevated, SYN.—lofty, tall, towering; eminent, exalted, high, proud. ANT.—small, stunted, tiny; base, low, mean.

eliminate, SYN.—dislodge, eject, eradicate, erase, exclude, expel; extirpate, oust, remove. ANT.—accept, admit, include, involve.

elongate, SYN.—distend, distort, expand, extend, lengthen, protract, spread, strain, stretch. ANT.—contract, loosen, shrink, slacken, tighten.

elucidate, SYN.—clarify, decipher, explain, expound, illustrate, interpret, resolve, unfold, unravel. ANT.—baffle, confuse, darken, obscure.

elude, SYN.—avert, avoid, dodge, escape, eschew, forbear, forestall, free, shun, ward. ANT.—

confront, encounter, meet, oppose.

emanate, SYN.—belch, breathe, discharge, eject, emit, expel, hurl, shed, shoot, spurt, vent.

emancipate, SYN.—deliver, discharge, free, let go, liberate, release, set free. ANT.—confine, imprison, oppress, restrict, subjugate.

embarrass, SYN.—abash, discomfit, distress, entangle, fluster, hamper, hinder, mortify, perplex, rattle, trouble. ANT.—cheer, encourage, help, relieve.

embellish, SYN.—adorn, beautify, deck, decorate, enrich, garnish, ornament, trim. ANT.—debase, defame, expose, strip, uncover.

embody, SYN.—accommodate, comprise, contain, embrace, hold, include. ANT.—discharge, emit, exclude.

embrace, SYN.—clasp, hug; accept, adopt, espouse, receive, welcome; comprehend, comprise, contain, embody, include, incorporate, subsume. ANT.—reject, renounce, repudiate, scorn, spurn.

emerge, SYN.—appear, arise, arrive, emanate, issue. ANT.—disappear, vanish, withdraw.

emergency, SYN.—crisis, exigency, juncture, pass, pinch, strait, urgency.

eminence, SYN.—acclaim, credit, distinction, fame, glory, honor, notoriety, renown, reputation. ANT.—disrepute, ignominy, infamy, obscurity.

eminent, SYN.—conspicuous, distinguished, elevated, famous, glorious, illustrious, noted, prominent, renowned. ANT.—common, obscure, ordinary, unimportant, unknown.

emit, SYN.—belch, breathe, discharge, eject, emanate, expel, hurl, shed, shoot, spurt, vent.

emotion, SYN.—affection, agitation, feeling, passion, perturbation, sentiment, trepidation, turmoil. ANT.—calm, dispassion, indifference, restraint, tranquility.

employ, SYN.—apply, avail, busy, devote, occupy, use, utilize. ANT.—banish, discard, discharge, reject.

employment, SYN.—business, engagement, function, occupation, service, vocation, work. ANT.—idleness, leisure, slothfulness.

empty, SYN.—barren, devoid, hollow, senseless, unfilled, unfurnished, unoccupied, vacant, vacuous, vain, void, worthless. ANT.—full, inhabited, occupied, replete, supplied.

enclose, SYN.—bound, circumscribe, confine, encompass, envelop, fence, limit, surround. ANT.—develop, distend, enlarge, expand, expose, open.

encounter, SYN.—battle, collision, combat, conflict, duel, fight, struggle; contention, controversy, discord, inconsistency, interference, opposition, variance. ANT.—amity, concord, consonance, harmony.

encounter, SYN.—collide, confront, engage, find, greet, intersect, meet; experience, suffer, undergo. ANT.—cleave, disperse, part, scatter, separate.

encourage, SYN.—animate, cheer, countenance, embolden, exhilarate, favor, hearten, impel, incite, inspirit, urge; foster, promote, sanction, stimulate, support. ANT.—deject, deter, discourage, dispirit, dissuade.

encroach, SYN.—attack, infringe, intrude, invade, penetrate, trespass, violate. ANT.—abandon, evacuate, relinquish, vacate.

end, SYN.—aim, cessation, close, completion, conclusion, expiration, extremity, finish, object, purpose, result, termination, terminus, tip. ANT.—beginning, commencement, inception, introduction.

endanger, SYN.—expose, hazard, jeopardize, peril, risk. ANT.—insure, protect, secure.

endeavor, SYN.—attempt, effort, essay, exertion, trial; labor, pains, strain, strife, struggle, toil trouble.

endless, SYN.—boundless, eternal, illimitable, immeasurable, immense, infinite, interminable, unbounded, unlimited, vast. ANT.—bounded, circumscribed, confined, finite, limited.

endorsement, SYN.—approbation, approval, assent, commendation, consent, praise, sanction, support. ANT.—censure, reprimand, reproach, stricture.

endurance, SYN.—composure, forbearance, fortitude, long-suffering, patience, perseverance, resignation. ANT.—impatience, nervousness, restlessness, unquiet.

endure, SYN.—bear, brook, experience, suffer, sustain, tolerate, undergo; abide, continue, last, persist, remain. ANT.—fail, falter, succumb; disperse, wane.

enduring, SYN.—abiding, ceaseless, constant, continual, faithful, fixed, immutable, invariant, permanent, perpetual, persistent, unalterable, unchanging, unwavering. ANT.—fickle, mutable, vacillating, wavering.

enemy, SYN.—adversary, antagonist, competitor, foe, opponent, rival. ANT.—accomplice, ally, comrade, confederate, friend.

energetic, SYN.—active, animated, blithe, brisk,

frolicsome, lively, spirited, sprightly, supple, vigorous, vivacious. ANT.—dull, insipid, listless, stale, vapid.

energy, SYN.—dint, emphasis, force, intensity, might, potency, power, strength, vigor, coercion, compulsion, constraint, violence. ANT.—feebleness, frailty, impotence, weakness; persuasion.

enervation, SYN.—exhaustion, fatigue, languor, lassitude, tiredness, weariness. ANT.—freshness, rejuvenation, restoration, vigor, vivacity.

engage, SYN.—attach, bind, fasten, fetter, join, link, oblige, restrain, restrict, tie. ANT.—free, loose, unfasten, untie.

engender, SYN.—cause, create, fashion, form, formulate, generate, invent, make, originate, produce. ANT.—annihilate, demolish, destroy.

engross, SYN.—absorb, assimilate, consume, engulf, imbibe, swallow up; engage, occupy. ANT.—discharge, dispense, emit, expel, exude.

engulf, SYN.—absorb, assimilate, consume, imbibe, swallow up; engage, engross, occupy. ANT.—discharge, dispense, emit, expel, exude.

enigma, SYN.—conundrum, mystery, problem, puzzle, riddle. ANT.—answer, clue, key, resolution, solution.

enjoyment, SYN.—bliss, ecstasy, gladness, happiness, joy, pleasure, rapture, transport. ANT.—annoyance, dejection, melancholy, misery, sorrow.

enlarge, SYN.—amplify, augment, broaden, dilate, distend, expand, increase, magnify, widen. ANT.—abridge, contract, diminish, restrict, shrink.

enlargement, SYN.—amplification, augmentation, broadening, dilation, distension, expansion, increase, magnification, widening. ANT.—abridgement, contraction, diminish, restriction, shrinkage.

enlighten, SYN.—brighten, clarify, elucidate, illumine, illustrate, irradiate. ANT.—complicate, confuse, darken, obfuscate, obscure.

enmity, SYN.—animosity, antagonism, antipathy, hatred, hostility, ill will, invidiousness, malignity. ANT.—affection, cordiality, friendliness, good will, love.

ennoble, SYN.—aggrandize, consecrate, dignify, elevate, erect, exalt, extol, glorify, hallow, raise. ANT.—debase, degrade, dishonor, humble, humiliate.

enormous, SYN.—colossal, elephantine, gargantuan, gigantic, huge, immense, large, prodigious, vast. ANT.—diminutive, little, minute, small, tiny.

enough, SYN.—adequate, ample, capable, commensurate, fitting, satisfactory, sufficient, suitable. ANT.—deficient, lacking, scant.

ensue, SYN.—follow, succeed, come next; accompany, attend; result. ANT.—precede; guide, lead; avoid, elude, flee; cause.

entangle, SYN.—embrace, embroil, envelop, implicate, include, incriminate, involve. ANT.—disconnect, disengage, extricate, separate.

entente, SYN.—alliance, association, coalition, combination, confederacy, federation, league, partnership, union; compact, covenant, treaty. ANT.—divorce, schism, separation.

enterprise, SYN.—art, business, commerce, employment, engagement, job, occupation, profession, trade, trading, vocation, work. ANT.—avocation, hobby, pastime.

enterprising, SYN.—adventurous, bold, chivalrous, daring, foolhardy, precipitate, rash. ANT.—cautious, hesitating, timid.

entertain, SYN.—consider, contemplate, harbor, hold; amuse, beguile, cheer, delight, divert, gladden, please, regale.

ANT.—annoy, bore, disgust, disturb, repulse.

entertainment, SYN.—amusement, diversion, fun, game, pastime, play, recreation, sport. ANT.—boredom, labor, toil, work.

enthusiasm, SYN.—ardor, devotion, earnestness, excitement, fanaticism, fervency, fervor, inspiration, intensity, vehemence, warmth, zeal. ANT.—apathy, detachment, ennui, indifference, unconcern.

enthusiastic, SYN.—anxious, ardent, avid, eager, fervent, hot, impassioned, impatient, keen, yearning. ANT.—apathetic, indifferent, unconcerned, uninterested.

entice, SYN.—allure, attract, captivate, charm, enchant, fascinate, lure. ANT.—alienate, deter, repel, repulse.

entire, SYN.—all, complete, intact, integral, perfect, total, undivided, unimpaired, whole. ANT.—defective, deficient, incomplete, partial.

entrance, SYN.—doorway, entry, inlet, opening, portal. ANT.—departure, exit.

entreat, SYN.—adjure, ask, beg, beseech, crave, implore, importune, petition, pray, request, solicit, supplicate. ANT.—bestow, cede, favor, give, grant.

entrust, SYN.—commend,

commit, consign, relegate, trust; bind, obligate, pledge. ANT.—mistrust, release, renounce; free, loose.

envy, SYN.—covetousness, jealousy, spitefulness. ANT.—generosity, geniality, indifference.

episode, SYN.—circumstance, event, happening, incident, issue; occurrence.

epoch, SYN.—age, antiquity, date, era, generation, period, time.

equal, SYN.—alike, commensurate, equitable, equivalent, even, identical, like, same, uniform, unvarying. ANT.—different, disparate, dissimilar, diverse.

equilibrium, SYN.—balance, composure, poise, stability, steadiness; proportion, symmetry. ANT.—fall, imbalance, instability, unsteadiness.

equip, SYN.—endow, fit, fit out, furnish, provide, supply. ANT.—denude, despoil, divest, strip.

equitable, SYN.—fair, honest, impartial, just, reasonable, unbiased ANT — dishonorable, fraudulent, partial.

equity, SYN.—fairness, impartiality, justice, justness, law, rectitude, right. ANT.—inequity, partiality, unfairness, wrong.

equivalent, SYN.—coincident, equal, identical, indistinguishable, like,

same. ANT.—contrary, disparate, dissimilar, distinct, opposed.

era, SYN.—age, antiquity, date, epoch, generation, period, time.

eradicate, SYN.—eliminate, erase, exclude, expel, extirpate, oust, remove. ANT.—accept, admit, include, involve.

erase, SYN.—cancel, cross out, delete, eliminate, expunge, obliterate; abolish, abrogate, annul, invalidate, nullify, quash, repeal, rescind, revoke. ANT.—confirm, enact, enforce, perpetuate.

erect, SYN.—unbent, upright; straight, vertical. ANT.—circuitous, winding; bent, crooked.

erroneous, SYN.—amiss, askew, awry, fallacious, false, faulty, inaccurate, incorrect, mistaken, unprecise, untrue, wrong; improper, inappropriate, unsuitable; aberrant, bad, criminal, evil, immoral, iniquitous, reprehensible. ANT.—correct, right, true; suitable, proper.

error, SYN.—blunder, fallacy, fault, inaccuracy, mistake, slip. ANT.—accuracy, precision, truth.

erudition, SYN.—information, insight, intelligence, judgment, knowledge, learning, reason, sagacity, sageness, sense, wisdom. ANT.—foolishness, ignorance, nonsense, stupidity.

escape, SYN.—abscond, decamp, flee, fly; avert, avoid, elude, evade, shun. ANT.—catch, confront, face, invite, meet.

eschew, SYN.—avert, avoid, dodge, escape, elude, forbear, forestall, free, shun, ward. ANT.—confront, encounter, meet, oppose.

escort, SYN.—accompany, attend, follow, guard, lackey, protect, serve, tend, watch; be present, frequent.

essay, SYN.—composition, motive, subject, text, theme, thesis, topic.

essential, SYN.—basic, fundamental, important, indispensable, intrinsic, necessary, requisite, vital. ANT.—expendable, extrinsic, optional, peripheral.

establish, SYN.—form, found, institute, organize, raise; confirm, fix, ordain, sanction, settle, strengthen; prove, substantiate, verify. ANT.—abolish, demolish, overthrow, unsettle, upset; dislike, scorn.

estate, SYN.—belongings, commodities, effects, goods, merchandise, possessions, property, stock, wares, wealth. ANT.—deprivation, destitution, poverty, privation, want.

esteemed, SYN.—beloved, dear, precious, valued. ANT.—despised, unwanted.

estimate, SYN.—appraise, access, assign, calculate, compute, evaluate, fix, levy, reckon, tax.

eternal, SYN.—ceaseless, deathless, endless, everlasting, immortal, infinite, perpetual, timeless, undying. ANT.—ephemeral, finite, mortal, temporal, transient.

eternally, SYN.—always, constantly, continually, ever, evermore, forever, incessantly, perpetually, unceasingly. ANT.—fitfully, never, occasionally, rarely, sometimes.

ethereal, SYN.—divine, ghostly, holy, immaterial, incorporeal, religious, sacred, spiritual, supernatural, unearthly, unworldly. ANT.—carnal, corporeal, material, mundane, physical.

ethical, SYN.—chaste, decent, good, honorable, just, moral, pure, right, righteous, scrupulous, virtuous. ANT.—amoral, libertine, licentious, sinful, unethical.

evade, SYN.—avert, avoid, escape, shun. ANT.—catch, confront, face, invite, meet.

evaluate, SYN.—appraise, assess, assign, calculate, compute, estimate, fix, levy, reckon, tax.

event, SYN.—circumstance, episode, happening, incident, issue; consequence, end, occurrence, outcome, result.

ever, SYN.—always, constantly, continually, eternally, evermore, forever, incessantly, perpetually, unceasingly. ANT.—fitfully, never, occasionally, rarely, sometimes.

everlasting, SYN.—ceaseless, deathless, endless, eternal, immortal, infinite, perpetual, timeless, undying. ANT.—ephemeral, finite, mortal, temporal, transient.

evidence, SYN.—confirmation, corroboration, demonstration, experiment, proof, test, testimony, trial, verification. ANT.—failure, fallacy, invalidity.

evident, SYN.—apparent, clear, conspicuous, indubitable, manifest, obvious, open, overt, patent, unmistakable. ANT.—concealed, covert, hidden, obscure.

evil, SYN.—bad, baleful, base, deleterious, immoral, iniquitous, noxious, pernicious, sinful, unsound, unwholesome, villainous, wicked. ANT.—excellent, good, honorable, moral, reputable.

evil, SYN.—crime, guilt, iniquity, offense, sin, transgression, ungodliness, vice, wickedness, wrong. ANT.—goodness, innocence, purity, righteousness, virtue.

evolve, SYN.—amplify, create, develop, elaborate, enlarge, expand, mature, unfold. ANT.—compress, contract, restrict, stunt, wither.

exact, SYN.—accurate, correct, definite, distinct, precise, strict, unequivocal. ANT.—erroneous, loose, rough, vague; careless, easy, informal.

exactness, SYN.—accuracy, fidelity, precision.

exaggerate, SYN.—amplify, caricature, embroider, enlarge, expand, heighten, magnify, overstate, stretch. ANT.—belittle, depreciate, minimize, understate.

exalt, SYN.—aggrandize, consecrate, dignify, elevate, ennoble, erect, extol, glorify, hallow, raise. ANT.—debase, degrade, dishonor, humble, humiliate.

exalted, SYN.—dignified, elevated, eminent, grand, illustrious, lofty, majestic, noble, stately. ANT.—base, low, mean, plebian, vile.

examination, SYN.—exploration, inquiry, interrogation, investigation, query, quest, question, research, scrutiny. ANT.—disregard, inactivity, inattention, negligence.

examine, SYN.—analyze, assess, audit, check, contemplate, dissect, inquire, interrogate, notice, question, quiz, review, scan, scrutinize, survey, view, watch. ANT.—disregard, neglect, omit, overlook.

example, SYN.—archetype, illustration, instance,

exasperate, SYN.—aggravate, annoy, chafe, embitter, inflame, irritate, nettle, provoke, vex. ANT.—appease, mitigate, palliate, soften.

exasperation, SYN.—annoyance, chagrin, irritation, mortification, pique, vexation. ANT.—appeasement, comfort, gratification, pleasure.

excellent, SYN.—conscientious, exemplary, honest, moral, pure, reliable, virtuous, worthy; admirable, commendable, genuine, good, precious, safe, sound, valid; fair, honorable, immaculate, auspicious, beneficial, favorable, profitable, useful; able, capable, efficient, expert, proficient, skillful.

exception, SYN.—exclusion, omission, preclusion; anomaly, deviation, unusual case; affront, objection, offense. ANT.—inclusion, rule, standard.

exceptional, SYN.—infrequent, occasional, strange, unusual; choice, incomparable, precious, rare, scarce, singular, uncommon, unique. ANT.—customary, frequent, ordinary, usual; abundant, commonplace, numerous, worthless.

excess, SYN.—extravagance, immoderation, intemperance, profusion, superabundance, superfluity, surplus. ANT.—dearth, deficiency, lack, paucity, want.

excessive, SYN.—abundant, copious, extravagant, exuberant, immoderate, improvident, lavish, luxuriant, overflowing, plentiful, prodigal, profuse, wasteful. ANT.—economical, meager, poor, skimpy, sparse.

exchange, SYN.—change, substitute; convert, modify, shift, transfigure, transform, vary, veer. ANT.—retain; continue, establish, preserve, settle, stabilize.

excite, SYN.—agitate, arouse, awaken, disquiet, disturb, incite, irritate, provoke, rouse, stimulate, stir up. ANT.—allay, calm, pacify, quell, quiet.

exclaim, SYN.—call out, cry, cry out, ejaculate, shout, vociferate. ANT.—intimate, whisper, write.

exclude, SYN.—bar, blackball, except, expel, hinder, omit, ostracize, prevent, prohibit, restrain, shut out. ANT.—accept, admit, include, welcome.

exculpation, SYN.—absolution, acquittal, amnesty, forgiveness, pardon, remission. ANT.—conviction, penalty, punishment, sentence.

excuse, SYN.—absolve, acquit, condone, exculpate, exempt, forgive, free, justify, overlook, pardon, remit. ANT.—convict, prosecute, punish, retaliate, revenge.

execrable, SYN.—abominable, detestable, foul, hateful, loathsome, odious, revolting, vile. ANT.—agreeable, commendable, delightful, pleasant.

execute, SYN.—accomplish, achieve, attain, complete, consummate, do, effect, finish, fulfill, perfect, perform. ANT.—block, defeat, fail, frustrate, spoil.

execution, SYN.—accomplishment, act, action, deed, doing, feat, operation, performance, transaction. ANT.—cessation, deliberation, inactivity, inhibition, intention.

exemplar, SYN.—copy, duplicate, facsimile, imitation, replica, reproduction, transcript. ANT.—original, prototype.

exemplary, SYN.—fancied, faultless, ideal, imaginary, perfect, supreme, unreal, utopian, visionary. ANT.—actual, faulty, imperfect, material, real.

exercise, SYN.—activity, application, drill, employment, exertion, lesson, operation, performance, practice, task, training, use. ANT.—idleness, indolence, relaxation, repose, rest.

exhaust, SYN.—fatigue, tire, tucker, wear out, weary. ANT.—amuse, invigorate, refresh, restore, revive.

exhausted, SYN.—faint, fatigued, spent, tired, wearied, weary, worn. ANT.—fresh, hearty, invigorated, rested.

exhaustion, SYN.—enervation, fatigue, languor, lassitude, tiredness, weariness. ANT.—freshness, rejuvenation, restoration, vigor, vivacity.

exhibit, SYN.—display, expose, flaunt, parade, reveal, show, spread out. ANT.—conceal, cover, disguise, hide.

exhibition, SYN.—array, display, exposition, show; demonstration, flourish, ostentation, parade, spectacle, splurge; entertainment, movie, performance, production.

exile, SYN.—banishment, deportation, expatriation, expulsion, extradition, ostracism, proscription. ANT.—admittance, recall, reinstatement, retrieval, welcome.

existence, SYN.—animation, being, buoyancy, life, liveliness, spirit, vigor, vitality, vivacity. ANT.—death, demise, dullness, languor, lethargy.

exoneration, SYN.—absolution, acquittal, amnesty, forgiveness, pardon, remission.

ANT.—conviction, penalty, punishment, sentence.

expand, SYN.—advance, develop, distend, enlarge, extend, germinate, grow, increase, mature, swell. ANT.—atrophy, contract, decay, diminish, shrink, wane.

expanse, SYN.—amount, area, compass, degree, extent, length, magnitude, measure, range, reach, scope, size, stretch.

expansion, SYN.—development, elaboration, unfolding, unraveling; evolution, growth, maturing, progress. ANT.—abbreviation, compression, curtailment.

expatriation, SYN.—banishment, deportation, exile, expulsion, extradition, ostracism, proscription. ANT.—admittance, recall, reinstatement, retrieval, welcome.

expect, SYN.—anticipate, awaite, contemplate, hope for. ANT.—despair of.

expectation, SYN.—anticipation, contemplation, foresight, forethought, hope, preconception, prescience, presentiment. ANT.—doubt, dread, fear, worry.

expedite, SYN.—accelerate, dispatch, facilitate, forward, hasten, hurry, push, quickness, rush, speed. ANT.—block, hinder, impede, retard, slow.

expedition, SYN.—cruise, jaunt, journey, passage, pilgrimage, tour, travel, trip, voyage.

expel, SYN.—banish, discharge, dismiss, disown, excommunicate, exile, expatriate, ostracize, oust, proscribe; dislodge, eject, eliminate, void. ANT.—admit, favor, include, recall.

expend, SYN.—avail, employ, exploit, manipulate, operate, utilize; exercise, exert, practice; consume, exhaust, use. ANT.—ignore, neglect, overlook, waste.

expense, SYN.—charge, cost, price, value, worth.

expensive, SYN.—costly, precious, valuable; profitable, useful. ANT.—cheap, mean, poor; trashy, worthless.

expert, SYN.—able, accomplished, adept, clever, competent, cunning, ingenious, practiced, proficient, skilled, skillful, versed. ANT.—awkward, bungling, clumsy, inexpert, untrained.

expire, SYN.—cease, decay, decease, decline, depart, die, fade, languish, perish, sink, wane, wither. ANT.—begin, flourish, grow, live, survive.

explain, SYN.—clarify, decipher, elucidate, expound, illustrate, interpret, resolve, unfold, unravel. ANT.—baffle, confuse, darken, obscure.

explanation, SYN.—alibi, apology, confession, defense, excuse, justification. ANT.—accusation, complaint, denial, dissimulation.

explicit, SYN.—clear, definitive, express, lucid, manifest, specific. ANT. — ambiguous, equivocal, implicit, obscure, vague.

exploit, SYN.—deed, feat; accomplishment, achievement, attainment, performance, realization. ANT.—neglect, omission; defeat, failure.

exploit, SYN.—avail, employ, manipulate, operate, use, utilize; exercise, exert, consume, exhaust, expend; handle, manage, treat. ANT.—ignore, neglect, overlook, waste.

exposed, SYN.—agape, ajar, open, unclosed, uncovered, unlocked; clear, passable, unobstructed; accessible, public, unrestricted.

expound, SYN.—clarify, elucidate, explain, illustrate, interpret, unfold, unravel. ANT.—baffle, confuse, darken, obscure.

express, SYN.—clear, definitive, explicit, lucid, manifest, specific. ANT. — ambiguous, equivocal, implicit, obscure, vague.

express, SYN.—affirm, assert, avow, claim, declare, explain, propound, recite, recount, say, specify, state, tell, utter.

ANT.—conceal, deny, imply, retract.

expressive, SYN.—animated, clear, fresh, graphic, lively, lucid, vivid. ANT.—dull, vague.

exquisite, SYN.—choice, dainty, delicate, elegant, fine, nice, pure, refined, splendid, subtle; beautiful, handsome, pretty; small, thin. ANT.—blunt, coarse, large, rough, thick.

extend, SYN.—distend, distort, elongate, expand, lengthen, protract, spread, strain, stretch. ANT.—contract, loosen, shrink, slacken, tighten.

extended, SYN.—drawn out, elongated, lasting, lengthy, lingering, long, prolix, prolonged, protracted, tedious, wordy. ANT.—abridged, brief, concise, short, terse.

extension, SYN.—amount, area, compass, degree, expanse, extent, length, magnitude, measure, range, reach, scope, size, stretch.

extensive, SYN.—broad, expanded, large, sweeping, vast, wide. ANT.—confined, narrow, restricted.

extent, SYN.—amount, area, compass, degree, expanse, length, magnitude, measure, range, reach, scope, size, stretch.

exterior, SYN.—countenance, mug, visage; cover, face, front, surface. ANT.—timidity; back, interior, rear.

extol, SYN.—celebrate, commend, glorify, honor, laud, praise. ANT.—disregard, overlook; decry, disgrace, dishonor, profane.

extract, SYN.—abandon, depart, desert, forsake, give up, go, quit, relinquish, renounce, retire, withdraw. ANT.—abide, remain, stay, tarry.

extradition, SYN.—banishment, deportation, exile, expatriation, expulsion, ostracism, proscription. ANT.—admittance, recall, reinstatement, retrieval, welcome.

extraneous, SYN.—adverse, alien, contrasted, foreign, irrelevant, remote, strange, unconnected. ANT.—akin, germane, kindred, relevant.

extraordinary, SYN.—exceptional, marvelous, peculiar, rare, remarkable, singular, uncommon, unusual, wonderful. ANT.—common, frequent, ordinary, usual.

extravagant, SYN.—abundant, copious, excessive, exuberant, immoderate, improvident, lavish, luxuriant, overflowing, plentiful, prodigal, profuse, wasteful. ANT.—economical, meager, poor, skimpy, sparse.

extreme, SYN.—acute, arduous, distressing, exacting, hard, harsh, intense, relentless, rigid, rigorous, severe, sharp, stern, stringent, unmitigated, unyielding.

exude, SYN.—discharge, dislodge, eject, eliminate, expel, void.

F

fabrication, SYN.—allegory, fable, falsehood, fiction, invention, narrative, novel, romance, story, tale. ANT.—fact, history, reality, truth, verify.

face, SYN.—countenance, mug, visage; assurance, audacity; cover, exterior, front, surface. ANT.—timidity; back, interior, rear.

facetiousness, SYN.—humor, irony, jocularity, joke, sarcasm, satire, waggery, wit. ANT.—gravity, seriousness, sorrow.

facilitate, SYN.—allay, alleviate, assuage, calm, comfort, ease, lighten, mitigate, pacify, relieve, soothe. ANT.—confound, distress, disturb, trouble, worry.

fact, SYN.—actuality, certainty, reality, truth; act, circumstance, deed, event, incident, occurrence. ANT.—fiction, supposition, theory, delusion, falsehood.

faculty, SYN.—ability, capability, capacity, power, skill, talent; magnitude, size, volume. ANT.—impotence, inability, incapacity, stupidity.

fail, SYN.—defeat, disappoint, foil, frustrate, hinder, thwart. ANT.—accomplish, fulfill, further, promote.

failure, SYN.—fiasco, miscarriage, default, dereliction, omission; decay, decline; deficiency, lack, loss, want. ANT.—achievement, success, victory; sufficiency.

faint, SYN.—dim, faded, indistinct, pale; feeble, languid, wearied; irresolute, timid, weak. ANT.—conspicuous, glaring; strong, vigorous; brave, forceful.

fair, SYN.—bright, clear, light; attractive, blond, comely, lovely; equitable, honest, impartial, just, reasonable, unbiased; average, mediocre, passable. ANT.—foul, ugly; dishonorable, fraudulent, partial; excellent, first-rate, worst.

faith, SYN.—confidence, credence, dependence, reliance, trust; belief, creed, doctrine, dogma, persuasion, religion, tenet; constancy, fidelity, loyalty. ANT.—doubt, incredulity, mistrust, skepticism; infidelity.

faithful, SYN.—constant, devoted, loyal, staunch, steadfast, true; accurate, reliable, trusty. ANT.—disloyal, false, fickle, treacherous, untrustworthy.

fall, SYN.—collapse, decline, decrease, descend, diminish, drop, sink, subside; stumble, topple, tumble; droop, extend downward, hang. ANT.—arise, ascend, climb, mount, soar; steady.

fame, SYN.—acclaim, credit, distinction, eminence, glory, honor, notoriety, renown, reputation. ANT.—disrepute, ignominy, infamy, obscurity.

familiar, SYN.—acquainted, aware, cognizant, conversant, intimate, knowing, versed; affable, amicable, close, courteous, friendly, informal, sociable, unreserved. ANT.—affected, cold, distant, reserved, unfamiliar.

familiarity, SYN.—acquaintance, fellowship, friendship, sociability; frankness, informality, intimacy, liberty, unreserve. ANT.—constraint, distance, haughtiness, presumption, reserve.

famous, SYN.—celebrated, distinguished, eminent, glorious, illustrious, noted, renowned; well-known. ANT.—hidden, ignominious, infamous, obscure, unknown.

fanatical, SYN.—bigoted, dogmatic, illiberal, intolerant, narrowminded, prejudiced. ANT.—liberal, progressive, radical, tolerant.

fantasy, SYN.—caprice, dream, fancy, hallucination, illusion, imagination, whim.

farewell, SYN.—departure, good-by, leave-taking, valediction. ANT.—greeting, salutation, welcome.

fast, SYN.—expeditious, fleet, quick, rapid, speedy, swift; constant, firm, inflexible, secure, solid, stable, steadfast, steady, unswerving, unyielding. ANT.—slow, sluggish; insecure, loose, unstable, unsteady.

fasting, SYN.—abstention, continence, forbearance. ANT.—excess, gluttony, greed, intoxication, self-indulgence.

fat SYN.—chubby, corpulent, obese, paunchy, plump, portly, pudgy, rotund, stocky, stout, thickset. ANT.—gaunt, lean, slender, slim, thin.

fate, SYN.—consequence, doom, fortune, lot, portion; destiny, issue, necessity, outcome, result.

fatigue, SYN.—enervation, exhaustion, languor, lassitude, tiredness, weariness. ANT.—freshness, rejuvenation, restoration, vigor, vivacity.

fault, SYN.—blemish, defect, error, failure, flaw, imperfection, mistake, omission, shortcoming, vice. ANT.—completeness, correctness, perfection.

fear, SYN.—alarm, apprehension, consternation, cowardice, dismay, dread, fright, horror, panic, scare, terror, timidity, trepidation. ANT.—assurance, boldness, bravery, courage, fearlessness.

feat, SYN.—accomplishment, act, action, deed, doing, execution, operation, performance, transaction. ANT.—cessation, deliberation, inactivity, intention.

feeble, SYN.—decrepit, delicate, enervated, exhausted, faint, forceless, impaired, infirm, languid, powerless, puny, weak. ANT.—forceful, lusty, stout, strong, vigorous.

feeling, SYN.—sensation; affection, emotion, passion, sensibility, sentiment, tenderness; impression, opinion. ANT.—anesthesia; coldness, imperturbability, insensibility; fact.

fellowship, SYN.—brotherhood, brotherliness, kindness, solidarity; association, clan, fraternity, society. ANT.—acrimony, discord, opposition, strife.

feminine, SYN.—female, girlish, ladylike, maidenly, womanish, womanly. ANT.—male, manly, mannish, masculine, virile.

fertile, SYN.—bountiful, fecund, fruitful, luxuriant, plenteous, productive, prolific, rich, teeming. ANT.—barren, impotent, sterile, unproductive.

festival, SYN.—banquet, celebration, entertainment, feast, regalement.

fickle, SYN.—capricious,

changeable, fitful, inconstant, restless, unstable, variable. ANT.—constant, reliable, stable, steady, trustworthy.

fiction, SYN.—allegory, fable, fabrication, falsehood, invention, narrative, novel, romance, story, tale. ANT.—fact, history, reality, truth, verity.

fidelity, SYN.—allegiance, constancy, devotion, faithfulness, fealty, loyalty; accuracy, exactness, precision. ANT.—disloyalty, faithlessness, perfidy, treachery.

fight, SYN.—battle, brawl, combat, conflict, contend, dispute, encounter, quarrel, scuffle, skirmish, squabble, struggle, wrangle.

fill, SYN.—fill up, occupy, pervade; furnish, replenish, stock, store, supply; content, glut, gorge, sate, satiate, satisfy, stuff. ANT.—deplete, drain, empty, exhaust, void.

final, SYN.—concluding, conclusive, decisive, ending, eventual, last, latest, terminal, ultimate. ANT.—first, inaugural, incipient, original, rudimentary.

fine, SYN.—choice, dainty, delicate, elegant, exquisite, nice, pure, refined, splendid, small, thin. ANT.—blunt, coarse, large, rough, thick.

finish, SYN.—accomplish, achieve, close, complete, conclude, consummate,

do, end, execute, fulfill, get done, perfect, perform, terminate.

fire, SYN.—blaze, burning, combustion, conflagration, flame, glow, heat, warmth; ardor, fervor, intensity, passion, vigor. ANT.—cold; apathy, quiescence.

first, SYN.—beginning, earliest, initial, original, primary, prime, primeval, primitive, pristine; chief, foremost. ANT.—hindmost, last, latest, least, subordinate.

fit, SYN.—accommodate, adapt, adjust, conform, suit. ANT.—disturb, misapply, misfit.

fitful, SYN.—capricious, changeable, fickle, inconstant, restless, unstable, variable. ANT.—constant, reliable, stable, steady, trustworthy.

fix, SYN.—affix, attach, bind, fasten, link, place, set, stick, tie; define, determine, establish, limit, set, settle; adjust, mend, rectify, regulate, repair. ANT.—displace, remove, unfasten; alter, change, disturb, modify; damage, mistreat.

flat, SYN.—even, horizontal, level, plane, smooth; dull, insipid, stale, tasteless, vapid. ANT.—broken, hilly, irregular, sloping; exciting, racy, savory, tasty.

flee, SYN.—abscond, decamp, escape, fly, hasten, run away. ANT.—appear, arrive, remain, stay.

flexible, SYN.—compliant, ductile, elastic, lithe, pliable, pliant, resilient, supple, tractable. ANT.—brittle, hard, rigid, stiff, unbending.

flow, SYN.—gush, run, spout, spurt, stream; come, emanate, issue, originate, proceed, result; abound, be copious.

fluctuate, SYN.—change, hesitate, oscillate, undulate, vacillate, vary, waver. ANT.—adhere, decide, persist, resolve, stick.

fly, SYN.—flit, float, flutter, glide, hover, mount, sail, soar; dart, rush, shoot, spring; abscond, decamp, escape, flee, run away. ANT.—descend, fall, plummet, sink.

follow, SYN.—succeed, come next; comply, heed, obey, observe; adopt, copy, imitate; accompany, attend; chase, pursue, trail; ensue, result. ANT.—precede; guide, lead; avoid, elude, flee; cause.

follower, SYN.—adherent, attendant, devotee, disciple, henchman, partisan, successor, supporter, votary. ANT.—chief, head, leader, master.

folly, SYN.—foolishness, imbecility, silliness; absurdity, extravagance, imprudence, indiscretion. ANT.—sense, wisdom; judgment, prudence, reasonableness.

food, SYN.—diet, edibles, fare, feed, meal, nutriment, provisions, rations, repast, sustenance, viands, victuals. ANT.—drink, hunger, starvation, want.

fool, SYN.—buffoon, clown, harlequin, jester; blockhead, dolt, dunce, idiot, imbecile, nincompoop, numbskull, oak, simpleton. ANT.—genius, philosopher, sage, scholar.

foolish, SYN.—absurd, asinine, brainless, crazy, idiotic, irrational, nonsensical, preposterous, ridiculous, senseless, silly, simple. ANT.—judicious, prudent, sagacious, sane, wise.

forbearance, SYN.—abstention, abstinence, continence, moderation, self-denial. ANT.—excess, gluttony, greed, intoxication, self-indulgence.

force, SYN.—dint, emphasis, energy, intensity, might, potency, power, strength, vigor; coercion, compulsion, constraint, violence. ANT.—feebleness, frailty, impotence, weakness; persuasion.

form, SYN.—construct, create, fashion, forge, make, mold, produce, shape; compose, constitute, make up; arrange, combine, organize; devise, frame, invent. ANT.—destroy, disfigure, dismantle, misshape, wreck.

formal, SYN.—affected, ceremonious, correct, decorous, exact, methodical, precise, proper, regular, solemn, stiff; external, outward, perfunctory. ANT.—easy, natural, unconstrained, unconventional; heartfelt.

fortuitous, SYN.—advantageous, auspicious, benign, favored, felicitous, fortunate, happy, lucky, propitious, successful. ANT.—cheerless, condemned, ill-fated, persecuted, unlucky.

fortunate, SYN.—advantageous, auspicious, benign, favored, felicitous, fortunate, happy, lucky, propitious, successful. ANT.—cheerless, condemned, ill-fated, persecuted, unlucky.

forward, SYN.—advance, aggrandize, elevate, further, promote; bring forward. ANT.—hinder, oppose, retard, retreat, withhold.

foul, SYN.—dirty, filthy, grimy, muddy, soiled, squalid; indecent, nasty, obscene; base, contemptible, despicable, low, mean, pitiful, shabby. ANT.—clean, neat, presentable; pure, wholesome.

foundation, SYN.—base, basis, bottom, ground, groundwork, root, substructure, support, underpinning. ANT.—building, cover, superstructure, top.

fragile, SYN.—breakable, brittle, delicate, feeble, frail, infirm, weak. ANT.—durable, hardy, strong, sturdy, tough.

fraud, SYN.—artifice, cheat, chicanery, deceit, deception, duplicity, guile, imposition, imposture, swindle, trick. ANT.—fairness, honesty, integrity, sincerity.

fray, SYN.—battle, combat, conflict, contest, fight, skirmish, strife, struggle. ANT.—agreement, concord, peace, truce.

free, SYN.—autonomous, emancipated, exempt, freed, independent, liberated, unconfined, unrestricted; clear, loose, open, unfastened, unobstructed; immune; careless, easy, familiar, frank; artless, bounteous, bountiful, generous, liberal, munificent. ANT.—confined, restrained, restricted; blocked, clogged, impeded; subject; illiberal, parsimonious, stingy.

freedom, SYN.—exemption, familiarity, immunity, independence, liberation, liberty, license, privilege, unrestraint. ANT.—bondage, compulsion, constraint, necessity, servitude.

frequent, SYN.—common, general, habitual, often, persistent, usual. ANT.—exceptional, rare, scanty, solitary, unique.

fresh, SYN.—modern, new, novel, recent; additional,

further; brisk, cool, refreshing; artless, green, inexperienced, natural, raw. ANT.—decayed, faded, hackneyed, musty, stagnant.

friend, SYN.—companion, comrade, crony, intimate; advocate, defender, patron, supporter, well-wisher; ally, associate. ANT.—adversary, enemy, stranger.

friendly, SYN.—affable, amicable, companionable, genial, kindly, neighborly, sociable, social. ANT.—antagonistic, cool, distant, hostile, reserved.

friendship, SYN.—acquaintance, cognizance, companionship, familiarity, fellowship, intimacy, knowledge. ANT.—ignorance, inexperience, unfamiliarity.

frighten, SYN.—affright, alarm, appal, astound, daunt, dismay, horrify, intimidate, scare, startle, terrify, terrorize. ANT.—allay, compose, embolden, reassure, soothe.

frugal, SYN.—economical, parsimonious, provident, saving, sparing, stingy, temperate, thrifty. ANT.—extravagant, intemperate, self-indulgent, wasteful.

fruitful, SYN.—bountiful, fecund, fertile, luxuriant, plenteous, productive, prolific, rich, teeming. ANT.—barren, impotent, sterile, unproductive.

frustrate, SYN.—baffle, balk, circumvent, defeat, disappoint, foil, hinder, outwit, prevent, thwart. ANT.—accomplish, fulfill, further, promote.

full, SYN.—crammed, filled, gorged, packed, replete, satiated, soaked; ample, complete, copious, entire, extensive, perfect, plentiful, sufficient; baggy, flowing, loose, voluminous; circumstantial, detailed, exhaustive. ANT.—depleted, devoid, empty, vacant; insufficient, lacking, partial.

funny, SYN.—amusing, comical, droll, farcical, humorous, laughable, ludicrous, ridiculous, witty; curious, odd, queer. ANT.—melancholy, sad, serious, sober, solemn.

furnish, SYN.—endow, equip, fit, fit out, provide, supply; afford, give, produce, yield. ANT.—denude, despoil, divest, strip.

G

gain, SYN.—account, advantage, avail, behalf, benefit, favor, good, interest, profit, service. ANT.—calamity, distress, handicap, trouble.

gain, SYN.—achieve, acquire, attain, earn, get, obtain, procure, reach, secure, win; benefit, net, profit. ANT.—forfeit, lose, surrender.

game, SYN.—amusement,

contest, diversion, fun, match, merriment, pastime, play, recreation, sport. ANT.—business.

gap, SYN.—abyss, aperture, cavity, chasm, gulf, hole, opening, pore, void.

garb, SYN.—apparel, array, attire, clothes, clothing, drapery, dress, garments; raiment, vestments, vesture. ANT.—nakedness, nudity.

garments, SYN.—apparel, array, attire, clothes, clothing, drapery, dress, garb, raiment, vestments, vesture. ANT.—nakedness, nudity.

garnish, SYN.—adorn, beautify, deck, decorate, embellish, enrich, ornament, trim. ANT.—debase, defame, expose, strip, uncover.

garrulous, SYN.—chattering, chatty, communicative, glib, loquacious, talkative, verbose, voluble. ANT.—laconic, reticent, silent, taciturn, uncommunicative.

gather, SYN.—accumulate, amass, assemble, collect, congregate, convene, muster; cull, garner, glean, harvest, pick, reap, conclude, deduce, infer, judge. ANT.—disband, disperse, distribute, scatter, separate.

gaunt, SYN.—attenuated, diaphanous, diluted, emaciated, fine, flimsy, gauzy, gossamer, lank, lean, meager, narrow, rare, scanty, scrawny, skinny, slender, slight, slim, spare, tenuous, thin. ANT.—broad, bulky, fat, thick, wide.

gay, SYN.—cheerful, glad, happy, jolly, joyful, lighthearted, merry, sprightly. ANT.—depressed, glum, mournful, sad, sullen.

gaze, SYN.—behold, discern, eye, glance, look, see, stare, survey, view, watch, witness; appear, seem; examine, inspect, observe, regard. ANT.—avert, hide, miss, overlook.

general, SYN.—common, customary, ordinary, popular, prevalent, regular, universal, usual; indefinite, inexact, vague. ANT.—exceptional, rare, singular; definite, particular, specific.

generate, SYN.—afford, bear, bestow, breed, impart, pay, produce, supply; accord, allow, concede, grant, permit; abdicate, accede, acquiesce, capitulate, cede, quit, relent, relinquish, resign, submit, succumb, surrender, waive, yield. ANT.—deny, dissent, oppose, refuse; assert, resist, strive, struggle.

generation, SYN.—age, dotage, senescence, senility, seniority; antiquity, date, epoch, era, period, time. ANT.—childhood, infancy, youth.

generosity, SYN.—altruism, beneficence, benevolence, charity, humanity, kindness, liberality, magnanimity, philanthropy, tenderness. ANT.—cruelty, inhumanity, malevolence, selfishness, unkindness.

generous, SYN.—beneficent, bountiful, giving, liberal, magnanimous, munificent, openhanded, unselfish. ANT.—covetous, greedy, miserly, selfish, stingy.

genius, SYN.—ability, aptitude, creativity, faculty, gift, inspiration, intellect, originality, sagacity, talent; adept, intellectual, master, proficient. ANT.—ineptitude, obtuseness, shallowness, stupidity; dolt, dullard, moron.

genre, SYN.—caste, category, class, denomination, kind; grade, order, rank, set; elegance, excellence.

gentle, SYN.—benign, calm, docile, mild, peaceful, placid, relaxed, serene, soft, soothing, tame, tractable. ANT.—fierce, harsh, rough, savage, violent.

genuine, SYN.—authentic, bona fide, legitimate, proven, real, sincere, true, unadulterated, unaffected, veritable. ANT.—artificial, bogus, counterfeit, false, sham.

genus, SYN.—breed, character, family, kind, race, sort, species, stock, strain, type, variety.

germ, SYN.—contagion, infection, pest, virus; ail-ment, contamination, disease, poison, pollution, taint.

gesture, SYN.—emblem, indication, mark, note, omen, portent, proof, sign, signal, symbol, symptom, token.

get, SYN.—achieve, acquire, attain, earn, gain, obtain, procure, receive, secure. ANT.—forfeit, leave, lose, renounce, surrender.

ghost, SYN.—apparition, phantom, shade, spectre, spirit, spook.

gift, SYN.—benefaction, bequest, boon, charity, donation, endowment, favor, grant, gratuity, largess, present; aptitude, faculty, genius, talent. ANT.—deprivation, earnings, loss, purchase; incapacity, ineptitude, stupidity.

gigantic, SYN.—colossal, elephantine, enormous, gargantuan, huge, immense, large, prodigious, vast. ANT.—diminutive, little, minute, small, tiny.

giggle, SYN.—cackle, chuckle, guffaw, jeer, laugh, mock, roar, scoff, snicker, titter.

gist, SYN.—acceptation, connotation, drift, explanation, implication, import, intent, interpretation, meaning, purport, purpose, sense, significance, signification.

give, SYN.—bestow, confer, contribute, deliver, donate, furnish, grant, impart, present, provide, supply. ANT.—keep, retain, seize, withdraw.

glad, SYN.—cheerful, delighted, exulting, gratified, happy, joyous, lighthearted, merry, pleased. ANT.—dejected, depressed, despondent, melancholy, sad.

gladness, SYN.—beatitude, blessedness, bliss, contentment, delight, felicity, happiness, pleasure, satisfaction, wellbeing, ANT.—despair, grief, misery, sadness, sorrow.

glance, SYN.—behold, discern, eye, gaze, look, scan, see, stare, survey, view, watch, witness, appear, seem; examine, inspect, observe, regard. ANT.—avert, hide, miss, overlook.

gleam, SYN.—beam, blaze, flash, flicker, glare, glimmer, glisten, glitter, glow, radiate, scintillate, shimmer, shine, sparkle, twinkle.

glib, SYN.—flat, level, plain, polished, sleek, stick; diplomatic, smooth, suave, urbane. ANT.—bluff; blunt, harsh, rough, rugged.

gloom, SYN.—blackness, bleakness, darkness, obscurity, shadow; dejection, depression, despondency, melancholy, misery, sadness, woe. ANT.—exultation, frivolity, joy, light, mirth.

gloomy, SYN.—dejected, depressed, despondent, disconsolate, dismal, dispirited, doleful, glum,

melancholy, moody, sad, somber, sorrowful; grave, pensive. ANT.—cheerful, happy, joyous, merry.

glorify, SYN.—adore, consecrate, dignify, enshrine, enthrone, exalt, extol, hallow, honor, revere, venerate. ANT.—abuse, debase, degrade, dishonor, mock.

glorious, SYN.—elevated, exalted, grand, high, lofty, majestic, noble, raised, splendid, sublime, supreme. ANT.—base, ignoble, low, ordinary, ridiculous.

glory, SYN.—admiration, adoration, deference, dignity, esteem, fame, homage, honor, praise, renown, respect, reverence, worship. ANT.—contempt, derision, disgrace, dishonor, reproach.

glow, SYN.—beam, blaze, flash, flicker, glare, glimmer, glisten, glitter, radiate, scintillate, shimmer, shine, sparkle, twinkle.

glowing, SYN.—ardent, eager, enthusiastic, fervent, fervid, fiery, hot, impassioned, intense, keen, passionate, vehement, zealous. ANT.—apathetic, cool, indifferent, nonchalant.

glum, SYN.—crabbed, dour, fretful, gloomy, moody, morose, sulky, surly. ANT.—amiable, gay, joyous, merry, pleasant.

glut, SYN.—fill, fill up, occupy, pervade; furnish, replenish, stock, store, supply; content, gorge, sate, satiate, satisfy, stuff. ANT.—deplete, drain, empty, exhaust, void.

gluttony, SYN.—devouring, insatiability, ravenousness, voraciousness. ANT.—fullness, satisfaction.

go, SYN.—depart, exit, fade, flee, leave, move, proceed, quit, retire, vanish, walk, withdraw. ANT.—arrive, come, enter, stand, stay.

goal, SYN.—aim, ambition, aspiration, craving, desire, hope, longing, objective, passion.

godlike, SYN.—celestial, divine, heavenly, holy, superhuman, supernatural, transcendent. ANT.—blasphemous, diabolical, mundane, profane, wicked.

good, SYN.—conscientious, exemplary, honest, moral, pure, reliable, virtuous, worthy; admirable, commendable, excellent, genuine, precious, safe, sound, valid; benevolent, gracious, humane, kind; agreeable, cheerful, friendly, genial, pleasant; fair, honorable, immaculate; auspicious, beneficial, favorable, profitable, useful; able, capable, efficient, expert, proficient, skillful; adequate, ample, sufficient.

govern, SYN.—administer, command, control, direct, manage, oversee, regulate, reign, rule, supervise, sway. ANT.—acquiesce, assent, obey, submit, yield.

grace, SYN.—attractiveness, beauty, charm, comeliness, elegance, fairness, handsomeness, loveliness, pulchritude. ANT.—deformity, disfigurement, eyesore, homeliness, ugliness.

graceful, SYN.—beautiful, comely, elegant, flowing, fluid, lithe, natural, supple. ANT.—awkward, clumsy, deformed, gawky, ungainly.

gracious, SYN.—agreeable, amiable, engaging, friendly, good-natured, pleasing. ANT.—churlish, disagreeable, hateful, ill-natured, surly.

grade, SYN.—caste, category, denomination, genre, kind; order, rank, set; elegance, excellence.

gradual, SYN.—dawdling, delaying, deliberate, dull, laggard, leisurely, sluggish, slow, tired. ANT.—fast, quick, rapid, speedy, swift.

grandiose, SYN.—august, dignified, grand, high, imposing, lofty, magnificent, majestic, noble, pompous, stately, sublime. ANT.—common, humble, lowly, ordinary, undignified.

grant, SYN.—allot, apportion, deal, dispense, distribute, divide, mete; allocate, appropriate, assign, give, measure. ANT.—confiscate, keep, refuse, retain, withhold.

graph, SYN.—cabal, conspiracy, design, intrigue, machination, plan, plot, scheme, stratagem; chart, diagram, sketch.

grasp, SYN.—apprehend, arrest, capture, clutch, catch, grip, lay hold of, seize, snare, trap. ANT.—liberate, lose, release, throw.

grateful, SYN.—appreciative, beholden, indebted, obliged, thankful. ANT.—thankless, unappreciative.

gratifying, SYN.—comfort, consolation, contentment, ease, enjoyment, relief, solace, succor. ANT.—affliction, discomfort, misery, suffering, torment, torture.

grating, SYN.—coarse, gruff, harsh, jarring, rigorous, rough, rugged, severe, strict, stringent. ANT.—gentle, melodious, mild, smooth, soft.

grave, SYN.—consequential, important, momentous, serious, weighty; dignified, sedate, sober, solemn, staid, thoughtful. ANT.—insignificant, trifling, trivial; flighty, frivolous, light, merry.

great, SYN.—big, enormous, gigantic, huge, immense, large, vast; numerous, countless; celebrated, eminent, famed, illustrious, prominent, renowned; critical, important, momentous, serious, vital, weighty; august, dignified, elevated, grand, majestic, noble; excellent, fine, magnificent. ANT.—diminutive, little, minute, small; common, obscure, ordinary, unknown; menial, paltry.

greedy, SYN.—avaricious, covetous, grasping, rapacious, selfish; devouring, gluttonous, insatiable, ravenous, voracious. ANT.—generous, munificent; full, satisfied.

green, SYN.—modern, new, novel, recent; additional, further; brisk, cool, fresh, refreshing; artless, inexperienced, natural, raw. ANT.—decayed, faded, hackneyed, musty, stagnant.

greet, SYN.—accost, approach, hail, speak to. ANT.—avoid, pass by.

gregarious, SYN.—affable, civil, communicative, friendly, hospitable, outgoing, sociable. ANT.—antisocial, disagreeable, hermitic, inhospitable.

grief, SYN.—affliction, anguish, distress, heartache, lamentation, misery, mourning, sadness, sorrow, trial, tribulation, woe. ANT.—comfort, consolation, happiness, joy, solace.

grievance, SYN.—damage, detriment, harm, injury, mischief; injustice, prejudice, wrong. ANT.—benefit, improvement, repair.

grieve, SYN.—bemoan, bewail, deplore, lament, mourn, suffer, weep. ANT.—carouse, celebrate, rejoice, revel.

grieved, SYN.—afflicted, hurt, pained, sad, sorrowful, vexed; contrite, penitent, remorseful, repentant, sorry; beggarly, contemptible, mean, paltry, pitiable, pitiful, poor, shabby, vile, worthless, wretched. ANT.—cheerful, delighted, impenitent, splendid, unrepentant.

grip, SYN.—apprehend, arrest, capture, catch, clutch, grip, lay hold of, seize, snare, trap. ANT.—liberate, lose, release, throw.

gross, SYN.—aggregate, entire, total, whole; brutal, enormous, glaring, grievous, manifest, plain; coarse, crass, earthy, indelicate, obscene; rough, rude, vulgar, big, bulky, fat, great, large. ANT.—proper, refined; appealing, comely, delicate.

grouch, SYN.—complain, grumble, lament, murmur, protest, regret, remonstrate, repine, whine. ANT.—applaud, approve, praise, rejoice.

ground, SYN.—base, basis, bottom, foundation, groundwork, support, underpinning; assumption, postulate, premise, presumption, presupposition, principle. ANT.—derivative, implication,

superstructure, trimming.

groundwork, SYN.—base, basis, bottom, foundation, ground, support, underpinning; assumption, postulate, premise, presumption, presupposition, principle. ANT.—derivative, implication, superstructure, trimming.

group, SYN.—aggregation, assembly, band, brood, bunch, class, cluster, collection, crowd, flock, herd, horde, lot, mob, pack, party, set swarm, throng, troupe.

groveling, SYN.—abject, contemptible, despicable, dishonorable, base, ignoble, ignominious, low, lowly, mean, menial, servile, sordid, vile, vulgar. ANT.—esteemed, exalted, honored, lofty, noble, righteous.

grow, SYN.—advance, develop, distend, enlarge, expand, extend, germinate, increase, mature, swell. ANT.—atrophy, contract, decay, diminish, shrink, wane.

growth, SYN.—development, elaboration, expansion, unfolding, unraveling; evolution, maturing, progress. ANT.—abbreviation, compression, curtailment.

grudge, SYN.—animosity, enmity, ill will, malevolence, malice, malignity, rancor, spite. ANT.—affection, kindness, love, toleration.

gruff, SYN.—craggy, irregular, jagged, rugged, scabrous, scratchy, uneven; approximate, coarse, crude, cursory, imperfect, incomplete, unfinished, unpolished; harsh, severe, stormy, tempestuous, turbulent, violent; blunt, brusque, churlish, rough, rude, uncivil. ANT.—even, level, sleek, slippery, smooth; fine, finished, polished, refined; calm, placid, tranquil, unruffled; civil, courteous, gentle, mild.

guarantee, SYN.—bail, bond, earnest, guaranty, pawn, pledge, security, surety, token, warrant.

guard, SYN.—bulwark, fence, protection, refuge, safeguard, shelter, shield; defense, security.

guard, SYN.—cloak, clothe, conceal, cover, curtain, disguise, envelop, hide, mask, protect, screen, shield, shroud, veil. ANT.—bare, divulge, expose, reveal, unveil.

guess, SYN.—assume, believe, conjecture, estimate, reason, reckon, speculate, suppose, surmise, think.

guide, SYN.—conduct, direct, escort, lead, steer; control, manage, regulate, supervise.

guile, SYN.—beguilement, cheat, chicanery, cunning, deceitfulness, deception, duplicity, fraud, sham, trick, wiliness.

ANT.—candor, honesty, openness, sincerity, truthfulness.

guise, SYN.—advent, apparition, appearance, arrival; air, aspect, demeanor, look, manner, mien; fashion, pretense, semblance.

H

habit, SYN.—custom, fashion, practice, routine, usage, use, wont.

habitual, SYN.—common, frequent, general, often, persistent, usual. ANT.—exceptional, rare, scanty, solitary, unique.

hackneyed, SYN.—banal, common, ordinary, stale, stereotyped, trite. ANT.—fresh, modern, momentous, novel, stimulating.

hail, SYN.—accost, approach, greet, speak to. ANT.—avoid, pass by.

hale, SYN.—healthy, hearty, robust, sound, strong, well; hygienic, salubrious, salutary, wholesome. ANT.—delicate, diseased, frail, infirm; injurious, noxious.

hallow, SYN.—aggrandize, consecrate, dignify, elevate, ennoble, erect, exalt, extol, glorify, raise. ANT.—debase, degrade, dishonor, humble, humiliate.

hallucination, SYN.—aberration, fantasy, illusion, phantasm, vision.

halt, SYN.—abstain, arrest, bar, cease, check, close, cork, desist, discontinue, end, hinder, impede, interrupt, obstruct, plug, seal, stop, terminate. ANT.—begin, proceed, promote, speed, start.

handicap, SYN.—chastisement, fine, forfeiture, punishment, retribution; disadvantage, penalty. ANT.—compensation, pardon, remuneration, reward.

handsome, SYN.—beauteous, beautiful, charming, comely, elegant, fair, fine, lovely, pretty. ANT.—foul, hideous, homely, repulsive, unsightly.

handy, SYN.—accessible, adapted, advantageous, appropriate, commodious, convenient, favorable, fitting, suitable, timely. ANT.—awkward, inconvenient, inopportune, troublesome.

happen, SYN.—bechance, befall, betide, chance, occur, take place, transpire.

happiness, SYN.—beatitude, blessedness, bliss, contentment, delight, felicity, gladness, pleasure, satisfaction, wellbeing. ANT.—despair, grief, misery, sadness, sorrow.

happy, SYN.—blessed, cheerful, contented, delighted, fortunate, gay, glad, joyful, joyous, lucky, merry, opportune, propitious. ANT.—blue, depressed, gloomy, mo-rose.

harass, SYN.—aggravate, annoy, badger, bother, disturb, harry, irritate, molest, nag, pester, plague, provoke, tantalize, taunt, torment, vex, worry. ANT.—comfort, delight, gratify, please, soothe.

hard, SYN.—compact, firm, impenetrable, rigid, solid; arduous, burdensome, difficult, onerous, tough; intricate, perplexing, puzzling; cruel, harsh, rigorous, severe, stern, strict, unfeeling. ANT.—brittle, elastic, flabby, fluid, plastic, soft; easy, effortless, facile; simple; gentle, lenient, tender.

hardship, SYN.—examination, experiment, ordeal, proof, test; attempt, affliction, endeavor, essay, affliction, misery, misfortune, suffering, tribulation, trouble. ANT.—alleviation, consolation.

harm, SYN.—damage, detriment, evil, hurt, ill, infliction, injury, mischief, misfortune, mishap, wrong. ANT.—benefit, boon, favor, kindness.

harmful, SYN.—detrimental, damaging, deleterious, hurtful, injurious, mischievous. ANT.—advantageous, beneficial, helpful, profitable, salutary.

harmless, SYN.—certain, dependable, protected, reliable, secure, snug, trustworthy. ANT.—dangerous, hazardous, insecure, perilous, unsafe.

harmony, SYN.—accordance, coincidence, concord, concurrence, understanding, unison; bargain, compact, contract, covenant, pact, stipulation. ANT.—difference, disagreement, discord, dissension, variance.

harsh, SYN.—blunt, coarse, grating, gruff, jarring, rigorous, rough, rugged, severe, strict, stringent. ANT.—gentle, melodious, mild, smooth, soft.

harvest, SYN.—crop, fruit, proceeds, produce, product, reaping, result, store, yield.

harvest, SYN.—acquire, gain, garner, gather, glean, reap. ANT.—lose, plant, sow, squander.

hasten, SYN.—acclerate, expedite, hurry, precipitate, quicken, rush, speed. ANT.—delay, detain, hinder, retard, tarry.

hasty, SYN.—active, brisk, fast, lively, nimble, precipitate, quick, rapid, speedy, swift; excitable, impatient, irascible, sharp, testy, touchy. ANT.—slow, sluggish; dull.

hate, SYN.—abhor, abominate, despise, detest, dislike, loathe. ANT.—admire, approve, cherish, like, love.

hatred, SYN.—abhorrence, animosity, detestation, dislike, enmity, hostility; ill will, malevolence, rancor. ANT.—affection, attraction, friendship, love.

haughty, SYN.—arrogant, disdainful, overbearing, proud, stately, supercilious, vain, vainglorious. ANT.—ashamed, humble, lowly, meek.

have, SYN.—control, hold, occupy, own; affect, obtain, possess, seize. ANT.—abandon, lose, renounce, surrender.

hazard, SYN.—danger, jeopardy, peril, risk. ANT.—defense, immunity, protection, safety.

hazardous, SYN.—critical, dangerous, insecure, menacing, perilous, precarious, risky, threatening, unsafe. ANT.—firm, protected, safe, secure.

hazy, SYN.—ambiguous, dim, indefinite, indistinct, obscure, uncertain, unclear, undetermined, unsettled, vague. ANT.—clear, explicit, lucid, precise, specific.

head, SYN.—chief, commander, director, leader, master, principal, acme, crest, pinnacle, summit, top; crisis, culmination. ANT.—follower, subordinate, underling, base, bottom, foot.

healthy, SYN.—hale, hearty, robust, sound, strong, well; hygienic, salubrious, salutary, wholesome. ANT.—delicate, diseased, frail, infirm; injurious, noxious.

heap, SYN.—accrue, accumulate, amass, collect, gather, hoard, increase, store. ANT.—diminish, disperse, dissipate, scatter, waste.

hear, SYN.—harken, heed, listen, regard.

heart, SYN.—center, core, middle, midpoint, midst, nucleus. ANT.—border, boundary, outskirts, periphery, rim.

heartache, SYN.—affliction, anguish, distress, grief, lamentation, misery, mourning, sadness, sorrow, trial, tribulation, woe. ANT.—comfort, consolation, happiness, joy, solace.

heartbroken, SYN.—comfortless, disconsolate, distressed, forlorn, miserable, pitiable, wretched; abject, contemptible, despicable, low, mean, paltry, worthless. ANT.—contented, fortunate, happy; noble, significant.

hearten, SYN.—animate, cheer, countenance, embolden, encourage, exhilarate, favor, impel, incite, inspire, urge; foster, promote, sanction, stimulate, support. ANT.—deject, deter, discourage, dispirit, dissuade.

hearty, SYN.—ardent, cordial, earnest, gracious, sincere, sociable, warm. ANT.—aloof, cool, reserved, taciturn.

heavenly, SYN.—celestial,

divine, god-like, holy, superhuman, supernatural, transcendant. ANT.—blasphemous, diabolical, mundane, profane, wicked.

heavy, SYN.—massive, ponderous, weighty; burdensome, cumbersome, grievous, trying; gloomy, grave, serious, dull, sluggish. ANT.—animated, brisk, light.

heed, SYN.—alertness, attention, care, circumspection, consideration, mindfulness, notice, observance, watchfulness; application, contemplation, reflection, study. ANT.—disregard, indifference, negligence, omission, oversight.

heed, SYN.—consider, contemplate, deliberate, examine, meditate, ponder, reflect, study, weigh; esteem, regard, respect. ANT.—ignore, neglect, overlook.

heedless, SYN.—ignorant, blind, oblivious, sightless, unmindful, unseeing; headlong, rash. ANT.—aware, calculated, discerning, perceiving, sensible.

height, SYN.—acme, apex, culmination, peak, summit, zenith. ANT.—anticlimax, base, depth, floor.

heighten, SYN.—aggravate, increase, intensify, magnify, annoy, chafe, embitter, exasperate, inflame, irritate, nettle, provoke, vex. ANT.—

appease, mitigate, palliate, soften, soothe.

help, SYN.—abet, aid, assist, succor, support, uphold, facilitate, further, promote; mitigate, relieve, remedy. ANT.—impede, resist, thwart; hinder; afflict.

helpful, SYN.—advantageous, beneficial, good, profitable, salutary, serviceable, useful, wholesome. ANT.—deleterious, destructive, detrimental, harmful, injurious.

hence, SYN.—accordingly, consequently, so, thence, therefore.

heretic, SYN.—apostate, dissenter, nonconformist, schismatic, sectarian, sectary, unbeliever.

heroic, SYN.—adventurous, audacious, bold, brave, chivalrous, courageous, daring, dauntless, fearless, gallant, intrepid, magnanimous, valiant, valorous. ANT.—cowardly, cringing, fearful, timid, weak.

hesitant, SYN.—averse, disinclined, loath, reluctant, slow, unwilling. ANT.—disposed, eager, inclined, ready, willing.

hesitate, SYN.—delay, demur, doubt, falter, pause, scruple, stammer, stutter, vacillate, waver. ANT.—continue, decide, persevere, proceed, resolve.

hesitation, SYN.—ambiguity, distrust, doubt, incredulity, scruple, skepticism, suspense, suspicion, unbelief, uncertainty. ANT.—belief, certainty, conviction, determination, faith.

hidden, SYN.—concealed, dormant, inactive, latent, potential, quiescent, secret, undeveloped, unseen. ANT.—conspicuous, evident, explicit, manifest, visible.

hide, SYN.—cloak, conceal, cover, disguise, mask, screen, secrete, suppress, veil, withhold. ANT.—disclose, divulge, expose, reveal, show, uncover.

high, SYN.—lofty, tall, towering; elevated, eminent, exalted, proud. ANT.—small, stunted, tiny; base, low, mean.

hinder, SYN.—block, check, hamper, impede, obstruct, prevent, resist, restrain, retard, stop, thwart. ANT.—assist, expedite, facilitate, further, promote.

hint, SYN.—allusion, implication, insinuation, intimate, reminder. ANT.—affirmation, declaration, statement.

hire, SYN.—apply, avail, busy, devote, employ, occupy, use, utilize. ANT.—banish, discard, discharge, reject.

history, SYN.—account, chronicle, description, detail, narration, narrative, recital, relation; computation, reckoning, record. ANT.—caricature, confusion, distortion, misrepresentation.

hit, SYN.—beat, hurt, knock, pound, pummel, smite, strike.

hoard, SYN.—accrue, accumulate, amass, collect, gather, heap, increase, store. ANT.—diminish, disperse, dissipate, scatter, waste.

hoax, SYN.—antic, artifice, cheat, deception, device, fraud, guile, imposture, ploy, ruse, stratagem, stunt, subterfuge, wile. ANT.—candor, exposure, honesty, openness, sincerity.

hobbling, SYN.—crippled, defective, deformed, disabled, feeble, halt, lame, limping, maimed, unconvincing, unsatisfactory, weak. ANT.—agile, athletic, robust, sound, vigorous.

hold, SYN.—adhere, clasp, clutch, grasp, grip; have, keep, maintain, occupy, possess, retain, support; check, confine, curb, detain, restrain; accommodate, carry, contain, receive, stow. ANT.—abandon, relinquish, surrender, vacate.

hole, SYN.—abyss, aperture, cavity, chasm, gap, gulf; opening, pore, void.

hollow, SYN.—depressed, empty, unfilled, vacant, void; hypocritical, insincere, vain. ANT.—full, solid, sound; genuine, sincere.

holy, SYN.—blessed, consecrated, devout, divine, hallowed, pious, religious, sacred, saintly, spiritual. ANT.—evil, profane, sacrilegious, secular, worldly.

home, SYN.—abode, domicile, dwelling, habitat, hearth, quarters, residence, seat.

homely, SYN.—deformed, hideous, plain, repellent, repulsive, uncomely; disagreeable, illnatured, spiteful, surly, ugly, vicious. ANT.—attractive, beautiful, fair, handsome, pretty.

honest, SYN.—candid, conscientious, fair, honorable, ingenuous, just, scrupulous, sincere, trustworthy, truthful, upright. ANT.—deceitful, dishonest, fraudulent; lying, tricky.

honesty, SYN.—candor, fairness, frankness, integrity, justice, openness, rectitude, responsibility, sincerity, trustworthiness, uprightness. ANT.—cheating, deceit, dishonesty, fraud, trickery.

honor, SYN.—admiration, adoration, deference, dignity, esteem, fame, glory, homage, praise, renown, respect, reverence, worship. ANT.—contempt, derision, disgrace, dishonor, reproach.

honor, SYN.—admire, consider, heed, respect, revere, reverence, value, venerate. ANT.—abuse, despise, disdain, neglect, scorn.

honorable, SYN.—admirable, eminent, fair, honest, noble, respectable, true, trusty, upright, virtuous; creditable, esteemed, proper, reputable. ANT.—disgraceful, ignominious, infamous, shameful.

hope, SYN.—anticipation, expectancy, expectation; confidence, faith, optimism, trust. ANT.—despair, despondency, pessimism.

hopelessness, SYN.—depression, desperation, despondency, discouragement, gloom, pessimism. ANT.—confidence, elation, hope, optimism.

horde, SYN.—bevy, crowd, crush, host, masses, mob, multitude, populace, press, rabble, swarm, throng.

horrible, SYN.—appalling, awful, dire, dreadful, fearful, frightful, ghastly, hideous, horrid, repulsive, terrible. ANT.—beautiful, enchanting, enjoyable, fascinating, lovely.

horrid, SYN.—appalling, awful, dire, dreadful, fearful, frightful, ghastly, hideous, horrible, repulsive, terrible. ANT.—beautiful, enchanting, enjoyable, fascinating, lovely.

horror, SYN.—alarm, apprehension, awe, dread, fear, foreboding, reverence, terror. ANT.—

assurance, boldness, confidence, courage.

hostile, SYN.—adverse, antagonistic, inimical, opposed, unfriendly, warlike. ANT.—amicable, cordial, favorable.

hostility, SYN.—bitterness, enmity, grudge, hatred, malevolence, rancor, spite. ANT.—friendliness, good will, love.

hot, SYN.—burning, scalding, scorching, torrid, warm; ardent, fervent, fiery, hot-blooded, impetuous, intense, passionate; peppery, pungent. ANT.—cold, cool, freezing, frigid; apathetic, impassive, indifferent, passionless, phlegmatic; bland.

however, SYN.—but, nevertheless, notwithstanding, still, yet.

hue, SYN.—complexion, dye, paint, pigment, shade, stain, tincture, tinge, tint. ANT.—achromatism, paleness, transparency.

hug, SYN.—caress, coddle, cuddle, embrace, fondle, kiss, pet. ANT.—annoy, buffet, spurn, tease, vex.

huge, SYN.—ample, big, capacious, colossal, extensive, great, immense, large, vast, wide. ANT.—little, mean, short, small, tiny.

humane, SYN.—clement, compassionate, forbearing, forgiving, kind, lenient, merciful, tender, tolerant. ANT.—brutal, cruel, pitiless, remorseless, unfeeling.

humanity, SYN.—altruism, beneficence, benevolence, charity, generosity, humanity, kindness, liberality, magnanimity, philanthropy, tenderness. ANT.—cruelty, inhumanity, malevolence, selfishness, unkindness.

humble, SYN.—compliant, lowly, meek, modest, plain, simple, submissive, unassuming, unostentatious, unpretentious. ANT.—arrogant, boastful, haughty, proud, vain.

humble, SYN.—abase, abash, break, crush, degrade, humiliate, mortify, shame, subdue. ANT.—elevate, exalt, honor, praise.

humiliate, SYN.—abase, adulterate, alloy, corrupt, debase, defile, degrade, deprave, depress, impair, lower, pervert, vitiate. ANT.—enhance, improve, raise, restore, vitalize.

humiliation, SYN.—abashment, chagrin, mortification; disgrace, dishonor, disrepute, ignominy, odium, opprobrium, scandal, shame. ANT.—dignity, glory, honor, praise, renown.

humor, SYN.—facetiousness, irony, jocularity, joke, sarcasm, satire, waggery, wit; disposition, mood, temper, temperament. ANT.—gravity, seriousness, sorrow.

humorous, SYN.—amusing, comical, droll, farcical, funny, laughable, ludicrous, ridiculous, witty; curious, odd, queer. ANT.—melancholy, sad, serious, sober, solemn.

hunger, SYN.—relish, stomach, thirst, zest; craving, desire, inclination, liking, longing, passion. ANT.—disgust, distaste, renunciation, repugnance, satiety.

hunt, SYN.—examination, exploration, inquiry, investigation, pursuit, quest, search. ANT.—abandonment, cession, resignation.

hurl, SYN.—cast, fling, pitch, propel, throw, thrust, toss. ANT.—draw, haul, hold, pull, retain.

hurry, SYN.—accelerate, expedite, hasten, precipitate, quicken, rush, speed. ANT.—delay, detain, hinder, retard, tarry.

hurt, SYN.—damage, detriment, harm, mischief; grievance, injustice, prejudice, wrong. ANT.—benefit, improvement, repair.

hurt, SYN.—damage, disfigure, harm, impair, injure, mar, spoil, wound; abuse, affront, dishonor, insult, wrong. ANT.—ameliorate, benefit, help, preserve; compliment, praise.

hygienic, SYN.—hale, healthy, hearty, robust, sound, strong, well; salubrious, salutary, wholesome. ANT.—delicate, diseased, frail, infirm; injurious, noxious.

hypothesis, SYN.—conjecture, law, supposition, theory. ANT.—certainty, fact, proof.

I

idea, SYN.—abstraction, concept, conception, fancy, image, impression, notion, opinion, sentiment, thought. ANT.—entity, matter, object, substance, thing.

ideal, SYN.—exemplary, fancied, faultless, imaginary, perfect, supreme, unreal, utopian, visionary. ANT.—actual, faulty, imperfect, material, real.

identical, SYN.—coincident, equal, equivalent, indistinguishable, like, same. ANT.—contrary, disparate, dissimilar, distinct, opposed.

idiom, SYN.—dialect, diction, jargon, language, lingo, phraseology, slang, speech, tongue, vernacular. ANT.—babble, drivel, gibberish, nonsense.

idle, SYN.—dormant, inactive, indolent, inert, lazy, slothful, unemployed, unoccupied. ANT.—active, employed, industrious, occupied, working.

ignoble, SYN.—abject, base, contemptible, despicable, dishonorable, groveling, ignominious,

low, lowly, mean, menial, servile, sordid, vile, vulgar. ANT.—esteemed, exalted, honored, lofty, noble, righteous.

ignorant, SYN.—illiterate, uncultured, uneducated, uninformed, unlearned, unlettered, untaught. ANT.—cultured, educated, erudite, informed, literate.

ignore, SYN.—disregard, neglect, omit, overlook, skip, slight. ANT.—include, notice, regard.

ill-use, SYN.—abuse, asperse, defame, disparage, malign, revile, scandalize, traduce, vilify; misapply, misemploy, misuse. ANT.—cherish, honor, praise, protect, respect.

illegal, SYN.—criminal, illegitimate, illicit, outlawed, prohibited, unlawful. ANT.—honest, lawful, legal, permitted.

illiberal, SYN.—bigoted, dogmatic, fanatical, intolerant, narrow-minded, prejudiced. ANT.—liberal, progressive, radical, tolerant.

illuminate, SYN.—brighten, clarify, elucidate, enlighten, illumine, illustrate, irradiate. ANT.—complicate, confuse, darken, obfuscate, obscure.

illusion, SYN.—delusion, dream, fantasy, hallucination, mirage, phantom, vision. ANT.—actuality, reality, substance.

illusive, SYN.—deceitful,

illustration 103 immigration

deceptive, delusive, delusory, fallacious, false, misleading, specious. ANT.—authentic, genuine, honest, real, truthful.

illustration, SYN.—drawing, engraving, etching, image, likeness, painting, panorama, photograph, picture, portrait, portrayal, print, representation, scene, sketch, view.

illustrious, SYN.—celebrated, eminent, famed, great, prominent, renowned; critical, important, momentous, serious, vital, weighty; august, dignified, elevated, grand, majestic, noble; excellent, fine, magnificent. ANT.—diminutive, little, minute, small; common, obscure, ordinary, unknown; menial, paltry.

imagination, SYN.—conception, creation, fancy, fantasy, idea, invention, notion.

imaginative, SYN.—clever, creative, fanciful, inventive, mystical, poetical, visionary. ANT.—dull, literal, prosaic, unromantic.

imagine, SYN.—conceive, dream, fancy, picture, pretend; assume, believe, conjecture, guess, opine, suppose, surmise, think.

imbecile, SYN.—blockhead, dolt, dunce, fool, idiot, nincompoop, numbskull, oaf, simpleton. ANT.—

genius, philosopher, sage, scholar.

imitate, SYN.—ape, copy, counterfeit, duplicate, impersonate, mimic, mock, simulate. ANT.—alter, distort, diverge.

imitation, SYN.—copy, duplicate, exemplar, facsimile, replica, reproduction, transcript. ANT.—original, prototype.

immature, SYN.—boyish, callow, childish, childlike, girlish, juvenile, puerile, young, youthful. ANT.—aged, elderly, mature, old, senile.

immeasurable, SYN.—boundless, endless, eternal, illimitable, immense, infinite, interminable, unbounded, unlimited, vast. ANT.—bounded, circumscribed, confined, finite, limited.

immediately, SYN.—directly, forthwith, instantaneously, instantly, now, presently, promptly, straightaway. ANT.—distantly, hereafter, later, shortly, sometime.

immense, SYN.—colossal, elephantine, enormous, gargantuan, gigantic, huge, large, prodigious, vast. ANT.—diminutive, little, minute, small, tiny.

immerse, SYN.—dip, douse, dunk, plunge, sink, submerge; absorb, engage, engross. ANT.—elevate, recover, uplift.

immigration, SYN.—colonization, settlement. ANT.—emigration, exodus.

imminent, SYN.—approaching, impending, menacing, nigh, threatening. ANT.—afar, distant, improbable, remote, retreating.

immoderation, SYN.—excess, extravagance, intemperance, profusion, superabundance, superfluity, surplus. ANT.—dearth, deficiency, lack, paucity, want.

immoral, SYN.—antisocial, bad, corrupt, dissolute, indecent, licentious, profligate, sinful, unprincipled, vicious, wicked. ANT.—chaste, highminded, noble, pure, virtuous.

immortal, SYN.—ceaseless, deathless, endless, eternal, everlasting, infinite, perpetual, timeless, undying. ANT.—ephemeral, finite, mortal, temporal, transient.

immune, SYN.—exempt, free, freed; clear, loose, open, unfastened, unobstructed. ANT.—subject.

immutable, SYN.—abiding, ceaseless, constant, continual, enduring, faithful, fixed, invariant, permanent, perpetual, persistent, unalterable, unchanging, unwavering. ANT.—fickle, mutable, vacillating, wavering.

impair, SYN.—damage, deface, harm, hurt, injure, mar, spoil. ANT.—ameliorate, benefit, enhance, mend, repair.

impart, SYN.—communicate, convey, disclose, divulge, inform, notify, relate, reveal, tell, transmit. ANT.—conceal, hide, withhold.

impartial, SYN.—equitable, fair, honest, just, reasonable, unbiased. ANT.—dishonorable, fraudulent, partial.

impartiality, SYN.—disinterestedness, indifference, insensibility, neutrality, unconcern. ANT.—affection, ardor, fervor, passion.

impede, SYN.—bar, block, check, clog, delay, encumber, frustrate, hamper, hinder, interrupt, obstruct, restrain, retard, stop, thwart. ANT.—advance, assist, further, help, promote.

impel, SYN.—coerce, compel, constrain, drive, force, oblige. ANT.—convince, induce, persuade, prevent.

impending, SYN.—approaching, imminent, menacing, nigh, overhanging, threatening. ANT.—afar, distant, improbable, remote, retreating.

impenetrable, SYN.—compact, firm, hard, impenetrable, rigid, solid; arduous, burdensome, difficult, onerous, tough; intricate, perplexing, puzzling; cruel, harsh, rigorous, severe, stern, strict, unfeeling. ANT.—brittle, elastic, flabby, fluid, plastic, soft; easy, effortless, facile; simple; gentle, lenient, tender.

imperative, SYN.—cogent, compelling, critical, exigent, impelling, important, importunate, insistent, instant, necessary, pressing, serious, urgent. ANT.—insignificant, petty, trifling, trivial, unimportant.

imperceptible, SYN.—indistinguishable, invisible, undiscernible, unseen. ANT.—evident, perceptible, seen, visible.

imperfection, SYN.—blemish, defect, error, failure, fault, flaw, mistake, omission, shortcoming, vice. ANT.—completeness, correctness, perfection.

imperil, SYN.—endanger, hazard, jeopardize, peril, risk. ANT.—guard, insure.

impersonate, SYN.—ape, copy, duplicate, imitate, mimic, mock, simulate. ANT.—alter, distort, diverge, invent.

impertinence, SYN.—audacity, boldness, effrontery, impudence, insolence, presumption, rudeness, sauciness. ANT.—diffidence, politeness, subserviency, truckling.

impertinent, SYN.—abusive, arrogant, brazen, contemptuous, impudent, insolent, insulting, offensive, rude. ANT. — considerate, courteous, polite, respectful.

impetuous, SYN.—careless, hasty, heedless, impulsive, passionate, quick, rash. ANT.—calculating, cautious, reasoning.

implicate, SYN.—accuse, blame, censure, condemn, rebuke, reproach, upbraid. ANT.—absolve, acquit, exonerate.

implore, SYN.—adjure, ask, beg, beseech, crave, entreat, importune, petition, pray, request, solicit, supplicate. ANT.—bestow, cede, favor, give, grant.

imply, SYN.—connote, insinuate, involve, mean, signify, suggest. ANT.—assert, express, state.

impolite, SYN.—blunt, boorish, discourteous, impudent, insolent, rough, rude, saucy, surly, uncivil, vulgar; coarse, savage, unpolished, untaught. ANT.—civil, genteel, polished; courtly, dignified, noble, stately.

import, SYN.—emphasis, importance, influence, significance, stress, value, weight. ANT.—insignificance, triviality.

important, SYN.—consequential, critical, decisive, grave, influential, material, momentous, pressing, prominent, relevant, significant, weighty. ANT.—insignificant, irrelevant, mean, petty, trivial.

imposing, SYN.—august, dignified, grand, grandiose, high, lofty, magnificent, majestic, noble, pompous, stately, sublime. ANT.—common, humble, lowly, ordinary, undignified.

impression, SYN.—sensibility; feeling, opinion. ANT.—insensibility; fact.

impressive, SYN.—affecting, arresting, august, commanding, exciting, forcible, grandiose, imposing, majestic, moving, overpowering, remarkable, splendid, stirring, striking, thrilling, touching. ANT.—commonplace, ordinary, regular, unimpressive.

improve, SYN.—ameliorate, amend, better, help, rectify, reform. ANT.—corrupt, damage, debase, impair, vitiate.

improvement, SYN.—advance, advancement, betterment, development, growth, progress, progression. ANT.—decline, delay, regression, relapse, retrogression.

imprudent, SYN.—careless, heedless, inattentive, inconsiderate, indiscreet, reckless, thoughtless, unconcerned; desultory, inaccurate, lax, neglectful, negligent, remiss. ANT.—accurate, careful, meticulous.

impudence. SYN.—assurance, audacity, boldness, effrontery, impertinence, insolence, presumption, rudeness, sauciness. ANT.—diffidence, politeness, subserviency, truckling.

impudent, SYN.—bold, brazen, forward, insolent, pushy, rude; abrupt, conspicuous, prominent, striking. ANT.—cowardly, flinching, timid; bashful, retiring.

impulsive, SYN.—careless, hasty, heedless, impetuous, passionate, quick, rash. ANT.—calculating, cautious, reasoning.

impure, SYN.—contaminated, corrupt, corrupted, crooked, debased, depraved, dishonest, profligate, putrid, spoiled, tainted, unsound, venal, vitiated.

imputation, SYN.—arraignment, diary, incrimination, indictment. ANT.—exculpation, exoneration, pardon.

inability, SYN.—disability, handicap, impotence, incapacity, incompetence, weakness. ANT.—ability, capability, power, strength.

inaccurate, SYN.—amiss, askew, awry, erroneous, fallacious, false, faulty, incorrect, mistaken, unprecise, untrue. ANT.—correct, right, true.

inactive, SYN.—dormant, idle, indolent, inert, lazy, slothful, unemployed, unoccupied. ANT.—active, employed, industrious, occupied, working.

inadequate, SYN.—defective, deficient, incomplete, insufficient, lacking, scanty, short. ANT.—adequate, ample, enough, satisfactory, sufficient.

inane, SYN.—banal, commonplace, hackneyed, insipid, trite, vapid. ANT.—fresh, novel, original, stimulating, striking.

inanimate, SYN.—dead, deceased, defunct, departed, dull, gone, insensible, lifeless, spiritless, unconscious. ANT.—alive, animate, living, stirring.

inattentive, SYN.—absentminded, abstracted, distracted, preoccupied. ANT.—attending, attentive, watchful.

inaugurate, SYN.—arise, begin, commence, enter, initiate, institute, open, originate, start. ANT.—close, complete, end, finish, terminate.

inception, SYN.—beginning, commencement, opening, origin, outset, source, start. ANT.—close, completion, consummation, end, termination.

incessant, SYN.—ceaseless, constant, continual, continuous, endless, everlasting, perennial, perpetual, unceasing, uninterrupted, unremitting. ANT.—interrupted, occasional, periodic, rare.

incident, SYN.—circumstance, condition, event, fact, happening, occurrence, position, situation.

incidental, SYN.—accidental, casual, chance, contingent, fortuitous, undesigned, unintended. ANT.—calculated, decreed, intended, planned, willed.

incinerate, SYN.—blaze, burn, char, consume, scald, scorch, sear, singe. ANT.—extinguish, put out, quench.

incisive, SYN.—brief, compact, concise, condensed, neat, pithy, succinct, summary, terse. ANT.—lengthy, prolix, verbose, wordy.

incite, SYN.—arouse, cause, encourage, foment, goad, induce, instigate, provoke, stimulate, urge. ANT.—bore, pacify, quiet, soothe.

inclination, SYN.—bending, incline, leaning, slope; affection, attachment, bent, bias, desire, disposition, penchant, predilection, preference. ANT.—apathy, aversion, distaste, nonchalance, repugnance.

include, SYN.—accommodate, comprise, contain, embody, embrace, hold. ANT.—discharge, omit, exclude.

incompetency, SYN.—disability, handicap, impotence, inability, incapacity, weakness. ANT.—ability, capability, power, strength.

incongruous, SYN.—contradictory, contrary, discrepant, illogical, incompatible, inconsistent, irreconcilable, paradoxical. ANT.—compatible, congruous, consistent, correspondent.

inconsistency, SYN.—conflict, contention, controversy, discord, interference, opposition, variance. ANT.—amity, concord, consonance, harmony.

inconsistent, SYN.—changeable, fickle, fitful, shifting, unstable, vacillating, variable, wavering. ANT.—constant, stable, steady, unchanging, uniform.

increase, SYN.—accrue, amplify, augment, enhance, enlarge, expand, extend, grow, heighten, intensify, magnify, multiply, raise, wax. ANT.—atrophy, contract, decrease, diminish, reduce.

incriminate, SYN.—accuse, arraign, censure, charge, indict. ANT.—absolve, acquit, exonerate, release, vindicate.

incrimination, SYN.—accusation, arraignment, charge, imputation, indictment. ANT.—exculpation, exoneration, pardon.

indebted, SYN.—appreciative, beholden, grateful, obliged, thankful. ANT.—thankless, unappreciative.

indecent, SYN.—coarse, dirty, disgusting, filthy, gross, impure, lewd, obscene, offensive, pornographic, smutty. ANT.—decent, modest, pure, refined.

independence, SYN.—exemption, freedom, immunity, liberation, liberty, license, privilege, unrestraint. ANT.—bondage, compulsion, constraint, necessity, servitude.

independent, SYN.—autonomous, free, self-reliant, uncontrolled, unrestrained, unrestricted, voluntary. ANT.—contingent, dependent, enslaved, restricted.

indestructible, SYN.—abiding, changeless, constant, durable, enduring, fixed, lasting, permanent, stable, unchangeable. ANT.—ephemeral, temporary, transient, transitory, unstable.

indicate, SYN.—denote, designate, disclose, imply, intimate, manifest, reveal, show, signify, specify. ANT.—conceal, distract, divert, falsify, mislead.

indication, SYN.—emblem, gesture, mark, note, omen, portent, proof, sign, signal, symbol, symptom, token.

indict, SYN.—accuse, arraign, censure, charge, incriminate. ANT.—absolve, acquit, exonerate, release, vindicate.

indifference, SYN.—apathy, disinterestedness, impartiality, insensibility, neutrality, unconcern. ANT.—affection, ardor, fervor, passion.

indigence, SYN.—destitution, necessity, need,

penury, poverty, privation, want. ANT.—abundance, affluence, plenty, riches, wealth.

indigenous, SYN.—aboriginal, domestic, endemic, inborn, inherent, innate, native, natural.

indigent, SYN.—claiming, covetous, craving, demanding, desiring, lacking, needy, requiring, wanting, wishing.

indignation, SYN.—anger, animosity, choler, exasperation, fury, ire, irritation, passion, petulance, rage, resentment, temper, wrath. ANT.—conciliation, forbearance, patience, peace, self-control.

indignity, SYN.—abuse, affront, insolence, insult, offense. ANT.—apology, homage, salutation.

indirect, SYN.—circuitous, crooked, devious, distorted, erratic, roundabout, swerving, tortuous, wandering, winding; crooked, cunning, tricky. ANT.—direct, straight; honest, straightforward.

indiscretion, SYN.—absurdity, extravagance, folly, imprudence. ANT.—sense, wisdom, judgment, prudence, reasonableness.

indispensable, SYN.—basic, essential, fundamental, important, intrinsic, necessary, requisite, vital. ANT.—expendable, extrinsic, optional, peripheral.

indistinct, SYN.—abstruse,

ambiguous, cloudy, cryptic, dark, dim, dusky, enigmatic, mysterious, obscure, unintelligible, vague. ANT.—bright, clear, distinct, lucid.

indistinguishable, SYN.—coincident, equal, equivalent, identical, like, same. ANT.—contrary, disparate, dissimilar, distinct, opposed.

individual, SYN.—distinctive, marked, particular, separate, singular, special, specific, unique. ANT.—common, general, ordinary, universal.

individuality, SYN.—character, mark, sign, symbol.

indolent, SYN.—idle, inactive, inert, lazy, slothful, sluggish, supine, torpid. ANT.—active, alert, assiduous, diligent.

indomitable, SYN.—impregnable, insurmountable, invincible, invulnerable unassailable, unconquerable. ANT.—powerless, puny, vulnerable, weak.

induce, SYN.—cause, create, effect, evoke, incite, make, occasion, originate, prompt.

inducement, SYN.—cause, impulse, incentive, incitement, motive, principle, purpose, reason, spur, stimulus. ANT.—action, attempt, deed, effort, result.

indurate, SYN.—callous, hard, impenitent, insensible, insensitive, obdurate, tough, unfeeling. ANT. — compassionate, sensitive, soft, tender.

industrious, SYN.—active, assiduous, busy, careful, diligent, hard-working, patient, perseverant. ANT.—apathetic, careless, indifferent, lethargic, unconcerned.

inebriated, SYN.—drunk, drunken, high, intoxicated, tight, tipsy. ANT.—clear-headed, sober, temperate.

ineffective, SYN.—bending, fragile, frail, pliant, tender, yielding; debilitated, decrepit, delicate, feeble, impotent, infirm, illogical, inadequate, lame, poor, vague; irresolute, pliable, vacillating, wavering; assailable, defenseless, exposed, vulnerable, weak. ANT.—potent, powerful, robust, strong, sturdy.

inequity, SYN.—grievance, injury, injustice, unfairness, wrong. ANT.—equity, justice, lawfulness, righteousness.

inert, SYN.—dormant, idle, inactive, indolent, lazy, slothful. ANT.—active, industrious, occupied, working.

inertia, SYN.—idleness, inactivity, indolence, slothfulness, sluggishness, supineness, torpidity. ANT.—activity, alertness, assiduousness, diligence.

inevitable, SYN.—assured, certain, definite, fixed,

indubitable, positive, secure, sure, undeniable, unquestionable. ANT.—doubtful, probable, questionable, uncertain.

inexpensive, SYN.—cheap, low-priced, poor; beggarly, common, inferior, mean, shabby. ANT.—costly, dear, expensive.

inexplicable, SYN.—cabalistic, cryptic, dark, dim, enigmatical, hidden, incomprehensible, inscrutable, mysterious, mystical, obscure, occult, recondite, secret. ANT.—clear, explained, obvious, plain, simple.

infect, SYN.—befoul, contaminate, corrupt, defile, poison, pollute, sully, taint. ANT.—disinfect, purify.

infection, SYN.—contagion, germ, pest, virus; ailment, contamination, disease, poison, pollution, taint.

infectious, SYN.—catching, communicable, contagious, pestilential, virulent. ANT.—healthful, hygienic, noncommunicable.

inference, SYN.—conclusion, consequence, corollary, deduction, judgment, result. ANT.—assumption, foreknowledge, preconception, presupposition.

inferior, SYN.—lower, minor, poorer, secondary, subordinate. ANT.—better, greater, higher, superior.

infinite, SYN.—boundless,

endless, eternal, illimitable, immeasurable, immense, interminable, unbounded, unlimited, vast. ANT.—bounded, circumscribed, confined, finite, limited.

infirm, SYN.—decrepit, delicate, enervated, exhausted, faint, feeble, forceless, impaired, languid, powerless, puny, weak. ANT.—forceful, lusty, stout, strong, vigorous.

infirmity, SYN.—ailment, complaint, disease, disorder, illness, malady, sickness. ANT.—health, healthiness, soundness, vigor.

inflexible, SYN.—contumacious, determined, dogged, firm, headstrong, immovable, intractable, obdurate, obstinate, pertinacious, stubborn, uncompromising, unyielding. ANT.—amenable, compliant, docile, submissive, yielding.

influenced, SYN.—actuate, affect, bias, control, impel, incite, stir, sway.

influential, SYN.—consequential, critical, decisive, grave, important, material, momentous, pressing, prominent, relevant, significant, weighty. ANT.—insignificant, irrelevant, mean, petty, trivial.

inform, SYN.—acquaint, advise, apprise, enlighten, impart, instruct, notify, teach, tell, warn. ANT.—conceal, delude, distract, mislead.

informal, SYN.—easy, familiar, natural, simple, unofficial. ANT.—conceal, delude, distract, mislead.

informality, SYN.—acquaintance, familiarity, fellowship, friendship, sociability; frankness, intimacy, liberty, unreserve. ANT.—constraint, distance, haughtiness, presumption, reserve.

infrequent. SYN.—occasional, rare, strange, unusual. ANT.—customary, frequent, ordinary, usual; abundant, commonplace, numerous.

ingenious, SYN.—adroit, apt, clever, dexterous, quick, quick-witted, skillful, talented, witty; bright, sharp, smart. ANT.—awkward, bungling, clumsy, slow, unskilled; dull, foolish, stupid.

ingenuity, SYN.—aptitude, cleverness, cunning, faculty, ingeniousness, inventiveness, resourcefulness, skill. ANT.—clumsiness, dullness, ineptitude, stupidity.

ingenuous, SYN.—candid, frank, free, honest, open, plain, sincere, straightforward, truthful. ANT.—contrived, scheming, sly, wily.

inhabit, SYN.—absorb, dwell, fill, occupy, possess. ANT.—abandon, release, relinquish.

inherent, SYN.—congenital, inborn, inbred, innate, intrinsic, native, natural, real. ANT.—acquired, external, extraneous, extrinsic.

inhibit, SYN.—bridle, check, constrain, curb, hinder, hold back, limit, repress, restrain, stop, suppress. ANT.—aid, encourage, incite, loosen.

inhuman, SYN.—cruel; barbarous, brutal, ferocious, malignant, merciless, ruthless, savage. ANT.—benevolent, compassionate, forbearing, gentle, humane, kind, merciful.

inimical, SYN.—adverse, antagonistic, hostile, opposed, unfriendly, warlike. ANT.—amicable, cordial, favorable.

iniquitous, SYN.—bad, baleful, base, deleterious, evil, immoral, noxious, pernicious, sinful, unsound, unwholesome, villainous, wicked. ANT.—excellent, good, honorable, moral, reputable.

iniquity, SYN.—grievance, injury, injustice, unfairness, wrong. ANT.—equity, justice, lawfulness, righteousness.

initial, SYN.—beginning, earliest, first, original, primary, prime, primeval, primitive, pristine; chief, foremost. ANT.—hindmost, last, latest; least, subordinate.

initiate, SYN.—arise, begin, commence, enter, inaugurate, institute, open, originate, start. ANT.—close, complete, end, finish, terminate.

injure, SYN.—damage, disfigure, harm, hurt, impair, mar, spoil, wound; abuse, affront, dishonor, insult, wrong. ANT.—ameliorate, benefit, help, preserve; compliment, praise.

injurious, SYN.—damaging, deleterious, detrimental, harmful, hurtful, mischievous. ANT.—advantageous, beneficial, helpful, profitable, salutary.

injury, SYN.—damage, detriment, harm, mischief; grievance, injustice, prejudice, wrong. ANT.—benefit, improvement, repair.

injustice, SYN.—grievance, iniquity, injury, unfairness, wrong. ANT.—equity, justice, lawfulness, righteousness.

innate, SYN.—congenital, inborn, inbred, inherent, intrinsic, native, natural, real. ANT.—acquired, external, extraneous, extrinsic.

innocent, SYN.—blameless, faultless, innocuous, lawful, naive, pure, sinless, virtuous. ANT.—corrupt, culpable, guilty, sinful, unrighteous.

innocuous, SYN.—blameless, faultless, innocent, lawful, naive, pure, sinless, virtuous. ANT.—corrupt, culpable, guilty, sinful, unrighteous.

inquire, SYN.—ask, beg, claim, demand, entreat, invite, request, solicit; inquire, interrogate, query, question. ANT.—command, dictate, insist, order, reply.

inquiring, SYN.—curious, inquisitive, interrogative, meddling, nosy, peeping, peering, prying, searching, snoopy. ANT.—incurious, indifferent, unconcerned, uninterested.

inquiry, SYN.—examination, exploration, interrogation, investigation, query, quest, question, research, scrutiny. ANT.—disregard, inactivity, inattention, negligence.

inquisitive, SYN.—curious, inquiring, interrogative, meddling, nosy, peeping, peering, prying, searching, snoopy. ANT.—incurious, indifferent, unconcerned, uninterested.

insane, SYN.—crazy, delirious, demented, deranged, foolish, idiotic, imbecilic, mad, maniacal. ANT.—rational, reasonable, sane, sensible, sound.

insanity, SYN.—aberration, craziness, delirium, dementia, derangement, frenzy, lunacy, madness, mania.

insensitive, SYN.—callous, hard, impenitent, indurate, insensible, obdurate, tough, unfeeling. ANT. — compassionate, sensitive, soft, tender.

insight, SYN.—acumen, discernment, intuition, penetration, perspicuity. ANT.—obtuseness.

insignificant, SYN.—frivolous, paltry, petty, small, trifling, trivial, unimportant. ANT.—important, momentous, serious, weighty.

insinuate, SYN.—connote, imply, involve, mean, signify, suggest. ANT.—assert, express, state.

insipid, SYN.—dull, flat, stale, tasteless, vapid. ANT.—exciting, racy, savory, tasty.

insolence, SYN.—assurance, audacity, boldness, effrontery, impertinence, impudence, presumption, rudeness, sauciness. ANT.—diffidence, politeness, subserviency, truckling.

insolent, SYN.—abusive, arrogant, brazen, contemptuous, impertinent, impudent, insulting, offensive, rude. ANT.—considerate, courteous, polite, respectful.

inspect, SYN.—behold, discern, eye, gaze, glance, look, scan, see, stare, survey, view, watch, witness; examine, observe, regard. ANT.—avert, hide, miss, overlook.

inspection, SYN.—criticism, critique, examination, reconsideration, retrospect, retrospection, revision, review, survey.

inspiration, SYN.—ability, aptitude, creativity, fac-

instantaneous 114 intelligence

ulty, genius, gift, intellect, originality, sagacity, talent; adept, intellectual, master, proficient. ANT.—ineptitude, obtuseness, shallowness, stupidity; dolt, dullard, moron.

instantaneous, SYN.—abrupt, hasty, immediate, rapid, sudden, unexpected. ANT.—anticipated, gradual, slowly.

instantly, SYN.—directly, forthwith, immediately, instantaneously, now, presently, promptly, straightaway. ANT.—distantly, hereafter, later, shortly, sometime.

instinctive, SYN.—automatic, extemporaneous, impulsive, offhand, spontaneous, voluntary, willing. ANT.—compulsory, forced, planned, prepared, rehearsed.

institute, SYN.—establish, form, found, organize, raise; fix, ordain, sanction. ANT.—abolish, demolish, overthrow, unsettle, upset.

instruct, SYN.—educate, inculcate, inform, instill, school, teach, train, tutor. ANT.—misguide, misinform.

instruction, SYN.—admonition, advice, caution, counsel, exhortation, recommendation, suggestion, warning; information, intelligence, notification.

instrument, SYN.—agent, apparatus, channel, device, means, medium,

tool, utensil vehicle. ANT.—hindrance, impediment, obstruction, preventive.

insubordinate, SYN.—defiant, disobedient, forward, rebellious, refractory, undutiful, unruly. ANT.—compliant, dutiful, obedient, submissive.

insufficient, SYN.—deficient, inadequate, lacking, limited, short. ANT.—abundant, ample, big, extended, protracted.

insulation, SYN.—alienation, isolation, loneliness, quarantine, retirement, seclusion, segregation, solitude, withdrawal. ANT.—association, communion, connection, fellowship, union.

insult, SYN.—abuse, affront, indignity, insolence, offense. ANT.—apology, homage, salutation.

insult, SYN.—abuse, affront, dishonor, injure, wrong. ANT.—compliment, praise.

integrity, SYN.—candor, fairness, frankness, honesty, justice, openness, rectitude, responsibility, sincerity, trustworthiness, uprightness. ANT.—cheating, deceit, dishonesty, fraud, trickery.

intelligence, SYN.—ability, intellect, mind, reason, sense, understanding. ANT.—emotion, feeling, passion.

intelligent, SYN.—alert, astute, bright, clever, discerning, quick, smart; enlightened, intellectual, knowledgeable, well-informed. ANT.—dull, foolish, insipid, obtuse, slow, stupid.

intend, SYN.—contrive, delineate, design, devise, outline, plan, plot, prepare, project, scheme, sketch.

intense, SYN.—bright, brilliant, striking; animated, clear, expressive, fresh, graphic, lively, lucid, vivid. ANT.—dull, vague; dim, dreary, dusky.

intent, SYN.—design, intention, objective, purpose. ANT.—result; accidental, chance.

intensity, SYN.—activity, durability, force, fortitude, might, potency, power, stamina, toughness, vigor. ANT.—feebleness, frailty, infirmity, weakness.

intention, SYN.—design, intent, objective, purpose. ANT.—result; accident, chance.

intentional, SYN.—contemplated, deliberate, designed, intended, premeditated, studied, voluntary, willful. ANT.—accidental, fortuitous.

interfere, SYN.—interpose, interrupt, meddle, monkey, tamper.

interior, SYN.—inmost, inner, internal, inward. ANT.—adjacent, exterior, external, outer.

interject, SYN.—inject, insert, interpose, introduce, intrude. ANT.—avoid, disregard, overlook.

interminable, SYN.—boundless, endless, eternal, illimitable, immeasurable, immense, infinite, unbounded, unlimited, vast. ANT.—bounded, circumscribed, confined, finite, limited.

interpose, SYN.—inject, insert, interject, introduce, intrude; arbitrate, intercede, interfere, intervene, meddle, mediate. ANT.—avoid, disregard, overlook.

interpret, SYN.—construe, decipher, decode, elucidate, explain, explicate, render, solve, translate, unravel. ANT.—confuse, distort, falsify, misconstrue, misinterpret.

interrogate, SYN.—examine, inquire, question, quiz. ANT.—disregard, neglect, omit, overlook.

interrupt, SYN.—adjourn, defer, delay, discontinue, postpone, suspend, stay. ANT.—continue, maintain, persist, proceed, prolong.

intervene, SYN.—inject, insert, interject, introduce, intrude; arbitrate, intercede, interfere, interpose, meddle, mediate. ANT.—avoid, disregard, overlook.

intimacy, SYN.—acquaintance, familiarity, fellowship, friendship, sociability; frankness, informality, liberty, unreserve. ANT.—constraint, distance, haughtiness, presumption, reserve.

intimate, SYN.—affectionate, chummy, close, confidential, familiar, friendly, loving, near. ANT.—ceremonious, conventional, distant, formal.

intimation, SYN.—allusion, hint, implication, insinuation, reminder. ANT.—affirmation, declaration, statement.

intolerant, SYN.—bigoted, dogmatic, fanatical, illiberal, narrow-minded, prejudiced. ANT.—liberal, progressive, radical, tolerant.

intoxicated, SYN.—drunk, drunken, high, inebriated, tight, tipsy. ANT.—clear-headed, sober, temperate.

intrepid, SYN.—adventurous, audacious, bold, brave, courageous, daring, dauntless, fearless, brazen, forward, impudent, insolent, pushy, rude; abrupt, conspicuous, prominent, striking. ANT.—cowardly, flinching, timid; bashful, retiring.

intricate, SYN.—complex, complicated, compound, involved, perplexing. ANT.—plain, simple, uncompounded.

intrigue, SYN.—cabal, conspiracy, design, machination, plan, plot,

scheme, stratagem.

intrinsic, SYN.—congenital, inborn, inbred, inherent, innate, native, natural, real. ANT.—acquired, external, extraneous, extrinsic.

introduction, SYN.—beginning, forward, overture, preamble, preface, prelude, prologue, start. ANT.—completion, conclusion, end, epilogue, finale.

intrude, SYN.—attack, encroach, infringe, invade, penetrate, trespass, violate. ANT.—abandon, evacuate, relinquish, vacate.

intuition, SYN.—acumen, discernment, insight, penetration, perspicuity. ANT.—obtuseness.

invade, SYN.—attack, encroach, infringe, intrude, penetrate, trespass, violate. ANT.—abandon, evacuate, relinquish, vacate.

invalidate, SYN.—abolish, abrogate, annul, cancel, revoke. ANT.—continue, establish, promote, restore, sustain.

invasion, SYN.—aggression, assault, attack, onslaught. ANT.—defense, opposition, resistance, surrender.

invective, SYN.—abuse, aspersion, defamation, disparagement, insult, reproach, upbraiding. ANT. — commendation, laudation, plaudit.

invent, SYN.—conceive, concoct, contrive, design, devise, fabricate, frame. ANT.—copy, imitate, reproduce.

inventive, SYN.—clever, creative, fanciful, imaginative, mystical, poetical, visionary. ANT.—dull, literal, prosaic, unromantic.

inventiveness, SYN.—aptitude, cleverness, cunning, faculty, ingeniousness, ingenuity, resourcefulness, skill. ANT.—clumsiness, dullness, ineptitude, stupidity.

invert, SYN.—reverse, transpose, turn about; overturn, upset; countermand, repeal, rescind, revoke. ANT.—endorse, maintain, stabilize.

investigate, SYN.—examine, explore, ferret (out), hunt, look, probe, ransack, rummage, search, scour, scrutinize, seek.

investigation, SYN.—examination, exploration, inquiry, interrogation, query, quest, question, research, scrutiny. ANT.—disregard, inactivity, inattention, negligence.

invincible, SYN.—impregnable, indomitable, insurmountable, invulnerable, unassailable, unconquerable. ANT.—powerless, puny, vulnerable, weak.

invisible, SYN.—imperceptible, indistinguishable, undiscernible, unseen. ANT.—evident, perceptible, seen, visible.

involve, SYN.—embrace, embroil, entangle, envelop, implicate, include, incriminate. ANT.—disconnect, disengage, extricate, separate.

involved, SYN.—complex, complicated, compound, intricate, perplexing. ANT.—plain, simple, uncompounded.

invulnerable, SYN.—impregnable, indomitable, insurmountable, invincible, unassailable, unconquerable. ANT.—powerless, puny, vulnerable, weak.

ire, SYN.—anger, animosity, choler, exasperation, fury, indignation, irritation, passion, petulance, rage, resentment, temper, wrath. ANT.—conciliation, forbearance, patience, peace, self-control.

irk, SYN.—annoy, bother, chafe, disturb, inconvenience, irritate, molest, pester, tease, trouble, vex. ANT.—accommodate, console, gratify, soothe.

irrational, SYN.—absurd, foolish, inconsistent, nonsensical, preposterous, ridiculous, selfcontradictory, silly, unreasonable. ANT.—consistent, rational, reasonable, sensible, sound.

irregular, SYN.—aberrant, abnormal, capricious, devious, eccentric, unnatural, unusual, variable. ANT.—fixed, methodical, ordinary, regular, usual.

irrelevant, SYN.—alien, extraneous, foreign, remote, strange, unconnected. ANT.—akin, germane, kindred, relevant.

irresolute, SYN.—bending, fragile, frail, pliant, yielding; ineffective, pliable, vacillating, wavering. ANT.—potent, powerful, robust, strong, sturdy.

irritable, SYN.—choleric, excitable, fiery, hasty, hot, irascible, peevish, petulant, snappish, testy, touchy. ANT.—agreeable, calm, composed, tranquil.

irritate, SYN.—annoy, bother, chafe, disturb, inconvenience, irk, molest, pester, tease, trouble, vex. ANT.—accommodate, console, gratify.

irritation, SYN.—annoyance, chagrin, exasperation, mortification, pique, vexation. ANT.—appeasement, comfort, gratification, pleasure.

isolated, SYN.—alone, deserted, desolate, lonely, secluded, unaided; lone, only, single, sole, solitary. ANT.—accompanied, attended, surrounded.

isolation, SYN.—alienation, insulation, loneliness, quarantine, retirement, seclusion, segregation, separation, solitude, withdrawal. ANT.—association, communion, connection, fellowship, union.

issue, SYN.—come, emanate, flow, originate, proceed, result; abound, be copious.

J

jargon, SYN.—dialect, diction, idiom, language, lingo, phraseology, slang, speech, tongue, vernacular. ANT.—babble, drivel, gibberish, nonsense.

jealousy, SYN.—covetousness, envy, invidiousness, resentfulness, suspicion. ANT.—geniality, indifference, liberality, tolerance.

jeer, SYN.—deride, fleer, flout, gibe, mock, scoff, sneer, taunt. ANT.—compliment, flatter, laud, praise.

jeering, SYN.—derision, gibe, irony, mockery, raillery, ridicule, sarcasm, satire, sneering.

jeopardize, SYN.—chance, conjecture, dare, endanger, hazard, imperil, peril, risk, venture. ANT.—determine, guard, insure, know.

jester, SYN.—buffoon, clown, fool, harlequin. ANT.—genius, philosopher, sage, scholar.

job, SYN.—chore, labor, stint, task, toil, work, undertaking; business, employment, occupation, position, post, situation.

jocularity, SYN.—facetiousness, humor, joke, waggery, wit. ANT.—gravity, seriousness, sorrow.

join, SYN.—accompany, adjoin, associate, attach, combine, conjoin, connect, couple, go with, link, unite. ANT.—detach, disconnect, disjoin, separate.

jolly, SYN.—cheerful, gay, glad, happy, joyful, light-hearted, merry, sprightly. ANT.—depressed, glum, mournful, sad, sullen.

jolt, SYN.—jar, quake, rock, shake, sway, totter, waver.

journey, SYN.—cruise, expedition, jaunt, passage, pilgrimage, tour, travel. ANT.—stay, stop.

joy, SYN.—bliss, delight, ecstasy, felicity, happiness, pleasure, rapture, transport; elation, exultation, festivity, glee, merriment, mirth. ANT.—affliction, depression, despair, grief, sorrow.

joyful, SYN.—cheerful, contented, delighted, fortunate, gay, glad, happy, joyous, lucky, merry, opportune. ANT.—blue, depressed, gloomy, morose.

joyous, SYN.—blithe, cheerful, festive, gay, gleeful, hilarious, jolly, jovial, lively, merry, mirthful, sprightly. ANT.—gloomy, melancholy, morose, sad, sorrowful.

judge, SYN.—adjudicator, arbitrator, critic, justice, magistrate, referee, umpire.

judge, SYN.—decide, decree, determine; adjudicate, arbitrate, condemn, try, umpire; appreciate, consider, estimate, evaluate, measure, think.

judgment, SYN.—discernment, discrimination, intelligence, perspicacity, sagacity, understanding, wisdom. ANT.—arbitrariness, senselessness, stupidity, thoughtlessness.

jumble, SYN.—agitation, chaos, commotion, confusion, disarrangement, disarray, disorder, ferment, stir, tumult, turmoil. ANT.—certainty, order, peace, tranquility.

jumble, SYN.—amalgamate, blend, combine, commingle, compound, concoct, confound, fuse, mingle, mix. ANT.—divide, segregate, separate, sort.

jump, SYN.—bound, caper, hop, jerk, leap, skip, spring, start, vault.

just, SYN.—candid, conscientious, fair, honest, honorable, scrupulous, sincere, trustworthy, truthful, upright. ANT.—deceitful, dishonest, fraudulent, lying, tricky.

justice, SYN.—equity, fairness, impartiality, justness, law, rectitude, right. ANT.—inequity, partiality, unfairness, wrong.

justifiable, SYN.—admissible, allowable, fair, permissible, tolerable, warranted. ANT.—inadmissible, irrelevant, unsuitable.

justify, SYN.—absolve, defend, excuse, exonerate, support, uphold, vindicate. ANT.—blame, convict.

K

keen, SYN.—acute, cutting, penetrating, piercing, severe; astute, clever, cunning, quick, sharp, shrewd, wily, witty. ANT.—bland, blunt, gentle, shallow, stupid.

keep, SYN.—conserve, continue, maintain, preserve, save; confine, detain, hold, reserve, restrain, retain; execute, obey; celebrate, commemorate, honor, observe; guard, protect; support, sustain. ANT.—discard, reject; dismiss, relinquish; disobey, ignore; abandon, forsake, neglect.

kill, SYN.—assassinate, butcher, execute, massacre, murder, put to death, slaughter, slay. ANT.—animate, protect, resuscitate, save, vivify.

kind, SYN.—affable, benevolent, benign, compassionate, forbearing, gentle, good, humane, indulgent, kindly, merciful, sympathetic, tender, thoughtful. ANT.—cruel, inhuman, merciless, severe, unkind.

kind, SYN.—breed, character, family, genus, race, sort, species, stock, strain, type, variety.

kindred, SYN.—affinity, consanguinity, family, kinsfolk, relations, relationship, relatives. ANT.—disconnection, foreigners, strangers.

kiss, SYN.—caress, cuddle, embrace, fondle, pet. ANT.—annoy, buffet, spurn, tease, vex.

knack, SYN.—ability, adroitness, cleverness, deftness, dexterity, facility, ingenuity, readiness, skill, skillfullness. ANT.—awkwardness, clumsiness, inability, ineptitude.

know, SYN.—apprehend, ascertain, cognize, comprehend, discern, distinguish, perceive, recognize, understand. ANT.—dispute, doubt, ignore, suspect.

knowledge, SYN.—apprehension, cognizance, erudition, information, learning, lore, scholarship, science, understanding, wisdom. ANT.—ignorance, illiteracy, misunderstanding, stupidity.

L

labor, SYN.—drudgery, effort, endeavor, exertion, striving, task, toil, travail, work; childbirth, parturition. ANT.—

idleness, indolence, leisure, recreation.

lacking, SYN.—defective, deficient, inadequate, incomplete, insufficient, scanty, short. ANT.—adequate, ample, enough, satisfactory, sufficient.

ladylike, SYN.—female, feminine, girlish, maidenly, womanish, womanly. ANT.—male, manly, mannish, masculine, virile.

lame, SYN.—crippled, defective, deformed, disabled, feeble, halt, hobbling, limping, maimed, unconvincing, unsatisfactory, weak. ANT.—agile, athletic, robust, sound, vigorous.

lament, SYN.—bemoan, bewail, deplore, grieve, mourn, repine, wail, weep.

lamp, SYN.—beam, gleam, illumination, incandescence, light, luminosity, radiance, shine; enlightenment, insight, knowledge, understanding. ANT.—darkness, gloom, obscurity, shadow.

land, SYN.—continent, country, earth, field, ground, island, plain, region, soil, tract; domain, estate, farm, realm.

language, SYN.—cant, dialect, diction, idiom, jargon, lingo, phraseology, slang, speech, tongue, vernacular. SYN.—babble, drivel, gibberish, nonsense.

languid, SYN.—faint, feeble, wearied; irresolute, weak. ANT.—strong, vigorous; forceful.

languish, SYN.—droop, waste, wilt, wither, wizen; decline, fail, sink, weaken. ANT.—refresh, rejuvenate, renew, revive.

larceny, SYN.—burglary, larceny, pillage, plunder, robbery, theft.

large, SYN.—ample, big, capacious, colossal, extensive, great, huge, immense, vast, wide. ANT.—little, mean, short, small, tiny.

last, SYN.—concluding, extreme, final, hindmost, latest, terminal, ultimate, utmost. ANT.—beginning, first, foremost, initial, opening.

late, SYN.—delayed, overdue, slow, tardy; advanced, new, recent. ANT.—early, timely.

latent, SYN.—concealed, dormant, hidden, inactive, potential, quiescent, secret, undeveloped, unseen. ANT.—conspicuous, evident, explicit, manifest, visible.

laudation, SYN.—acclaim, applause, commendation, compliment, eulogy, extolling, flattery, glorification, praise. ANT.—censure, condemnation, criticizing, disparagement, reproach.

laugh, SYN.—cackle, chuckle, giggle, guffaw, jeer, mock, roar, scoff, snicker, titter.

lavish, SYN.—dissipate,

misuse, scatter, spend, squander, waste, wear out. ANT.—accumulate, conserve, economize, preserve, save.

law, SYN.—act, decree, edict, statute.

lawful, SYN.—allowable, authorized, constitutional, legal, legitimate, permissible, rightful. ANT.—criminal, illegal, illegitimate, illicit, prohibited.

lay, SYN.—earthly, laic, mundane, profane, secular, temporal, worldly. ANT.—ecclesiastical, religious, spiritual, unworldly.

lay, SYN.—arrange, deposit, dispose, place, put, set. ANT.—disarrange, disturb, mislay, misplace, remove.

lax, SYN.—careless, desultory, inaccurate, neglectful, negligent, remiss. ANT.—accurate, careful, meticulous.

lazy, SYN.—idle, inactive, indolent, inert, slothful, sluggish, supine, torpid. ANT.—active, alert, assiduous, diligent.

lead, SYN.—conduct, direct, escort, guide, steer; control, manage, regulate, supervise.

leader, SYN.—captain, chief, chieftain, commander, head, master, principal, ruler. ANT.—attendant, follower, servant, subordinate.

league, SYN.—alliance, association, coalition, combination, confedera-cy, entente, federation, partnership, union. ANT.—schism, separation.

lean, SYN.—bend, incline, sag, slant, slope, tend; depend, rely, trust. ANT.—erect, raise, rise, straighten.

leaning, SYN.—bent, bias, drift, inclination, predisposition, proclivity, proneness, propensity, tendency, trend. ANT.—aversion, deviation, disinclination.

leap, SYN.—bound, caper, hop, jerk, jump, skip, spring, start, vault.

learned, SYN.—deep, discerning, enlightened, intelligent, penetrating, profound, sagacious, sound; erudite, informed, knowing, scholarly, wise. ANT.—foolish, shallow, simple.

learning, SYN.—apprehension, cognizance, erudition, information, knowledge, lore, scholarship, science, understanding, wisdom. ANT.—ignorance, illiteracy, misunderstanding, stupidity.

leave, SYN.—abandon, depart, desert, forsake, give up, go, quit, relinquish, renounce, retire, withdraw. ANT.—abide, remain, stay, tarry.

lecture, SYN.—conference, discourse, discussion, report, speech, talk. ANT. — correspondence, meditation, silence, writing.

legal, SYN.—allowable, authorized, constitutional, lawful, legitimate, permissible, rightful. ANT.—criminal, illegal, illegitimate, illicit, prohibited.

legend, SYN.—allegory, chronicle, fable, fiction, myth, parable, saga. ANT.—fact, history.

legitimate, SYN.—authentic, bona fide, genuine, proven, real, sincere, true, unadulterated, veritable. ANT.—artificial, bogus, counterfeit, false, sham.

leisure, SYN.—calm, ease, peace, quiet, relaxation, repose, rest, tranquility; cessation, intermission, pause, respite. ANT.—agitation, commotion, disturbance, motion, tumult.

leisurely, SYN.—dawdling, delaying, deliberate, gradual, laggard, slow, sluggish. ANT.—fast, quick, rapid, speedy, swift.

lengthen, SYN.—draw, extend, prolong, protract, stretch. ANT.—contract, shorten.

leniency, SYN.—charity, clemency, compassion, forgiveness, grace, mercy, mildness, pity. ANT.—cruelty, punishment, retribution, vengeance.

lenient, SYN.—clement, compassionate, forbearing, forgiving, humane, kind, merciful, tender, tolerant. ANT.—brutal, cruel, pitiless, remorseless, unfeeling.

lessen, SYN.—curtail, decrease, deduct, diminish, reduce, remove, shorten, subtract. ANT.—amplify, enlarge, expand, grow, increase.

lethargy, SYN.—daze, drowsiness, insensibility, languor, numbness, stupefaction, stupor, torpor. ANT.—activity, alertness, liveliness, readiness, wakefulness.

letter, SYN.—mark, sign, symbol; letter, memorandum, message, note.

level, SYN.—even, flat, horizontal, plane, smooth. ANT.—broken, hilly, irregular, sloping.

levy, SYN.—assessment, custom, duty, exaction, excise, impost, rate, tax, toll, tribute. ANT.—gift, remuneration, reward, wages.

lewd, SYN.—coarse, dirty, disgusting, filthy, gross, impure, indecent, obscene, offensive, pornographic, smutty. ANT.—decent, modest, pure, refined.

liable, SYN.—accountable, amenable, answerable, exposed to, responsible, subject to. ANT.—exempt, free, immune, independent.

libel, SYN.—aspersion, backbiting, calumny, defamation, slander, vilification. ANT.—applause, commendation, defense, flattery, praise.

liberal, SYN.—broad, extensive, large, tolerant. ANT.—confined, narrow, restricted.

liberality, SYN.—altruism, beneficience, benevolence, charity, generosity, humanity, kindness, magnanimity, philanthropy. ANT.—cruelty, inhumanity, malevolence, selfishness.

liberate, SYN.—deliver, discharge, emancipate, free, let go, release, set free. ANT.—confine, imprison, oppress, restrict, subjugate.

liberated, SYN.—autonomous, emancipated, exempt, free, freed, independent, unconfined, unrestricted; loose, unfastened, unobstructed; immune; careless, easy, familiar, frank; liberal. ANT.—confined, restrained, restricted; blocked, clogged, impeded; subject.

liberty, SYN.—autonomy, freedom, independence, self-government; license, permission, privilege. ANT.—captivity, imprisonment, submission, constraint.

license, SYN.—exemption, familiarity, freedom, immunity, independence, liberation, liberty, privilege, unrestraint. ANT.—bondage, compulsion, constraint, necessity, servitude.

lie, SYN.—delusion, equivocation, falsehood, fib, fiction, illusion, untruth.

life, SYN.—animation, being, buoyancy, existence, liveliness, spirit, vigor, vitality, vivacity. ANT.—death, demise, dullness, languor, lethargy.

lifeless, SYN.—dead, deceased, defunct, departed, dull, gone, inanimate, insensible, spiritless, unconscious. ANT.—alive, animate, living, stirring.

lift, SYN.—elevate, erect, exalt, heave, heighten, hoist, lift, raise, uplift. ANT.—abase, depreciate, depress, destroy, hover.

light, SYN.—buoyant, effervescent, resilient; animated, blithe, cheerful, elated, hopeful, jocund, lively, spirited, sprightly, vivacious. ANT.—dejected, depressed, despondent, hopeless, sullen.

light, SYN.—beam, brightness, dawn, flame, gleam, illumination, incandescence, lamp, luminosity, radiance, shine; enlightenment, insight, knowledge, understanding. ANT.—darkness, gloom, obscurity, shadow.

like, SYN.—coincident, equal, equivalent, identical, indistinguishable, same. ANT.—contrary, disparate, dissimilar, distinct, opposed.

likeness, SYN.—analogy, correspondence, parity, resemblance, similarity, similitude. ANT.—difference, distinction, variance.

limit, SYN.—border, bound, boundary, confine, edge, extent, limitation, restraint, restriction, terminus. ANT.—boundlessness, endlessness, extension, infinity, vastness.

limpid, SYN.—clear, transparent; open, unobstructed. ANT.—foul.

lineage, SYN.—ancestry, clan, folk, nation, people, race, stock, strain, tribe.

linger, SYN.—abide, bide, delay, remain, rest, stay, tarry, wait. ANT.—expedite, hasten, leave.

link, SYN.—bond, connection, connective, coupler, juncture, tie, union. ANT.—break, gap, interval, opening, split.

link, SYN.—attach, conjoin, connect, couple, go with, join, unite. ANT.—detach, disconnect, disjoin, separate.

liquid, SYN.—flowing, fluent, juicy, watery. ANT.—congealed, gaseous, solid.

listen, SYN.—attend to, hear, hearken, heed, list, overhear. ANT.—be deaf to, disregard, ignore, reject, scorn.

little, SYN.—diminutive, insignificant, miniature, minute, petty, puny, slight, small, tiny, trivial, wee. ANT.—big, enormous, huge, immense, large.

lively, SYN.—active, animated, blithe, brisk, energetic, frolicsome, spirited, sprightly, supple, vigorous, vivaciousness; bright, clear, fresh, glowing, vivid. ANT.—dull, insipid, listless, stale, vapid.

liveliness, SYN.—activity, agility, briskness, energy, intensity, movement, quickness, rapidity, vigor. ANT.—dullness; idleness, inactivity, inertia, sloth.

load, SYN.—afflict, burden, encumber, oppress, overload, tax, trouble, weigh. ANT.—alleviate, console, ease, lighten, mitigate.

loathe, SYN.—abhor, abominate, despise, detest, dislike, hate. ANT.—admire, approve, cherish, like, love.

loathsome, SYN.—abominable, detestable, execrable, foul, hateful, odious, revolting, vile. ANT.—agreeable, commendable, delightful, pleasant.

locality, SYN.—district, environs, neighborhood; adjacency, nearness, vicinity. ANT.—distance, remoteness.

location, SYN.—area, locale, locality, place, region, site, situation, spot, station, vicinity.

lock, SYN.—bar, bolt, clasp, fastening, hook, latch, padlock; curl, ringlet, tress, tuft.

lofty, SYN.—grand, grandiose, high, imposing, magnificent, majestic, noble, pompous, stately, sublime. ANT.—common, humble, lowly, ordinary, undignified.

logical, SYN.—cogent, convincing, effective, efficacious, sound, strong, telling, valid, weighty. ANT.—spurious, weak.

lone, SYN.—deserted, desolate, isolated, lonely, secluded, unaided; alone, only, single, sole, solitary. ANT.—accompanied, attended, surrounded.

loneliness, SYN.—alienation, isolation, privacy, seclusion, solitude.

lonely, SYN.—deserted, desolate, isolated, secluded, unaided; alone, lone, only, single, sole, solitary. ANT.—accompanied, attended, surrounded.

long, SYN.—drawn out, elongated, extended, lasting, lengthy, lingering, prolix, prolonged, protracted, tedious, wordy. ANT.—abridged, brief, concise, short, terse.

look, SYN.—behold, discern, eye, gaze, glance, scan, see, stare, survey, view, watch, witness; appear, seem; examine, inspect, observe, regard. ANT.—avert, hide, miss, overlook.

loose, SYN.—disengaged, free, indefinite, lax, limp, slack, unbound, unfastened, untied, vague;

careless, dissolute, heedless, unrestrained, wanton. ANT.—fast, tied, tight; inhibited, restrained.

loss, SYN.—deficiency, failure, lack, want. ANT.—sufficiency.

lost, SYN.—adrift, astray, missing, consumed, destroyed, forefeited, misspent, used, wasted; absorbed, bewildered, confused, dazed, distracted, perplexed, preoccupied. ANT.—anchored, found, located.

lot, SYN.—doom, fate, fortune, portion; destiny, issue, outcome, result.

loud, SYN.—clamorous, deafening, noisy, resounding, sonorous, stentorian, vociferous. ANT.—dulcet, inaudible, quiet, soft, subdued.

love, SYN.—adoration, affection, attachment, devotion, endearment, fondness. ANT.—aversion, dislike, enmity, hatred, indifference.

loveliness, SYN.—attractiveness, beauty, charm, comeliness, elegance, fairness, grace, handsomeness, pulchritude. ANT.—deformity, disfigurement, eyesore, homeliness, ugliness.

lovely, SYN.—beauteous, beautiful, charming, comely, elegant, fair, fine, handsome, pretty. ANT.—foul, hideous, homely, repulsive, unsightly.

loving, SYN.—affectionate,

chummy, close, confidential, familiar, friendly, intimate, near. ANT. — ceremonious, conventional, distant, formal.

low, SYN.—abject, contemptible, despicable, dishonorable, groveling, ignoble, ignominious, lowly, mean, menial, servile, sordid, vile, vulgar. ANT.—esteemed, exalted, honored, lofty, noble, righteous.

lower, SYN.—inferior, minor, poorer, secondary, subordinate. ANT.—better, greater, higher, superior.

lower, SYN.—abase, adulterate, alloy, corrupt, debase, defile, degrade, deprave, depress, humiliate, impair, pervert, vitiate. ANT.—enhance, improve, raise, restore, vitalize.

loyal, SYN.—addicted, affectionate, ardent, attached, dedicated, devoted, earnest, faithful, fond, given up to, inclined, prone, true. ANT.—detached, disinclined, indisposed, untrammeled.

loyalty, SYN.—allegiance, constancy, devotion, faithfulness, fealty, fidelity. ANT.—disloyalty, falseness, perfidy, treachery.

lucid, SYN.—clear, limpid, transparent, distinct; evident, intelligible, manifest, obvious, plain, unmistakable, visible;

open, unobstructed. ANT.—ambiguous, obscure, unclear, vague.

lucky, SYN.—advantageous, auspicious, benign, favored, felicitous, fortuitous, fortunate, happy, propitious, successful. ANT.—cheerless, condemned, ill-fated, persecuted, unlucky.

luminous, SYN.—bright, brilliant, clear, gleaming, lucid, lustrous, radiant, shining. ANT.—dark, dull, gloomy, murky.

lunacy, SYN.—aberration, craziness, delirium, dementia, derangement, frenzy, insanity, madness, mania, psychosis. ANT.—rationality, sanity, stability.

lure, SYN.—drag, haul, pull, tow, tug; allure, attract, draw, entice, induce, persuade. ANT.—alienate, contract, drive, propel.

luscious, SYN.—delectable, delicious, delightful, palatable, savory, sweet, tasty. ANT.—acrid, distasteful, nauseous, unpalatable, unsavory.

lust, SYN.—appetite, aspiration, craving, desire, hungering, longing, urge, wish, yearning. ANT.—abomination, aversion, distaste, hate, loathing.

luster, SYN.—brightness, brilliance, brilliancy, effulgence, radiance, splendor. ANT.—darkness, dullness, gloom, obscurity.

M

mad, SYN.—angry, enraged, exasperated, furious, incensed, provoked, wrathful; crazy, delirious, demented, insane, lunatic, maniacal. ANT.—calm, happy, pleased; healthy, sane, sensible.

madness, SYN.—aberration, craziness, delirium, dementia, derangement, frenzy, insanity, lunacy, mania, psychosis. ANT.—rationality, sanity, stability.

magic, SYN.—black art, charm, conjuring, enchantment, legerdemain, necromancy, sorcery, voodoo, witchcraft, wizardry.

magistrate, SYN.—adjudicator, arbitrator, judge.

magnanimous, SYN.—beneficent, bountiful, generous, giving, liberal, munificent, openhanded, unselfish. ANT.—covetous, greedy, miserly, selfish, stingy.

magnify, SYN.—amplify, caricature, embroider, enlarge, exaggerate, expand, heighten, overstate, stretch. ANT.—belittle, depreciate, minimize, understate.

magnitude, SYN.—amplitude, area, bigness, bulk, dimensions, expanse, extent, greatness, largeness, mass, size, volume.

main, SYN.—cardinal, chief, essential, first, foremost, highest, leading, paramount, predominant, principal, supreme. ANT.—auxiliary, minor, subordinate, subsidiary, supplemental.

maintain, SYN.—continue, keep, preserve, support, sustain, uphold; affirm, allege, assert, claim, contend, declare, defend, justify, vindicate. ANT.—discontinue, neglect; deny, oppose, resist.

majestic, SYN.—august, dignified, grand, grandiose, high, imposing, lofty, magnificent, noble, pompous, stately, sublime. ANT.—common, humble, lowly, ordinary, undignified.

make, SYN.—assemble, build, cause, compel, construct, create, establish, execute, fashion, form, gain, manufacture, mold, produce, shape. ANT.—break, demolish, destroy, undo, unmake.

makeshift, SYN.—agent, alternate, deputy, lieutenant, proxy, representative, substitute, understudy; equivalent, expedient. ANT.—head, master, principal, sovereign.

malady, SYN.—ailment, complaint, disease, disorder, illness, infirmity, sickness. ANT.—health, healthiness, soundness, vigor.

malevolence, SYN.—animosity, enmity, grudge, ill will, malice, malignity, rancor, spite. ANT.—

affection, kindness, love, toleration.

malice, SYN.—animosity, enmity, grudge, ill will, malevolence, malignity, rancor, spite. ANT.—affection, kindness, love, toleration.

malicious, SYN.—bitter, evil-minded, hostile, malevolent, malignant, rancorous, spiteful, virulent, wicked. ANT.—affectionate, benevolent, benign, kind.

malign, SYN.—abuse, asperse, defame, disparage, ill-use, revile, scandalize, traduce, vilify; misapply, misemploy, misuse. ANT.—cherish, honor, praise, protect, respect.

malleable, SYN.—compassionate, flexible, gentle, lenient, meek, mellow, mild, soft, subdued, supple, tender, yielding. ANT.—hard, rigid, rough, tough, unyielding.

maltreatment, SYN.—abuse, aspersion, defamation, desecration, dishonor, disparagement, insult, invective, misuse, outrage, perversion, profanation, reproach, reviling, upbraiding. ANT.—approval, commendation, laudation, plaudit, respect.

manage, SYN.—command, control, direct, dominate, govern, regulate, rule, superintend; bridle, check, curb, repress, restrain. ANT.—abandon,

follow, forsake, ignore, submit.

maneuver, SYN.—action, agency, effort, enterprise, execution, instrumentality, operation, performance, proceeding, working. ANT.—cessation, inaction, inactivity, rest.

manifest, SYN.—clear, cloudless, fair, sunny; limpid, transparent; apparent, distinct, evident, intelligible, lucid, obvious, plain, unmistakable, visible; open, unobstructed. ANT.—cloudy, foul, overcast; ambiguous, obscure, unclear, vague.

manifest, SYN.—denote, designate, disclose, imply, indicate, intimate, reveal, show, signify, specify. ANT.—conceal, distract, divert, falsify, mislead.

manner, SYN.—custom, fashion, habit, method, mode, practice, style, way; air, behavior, conduct, demeanor, deportment.

many, SYN.—divers, manifold, multifarious, multitudinous, numerous, several, sundry, various. ANT.—few, infrequent, meager, scanty, scarce.

mar, SYN.—damage, deface, harm, hurt, impair, injure, spoil. ANT.—ameliorate, benefit, enhance, mend, repair.

marine, SYN.—maritime, nautical, naval, ocean, oceanic.

mark, SYN.—brand, scar, stain, stigma, trace, vestige; badge, label, sign; characteristic, feature, indication, property, symptoms, trait.

mark, SYN.—attend to, behold, descry, heed, note, notice, observe, perceive, recognize, regard, remark, see. ANT.—disregard, ignore, overlook, skip.

marriage, SYN.—espousal, matrimony, nuptials, union, wedding, wedlock. ANT.—celibacy, divorce, virginity.

marvelous, SYN.—exceptional, extraordinary, peculiar, rare, remarkable, singular, uncommon, unusual, wonderful. ANT.—common, frequent, ordinary, usual.

masculine, SYN.—bold, hardy, lusty, male, manly, mannish, robust, strong, vigorous, virile. ANT.—effeminate, emasculated, feminine, unmanly, weak, womanish.

mask, SYN.—cloak, conceal, cover, disguise, hide, screen, secrete, suppress, veil, withhold. ANT.—disclose, divulge, expose, reveal, show, uncover.

mass, SYN.—body, carcass, corpse, remains; form, frame, torso; bulk, corpus; aggregate, association, company, society. ANT.—intellect, mind, soul, spirit.

massacre, SYN.—butchery, carnage, pogrom, slaughter.

massacre, SYN.—assassinate, butcher, execute, kill, murder, put to death, slaughter, slay. ANT.—animate, protect, resuscitate, save, vivify.

massive, SYN.—heavy, ponderous, weighty; burdensome, cumbersome, grievous, trying; gloomy, grave, serious, dull, sluggish. ANT.—animated, brisk, light.

master, SYN.—chief; commander, employer, head, leader, lord, manager, overseer, ruler, teacher, holder, owner, proprietor; adept, expert. ANT.—servant, slave; amateur.

mastery, SYN.—ascendancy, domination, predominance, sovereignty, supremacy, sway, transcendence. ANT.—inferiority.

mate, SYN.—associate, attendant, colleague, companion, comrade, consort, crony, friend, partner. ANT.—adversary, enemy, stranger.

material, SYN.—bodily, corporeal, palpable, physical, sensible, tangible; essential, germane, important, momentous, relevant. ANT.—mental, metaphysical, spiritual; immaterial, insignificant.

material, SYN.—stuff, substance; cause, concern, matter, occasion, subject, theme, thing, topic; consequence, importance, moment. ANT.—

immateriality, phantom, spirit.

matrimony, SYN.—espousal, marriage, nuptials, union, wedding, wedlock. ANT.—celibacy, divorce, virginity.

matter, SYN.—material, stuff, substance; cause, concern, occasion, subject, theme, thing, topic; consequence, importance, moment. ANT.—immateriality, phantom, spirit.

mature, SYN.—complete, consummate, finished, full-grown, matured, mellow, ready, ripe, seasonable. ANT.—crude, green, immature, raw, undeveloped.

mature, SYN.—age, develop, perfect, ripen, season.

mean, SYN.—average, medium, middle; base, contemptible, despicable, low, sordid, vile, vulgar; malicious, nasty, offensive, selfish. ANT.—admirable, dignified, exalted, generous, noble.

meaning, SYN.—acceptation, connotation, drift, explanation, gist, implication, import; intent, interpretation, purport, purpose, sense, significance, signification.

means, SYN.—agent, apparatus, channel, device, instrument, medium, tool, utensil, vehicle. ANT.—hindrance, impediment, obstruction, preventive.

measure, SYN.—criterion, gauge, law, principle, proof, rule, standard, test, touchstone. ANT.—chance, fancy, guess, supposition.

meddle, SYN.—interfere, interpose, interrupt, mix in, monkey, tamper.

mediocre, SYN.—average, fair, intermediate, mean, median, medium, middling, moderate, ordinary. ANT.—exceptional, extraordinary, outstanding.

meditate, SYN.—conceive, imagine, picture, recall, recollect, remember; cogitate, contemplate, deliberate, muse, ponder, reason, reflect, speculate, think; apprehend, believe, consider, deem, esteem, judge, opine, reckon, regard, suppose; devise, intend, mean, plan, purpose. ANT.—conjecture, forget, guess.

meek, SYN.—docile, domestic, domesticated, gentle, subdued, submissive, tame; dull, flat, insipid, tedious. ANT.—fierce, savage, spirited, wild; animated, exciting, lively, spirited.

meet, SYN.—collide, confront, encounter, engage, find, greet, intersect; answer; fulfill, gratify, satisfy; experience, suffer, undergo. ANT.—cleave, disperse, part, scatter, separate.

melancholy, SYN.—dejected, depressed, despondent, disconsolate, dismal, dispirited, doleful, gloomy, glum, moody, sad, somber, sorrowful; grave, pensive. ANT.—cheerful, happy, joyous, merry.

melodramatic, SYN.—affected, artificial, ceremonious, dramatic, histrionic, showy, stagy, theatrical. ANT.—modest, subdued, unaffected, unemotional.

melody, SYN.—air, concord, harmony, strain, tune.

mellow, SYN.—complete, consummate, finished, full-grown, mature, matured, ready, seasonable, ANT.—crude, green, immature, raw, undeveloped.

member, SYN.—allotment, apportionment, division, fragment, moiety, piece, portion, scrap, section, segment, share; component, element, ingredient, organ, part; concern, faction, interest, party, side; character, lines, role. ANT.—entirety, whole.

memorandum, SYN.—indication, mark, sign, symbol, token; annotation, comment, letter, message, note, observation, remark.

memorial, SYN.—commemoration, memento, monument, remembrance, souvenir.

memory, SYN.—recollection, remembrance, reminiscence, retrospection; fame, renown, reputation. ANT.—forgetfulness, oblivion.

mend, SYN.—fix, patch, refit, repair, restore, sew; ameliorate, better, correct, improve, rectify, reform, remedy. ANT.—deface, destroy, hurt, injure, rend.

mendicant, SYN.—beggar, pauper, ragamuffin, scrub, starveling, tatterdemalion, vagabond, wretch.

mentality, SYN.—brain, faculties, intellect, intelligence, judgment, mind, psyche, reason, soul, spirit, understanding, wit; disposition, inclination, intention, liking, purpose, will, wish. ANT.—body, corporeality, materiality, matter.

mercenary, SYN.—avaricious, corrupt, greedy, sordid, venal. ANT.—generous, honorable, liberal.

merciful, SYN.—clement, compassionate, forbearing, forgiving, humane, kind, lenient, tender, tolerant. ANT.—brutal, cruel, pitiless, remorseless, unfeeling.

merciless, SYN.—barbarous, bestial, brute, brutish, carnal, coarse, cruel, ferocious, gross, inhuman, remorseless, rough, rude, ruthless, savage, sensual. ANT.—civilized, courteous, gentle, humane, kind.

mercy, SYN.—charity, clemency, compassion, forgiveness, grace, leniency, mildness, pity. ANT.—cruelty, punishment, retribution, vengeance.

merge, SYN.—amalgamate, blend, coalesce, combine, commingle, conjoin, consolidate, fuse, mingle, mix, unify, unite. ANT.—analyze, decompose, disintegrate, separate.

merit, SYN.—chastity, goodness, integrity, morality, probity, purity, rectitude, virginity; effectiveness, efficacy, force, power, strength; excellence, virtue, worth. ANT.—corruption, lewdness, sin, vice; fault.

merit, SYN.—achieve, acquire, attain, deserve, earn, gain, get, obtain, win. ANT.—consume, forfeit, lose, spend, waste.

merited, SYN.—adequate, condign, deserved, earned, proper, suitable. ANT.—improper, undeserved, unmerited.

merry, SYN.—blithe, cheerful, festive, gay, gleeful, hilarious, jolly, jovial, joyous, lively, mirthful, sprightly. ANT.—gloomy, melancholy, morose, sad, sorrowful.

message, SYN.—indication, mark, sign, symbol, token; annotation, comment, letter, memorandum, observation, remark.

mete, SYN.—allot, apportion, deal, dispense, distribute, divide; allocate, appropriate, assign, give, grant, measure. ANT.—confiscate, keep, refuse, retain, withhold.

method, SYN.—design, fashion, manner, mode, order, plan, procedure, system, way. ANT.—confusion, disorder.

methodical, SYN.—accurate, correct, definite, distinct, exact, precise, strict, unequivocal; ceremonious, formal, prim, rigid, stiff. ANT.—erroneous, loose, rough, vague; careless, easy, informal.

mettle, SYN.—boldness, bravery, chivalry, courage, fearlessness, fortitude, intrepidity, prowess, resolution. ANT.—cowardice, fear, pusillanimity, timidity.

microscopic, SYN.—fine, minute, tiny; detailed, exact, particular, precise. ANT.—enormous, huge, large; general.

middle, SYN.—center, core, heart, midpoint, midst, nucleus. ANT.—border, boundary, outskirts, periphery, rim.

might, SYN.—ability, force, potency, power, strength, vigor. ANT.—inability, weakness.

mighty, SYN.—athletic, cogent, concentrated, enduring, firm, forceful, forcible, fortified, hale, hardy, impregnable, potent, powerful, robust, sinewy, strong, sturdy, tough. ANT.—brittle, delicate, feeble, fragile, insipid.

mild, SYN.—bland, gentle, kind, meek, moderate, soft, soothing, tender. ANT.—bitter, fierce, harsh, rough, severe.

mimic, SYN.—ape, copy, counterfeit, duplicate, imitate, impersonate, mock, simulate. ANT.—alter, distort, diverge, invent.

mind, SYN.—brain, faculties, intellect, intelligence, judgment, mentality, psyche, reason, soul, spirit, understanding, wit; disposition, inclination, intention, liking, purpose, will, wish. ANT.—body, corporeality, materiality, matter.

mingle, SYN.—amalgamate, blend, coalesce, combine, commingle, conjoin, consolidate, fuse, mix, merge, unify, unite. ANT.—analyze, decompose, disintegrate, separate.

minimize, SYN.—belittle, curtail, deduct, diminish, lessen, reduce, shorten, subtract. ANT.—amplify, enlarge, expand, increase.

minor, SYN.—inferior, lower, poorer, secondary, subordinate. ANT.—better, greater, higher, superior.

minute, SYN.—fine, microscopic, tiny, detailed, exact, particular, precise. ANT.—enormous, huge, large; general.

miraculous, SYN.—marvelous, metaphysical, other-worldly, preternatural, spiritual, superhuman, supernatural, unearthly. ANT.—common, human, natural, physical, plain.

mirage, SYN.—delusion, dream, fantasy, hallucination, illusion, phantom, vision. ANT.—actuality, reality, substance.

miscarriage, SYN.—fiasco, failure; default, dereliction, omission; decay, decline; deficiency, lack, loss, want. ANT.—achievement, success, victory; sufficiency.

miscellaneous, SYN.—assorted, diverse, heterogeneous, indiscriminate, mixed, motley, sundry, varied. ANT.—alike, classified, homogeneous, ordered, selected.

mischief, SYN.—damage, detriment, evil, harm, hurt, ill, infliction, injury, misfortune, mishap, wrong. ANT.—benefit, boon, favor, kindness.

miserable, SYN.—comfortless, disconsolate, distressed, forlorn, heartbroken, pitiable, wretched; abject, contemptible, despicable, low, mean, paltry, worthless. ANT.—contented, fortunate, happy, noble, significant.

miserly, SYN.—acquisitive, avaricious, greedy, niggardly, parsimonious, penurious, stingy, tight. ANT.—altruistic, bountiful, extravagant, generous, munificent.

misery, SYN.—agony, anguish, distress, grief, sorrow, suffering, torment, tribulation, woe; calamity, disaster, evil, misfortune, trouble. ANT.—delight, elation, fun, joy, pleasure.

misfortune, SYN.—accident, adversity, affliction, calamity, catastrophe, disaster, distress, hardship, mishap, ruin. ANT.—blessing, comfort, prosperity, success.

mishap, SYN.—accident, calamity, casualty, disaster, misfortune. ANT.—calculation, design, intention, purpose.

misleading, SYN.—deceitful, deceptive, delusive, delusory, fallacious, false, illusive, specious. ANT.—authentic, genuine, honest, real, truthful.

miss, SYN.—fail, default, lack, lose, omit, want. ANT.—achieve, have, include, succeed, suffice.

mistake, SYN.—blunder, error, fallacy, fault, inaccuracy, slip. ANT.—accuracy, precision, truth.

mistaken, SYN.—amiss, askew, awry, erroneous, fallacious, false, faulty, inaccurate, incorrect, unprecise, untrue, wrong; improper, inappropriate, unsuitable; aberrant, bad, criminal, evil, immoral, iniquitous, reprehensible. ANT.—correct, right, true; suit-

able; proper.

misuse, SYN.—abuse, asperse, defame, disparage, ill-use, malign, revile, scandalize, traduce, vilify; misapply, misemploy. ANT.—cherish, honor, praise, protect, respect.

misuse, SYN.—despoil, destroy, devastate, pillage, plunder, ravage, ruin, sack, strip; consume, corrode, dissipate, lavish, scatter, spend, squander, waste, wear out; decay, diminish, dwindle, pine, wither. ANT.—accumulate, conserve, economize, preserve, save.

mitigate, SYN.—abate, allay, alleviate, assuage, diminish, extenuate, relieve, soften, solace, soothe. ANT.—aggravate, agitate, augment, increase, irritate.

mix, SYN.—alloy, amalgamate, blend, combine, commingle, compound, concoct, confound, fuse, jumble, mingle; associate, consort, fraternize, join. ANT.—dissociate, divide, segregate, separate, sort.

mixture, SYN.—assortment, change, difference, dissimilarity, diversity, heterogeneity, medley, miscellany, multifariousness, variety, variousness; breed, kind, sort, stock, strain, subspecies. ANT.—homogeneity, likeness, monotony, sameness, uniformity.

mob, SYN.—bevy, crowd, crush, horde, host, masses, multitude, populace, press, rabble, swarm, throng.

mock, SYN.—deride, fleer, flout, gibe, jeer, scoff, sneer, taunt. ANT.—compliment, flatter, laud, praise.

mockery, SYN.—banter, derision, gibe, irony, jeering, raillery, ridicule, sarcasm, satire, sneering.

mode, SYN.—design, fashion, manner, method, order, plan, procedure, system, way. ANT.—confusion, disorder.

model, SYN.—archetype, copy, example, mold, pattern, prototype, specimen, standard, type. ANT.—imitation, production, reproduction.

moderate, SYN.—abate, assuage, decrease, diminish, lessen, lower, reduce, suppress. ANT.—amplify, enlarge, increase, intensify.

moderation, SYN.—forbearance, self-denial, sobriety. ANT.—excess, gluttony, greed, intoxication, self-indulgence.

modern, SYN.—contemporary, current, new, novel, present, recent. ANT.—ancient, antiquated, bygone, old, past.

modest, SYN.—bashful, humble, meek, reserved, shy, unassuming, unpretentious, virtuous. ANT.—arrogant, bold, conceited, forward, immodest, ostentatious, proud.

modification, SYN.—alteration, alternation, change, mutation, substitution, variation, variety, vicissitude. ANT.—monotony, stability, uniformity.

modify, SYN.—change, exchange, substitute; alter, convert, shift, transfigure, transform, vary, veer. ANT.—retain; continue, establish, preserve, settle, stabilize.

moiety, SYN.—allotment, apportionment, division, fragment, part, piece, portion, scrap, section, segment, share. ANT.—entirety, whole.

mold, SYN.—construct, create, fashion, forge, form, make, produce, shape; compose, constitute, make up; arrange, combine, organize; devise, frame, invent. ANT.—destroy, disfigure, dismantle, misshape, wreck.

molest, SYN.—annoy, bother, chafe, disturb, inconvenience, irk, irritate, pester, tease, trouble, vex. ANT.—accommodate, console, gratify, soothe.

momentary, SYN.—brief, compendious, concise, curt, laconic, pithy, short, succinct, terse; fleeting, passing, transient. ANT.—extended, lengthy, long, prolonged, protracted.

momentous, SYN.—consequential, critical, decisive, grave, important, influential, material, pressing, prominent, relevant, significant, weighty. ANT.—insignificant, irrelevant, mean, petty, trivial.

monastery, SYN.—abbey, cloister, convent, hermitage, nunnery, priory.

monkey, SYN.—interfere, interpose, interrupt, meddle, mix in, tamper.

monotonous, SYN.—boring, burdensome, dilatory, dreary, dull, humdrum, irksome, slow, sluggish, tardy, tedious, tiresome, uninteresting, wearisome. ANT.—amusing, entertaining, exciting, interesting, quick.

monument, SYN.—commemoration, memento, memorial, remembrance, souvenir.

mood, SYN.—disposition, temper, temperament; facetiousness, irony, jocularity, joke, sarcasm, satire, waggery, wit. ANT.—gravity, seriousness, sorrow.

moody, SYN.—crabbed, dour, fretful, gloomy, glum, morose, sulky, surly. ANT.—amiable, gay, joyous, merry, pleasant.

moody, SYN.—dejected, depressed, despondent, disconsolate, dismal, dispirited, doleful, gloomy, glum, melancholy, sad, somber, sorrowful; grave, pensive. ANT.—cheerful, happy, joyous, merry.

moral, SYN.—chaste, decent, ethical, good, honorable, just, pure, right, righteous, scrupulous, virtuous. ANT.—amoral, libertine, licentious, sinful, unethical.

morality, SYN.—chastity, goodness, integrity, probity, purity, rectitude; virginity, virtue; effectiveness, efficacy, force, power, strength; excellence merit, worth. ANT.—corruption, lewdness, sin, vice; fault.

morose, SYN.—crabbed, dour, fretful, gloomy, glum, moody, sulky, surly. ANT.—amiable, gay, joyous, merry, pleasant.

morsel, SYN.—amount, bit, fraction, fragment, part, piece, portion, scrap. ANT.—all, entirety, sum, total, whole.

mortal, SYN.—deadly, destructive, fatal, final; human. ANT.—life-giving; divine, immortal.

mortify, SYN.—abase, abash, break, crush, degrade, humiliate, humble, shame, subdue. ANT.—elevate, exalt, honor, praise.

motion, SYN.—action, activity, change, gesture, move, movement; proposal, proposition. ANT.—equilibrium, immobility, stability, stillness.

motive, SYN.—cause, impulse, incentive, incitement, inducement, principle, purpose, reason, spur, stimulus. ANT.—

action, attempt, deed, effort, result.

motley, SYN.—assorted, diverse, heterogeneous, indiscriminate, miscellaneous, mixed, sundry, varied. ANT.—alike, varclassified, homogeneous, ordered.

motto, SYN.—adage, aphorism, apothegm, byword, maxim, proverb, saw, saying.

mount, SYN.—ascend, climb, rise, scale, soar, tower. ANT.—descend, fall, sink.

mourn, SYN.—bemoan, bewail, deplore, grieve, lament, suffer, weep. ANT.—carouse, celebrate, rejoice, revel.

mourning, SYN.—affliction, anguish, distress, heartache, lamentation, grief, misery, sadness, sorrow, trial, tribulation, woe. ANT.—comfort, consolation, happiness, joy, solace.

move, SYN.—actuate, agitate, drive, impel, induce, instigate, persuade, propel, push, shift, stir, transfer. ANT.—deter, halt, rest, stay, stop.

movement, SYN.—action, activity, change, gesture, motion, move, proposal, proposition. ANT.—equilibrium, immobility, stability, stillness.

muddled, SYN.—bewildered, confused, deranged, disconcerted, disordered, disorganized, indistinct, mixed,

perplexed. ANT.—clear, lucid, obvious, organized, plain.

multifarious, SYN.—divers, manifold, many, multitudinous, numerous, several, sundry, various. ANT.—few, infrequent, meager, scanty, scarce.

multitude, SYN.—army, crowd, host, legion, mob. ANT.—few, handful, paucity, scarcity.

mundane, SYN.—earthly, laic, lay, profane, secular, temporal, worldly. ANT.—ecclesiastical, religious, spiritual, unworldly.

munificent, SYN.—generous; full, satisfied. ANT.—avaricious, covetous, grasping, rapacious, selfish; devouring, gluttonous, insatiable, ravenous, voracious.

murder, SYN.—assassinate, butcher, execute, kill, massacre, put to death, slaughter, slay. ANT.—animate, protect, resuscitate, save, vivify.

murmur, SYN.—complain, grumble, lament, protest, regret, remonstrate, repine, whine. ANT.—applaud, approve, praise, rejoice.

music, SYN.—consonance, harmony, melody, symphony.

muster, SYN.—accumulate, amass, assemble, collect, congregate, convene, gather; cull, garner, glean, harvest, pick, reap; conclude, deduce, infer, judge. ANT.—disband, disperse, distribute, scatter, separate.

mute, SYN.—calm, dumb, hushed, noiseless, peaceful, quiet, silent, still, taciturn, tranquil. ANT.—clamorous, loud, noisy, raucous.

mutiny, SYN.—coup, insurrection, overthrow, rebellion, revolt, revolution, uprising.

mutual, SYN.—common, correlative, interchangeable, joint, reciprocal, shared. ANT.—dissociated, separate, unrequited, unshared.

mysterious, SYN.—cabalistic, cryptic, dark, dim, enigmatical, hidden, incomprehensible, inexplicable, inscrutable, mystical, obscure, occult, recondite, secret. ANT.—clear, explained, obvious, plain, simple.

mystery, SYN.—conundrum, enigma, problem, puzzle, riddle. ANT.—answer, clue, key, resolution, solution.

mystical, SYN.—cabalistic, cryptic, dark, dim, enigmatical, hidden, incomprehensible, inexplicable, inscruh able, mysterious, obscure, occult, recondite, secret. ANT.—clear, explained, obvious, plain, simple.

myth, SYN.—allegory, chronicle, fable, fiction, legend, parable, saga. ANT.—fact, history.

N

nag, SYN.—aggravate, annoy, badger, bother, disturb, harass, harry, irritate, molest, pester, plague, provoke, tantalize, taunt, tease, torment, vex, worry. ANT.—comfort, delight, gratify, please, soothe.

naive, SYN.—artless, candid, frank, ingenuous, innocent, natural, open, simple, unsophisticated. ANT.—crafty, cunning, sophisticated, worldly.

naked, SYN.—bare, exposed, nude, stripped, unclad, uncovered; bald, barren, unfurnished; mere, plain, simple; defenseless, open, unprotected. ANT.—clothed, covered, dressed; concealed; protected.

name, SYN.—appellation, denomination, designation, epithet, style, surname, title; character, reputation, repute; distinction, eminence, fame, renown. ANT.—misnomer, namelessness; anonymity.

name, SYN.—appoint, call, christen, denominate, entitle, mention, specify. ANT.—hint, miscall, misname.

nap, SYN.—catnap, doze, drowse, nod, repose, rest, sleep, slumber, snooze.

narrate, SYN.—declaim, deliver, describe, detail, mention, recite, recapitulate, rehearse, relate, repeat, tell.

narrative, SYN.—account, chronicle, description, detail, history, narration, recital, relation; record. ANT.—caricature, confusion, distortion, misrepresentation.

narrow, SYN.—bigoted, dogmatic, fanatical, illiberal, intolerant, narrowminded, prejudiced. ANT.—liberal, progressive, radical, tolerant.

nasty, SYN.—malicious, mean, offensive, selfish. ANT.—admirable, dignified, exalted, generous, noble.

nation, SYN.—commonwealth, community, kingdom, nationality, people, realm, state.

native, SYN.—aboriginal, domestic, endemic, inborn, indigenous, inherent, innate, natural.

natural, SYN.—characteristic, inherent, innate, native, original; normal, regular; genuine, ingenuous, real, simple, spontaneous, unaffected. ANT.—abnormal, artificial, irregular; forced, formal.

nature, SYN.—character, disposition, individuality, kind, reputation, repute, sort.

nautical, SYN.—marine, maritime, naval, ocean, oceanic.

naval, SYN.—marine, maritime, nautical, ocean, oceanic.

near, SYN.—adjacent, bordering, close, neighbor-

ing, nigh, proximate; approaching, imminent, impending; dear, familiar, intimate. ANT.—distant, far, removed.

neat, SYN.—clear, nice, orderly, precise, spruce, tidy, trim. ANT.—dirty, disheveled, sloppy, slovenly, unkempt.

necessary, SYN.—inevitable, unavoidable, essential, expedient, indispensable, needed, requisite. ANT.—accidental, casual; contingent, nonessential, optional.

necessity, SYN.—compulsion, constraint, destiny, fate; requirement, requisite; exigency, indigence, need, poverty, want. ANT.—choice, freedom, luxury, option, uncertainty.

necromancy, SYN.—black art, charm, conjuring, enchantment, legerdemain, magic, sorcery, voodoo, witchcraft, wizardy.

need, SYN.—claim, covet, crave, demand, desire, lack, require, want, wish.

needed, SYN.—essential, expedient, indispensable, necessary, requisite. ANT.—contingent, nonessential, optional.

neglect, SYN.—carelessness, default, disregard, failure, heedlessness, negligence, omission, oversight, slight, thoughtlessness. ANT.—attention, care, diligence, watchfulness.

neglect, SYN.—disregard,

ignore, omit, overlook, slight, ANT.—do, guard, perform, protect, satisfy.

negligent, SYN.—careless, heedless, imprudent, inattentive, inconsiderate, reckless, thoughtless, unconcerned; desultory, inaccurate, lax, neglectful, remiss. ANT.—accurate, careful, meticulous, nice.

neighborhood, SYN.—district, environs, locality; adjacency, nearness, vicinity. ANT.—distance, remoteness.

neighborly, SYN.—affable, amicable, companionable, friendly, genial, kindly, sociable, social. ANT.—antagonistic, cool, distant, hostile, reserved.

new, SYN.—fresh, late, modern, newfangled, novel, original, recent. ANT.—ancient, antiquated, archaic, obsolete, old.

news, SYN.—advice, copy, information, intelligence, message, report, tidings.

niggardly, SYN.—acquisitive, avaricious, greedy, miserly, parsimonious, penurious, stingy, tight. ANT.—altruistic, bountiful, extravagant, generous, munificent.

nigh, SYN.—adjacent, bordering, close, near, neighboring, proximate; approaching, imminent, impending. ANT.—distant, far, removed.

nimble, SYN.—active, agile, alert, brisk, flexible, live-

ly, quick, spry, supple. ANT.—clumsy, heavy, inert, slow, sluggish.

noble, SYN.—dignified, elevated, eminent, exalted, grand, illustrious, lofty, majestic, stately. ANT.—base, low, mean, plebian, vile.

noise, SYN.—babel, clamor, cry, din, outcry, racket, row, sound, tumult, uproar. ANT.—hush, quiet, silence, stillness.

noisy, SYN.—clamorous, deafening, loud, resounding, sonorous, stentorian, vociferous. ANT.—dulcet, inaudible, quiet, soft, subdued.

nonplus, SYN.—bewilder, confound, confuse, dumfound, mystify, perplex, puzzle. ANT.—clarify, explain, illumine, instruct, solve.

nonsensical, SYN.—absurd, foolish, inconsistent, irrational, preposterous, ridiculous, self-contradictory, silly, unreasonable. ANT.—consistent, rational, reasonable, sensible, sound.

normal, SYN.—customary, natural, ordinary, regular, steady, uniform, unvaried. ANT.—abnormal, erratic, exceptional, rare, unusual.

nosy, SYN.—curious, inquiring, inquisitive, interrogative, meddling, peeping, peering, prying, searching, snoopy. ANT.—incurious, indifferent, unconcerned, uninterested.

note, SYN.—indication, mark, sign, symbol, token; annotation, comment, letter, memorandum, message, observation, remark.

noted, SYN.—celebrated, distinguished, eminent, famous, glorious, illustrious, renowned, well-known. ANT.—hidden, ignominious, infamous, obscure, unknown.

notice, SYN.—attend to, behold, descry, heed, mark, note, observe, perceive, recognize, regard, remark, see. ANT.—disregard, ignore, overlook, skip.

notify, SYN.—acquaint, advise, apprise, enlighten, impart, inform, instruct, teach, tell, warn. ANT.—conceal, delude, distract, mislead.

notion, SYN.—abstraction, concept, conception, fancy, idea, image, impression, opinion, sentiment, thought. ANT.—entity, matter, object, substance, thing.

novel, SYN.—allegory, fable, fabrication, fiction, invention, narrative, romance, story, tale. ANT.—fact, history, reality, truth, verity.

novice, SYN.—amateur, apprentice, beginner, dabbler, dilettante, learner, neophyte. ANT.—adept, authority, expert, master, professional.

now, SYN.—present, today.

nude, SYN.—bare, exposed, naked, stripped, unclad, uncovered; mere, plain, simple; defenseless, open, unprotected. ANT.—clothed, covered, dressed; concealed; protected.

nullify, SYN.—cancel, cross out, delete, eliminate, erase, expunge, obliterate; abolish, abrogate, annul, invalidate, quash, repeal, rescind, revoke. ANT.—confirm, enact, enforce, perpetuate.

number, SYN.—aggregate, amount, quantity, sum, volume. ANT.—nothing, nothingness, zero.

numerous, SYN.—divers, manifold, many, multifarious, multitudinous, several, sundry, various. ANT.—few, infrequent, meager, scanty, scarce.

nuptials, SYN.—espousal, marriage, matrimony, union, wedding, wedlock. ANT.—celibacy, divorce, virginity.

nurture, SYN.—appreciate, cherish, hold dear, prize, treasure, value; foster, sustain. ANT.—dislike, disregard, neglect; abandon, reject.

nutriment, SYN.—diet, edibles, fare, feed, food, meal, provisions, rations, repast, sustenance, viands, victuals. ANT.—drink, hunger, starvation, want.

O

obdurate, SYN.—callous, hard, impenitent, indurate, insensible, insensitive, tough, unfeeling. ANT.— compassionate, sensitive, soft, tender.

obedient, SYN.—compliant, deferential, dutiful, submissive, tractable, yielding. ANT.—insubordinate, intractable, obstinate, rebellious.

obese, SYN.—chubby, corpulent, fat, paunchy, plump, portly, pudgy, rotund, stocky, stout, thickset. ANT.—gaunt, lean, slender, slim, thin.

object, SYN.—article, particular, thing; aim, design, end, goal, intention, mark, objective, purpose. ANT.—acquiesce, approve, assent, comply, concur.

objection, SYN.—challenge, difference, disagreement, dissent, dissentience, noncompliance, nonconformity, protest, recusancy, rejection, remonstrance, variance. ANT.— acceptance, agreement, assent, compliance.

objective, SYN.—aim, ambition, aspiration, craving, desire, goal, hope, longing, passion.

obligate, SYN.—commit, pledge. ANT.—free, loose.

obligation, SYN.—accountability, bond, compulsion, contract, duty, engagement, responsibility. ANT.—choice, exemption, freedom.

oblige, SYN.—coerce, compel, constrain, drive, enforce, force, impel.

ANT.—allure, convince, induce, persuade, prevent.

obliterate, SYN.—annihilate, demolish, destroy, devastate, eradicate, exterminate, extinguish, ravage, raze, ruin, wreck. ANT.—construct, establish, make, preserve, save.

oblivious, SYN.—blind, ignorant, sightless, undiscerning, unmindful, unseeing; headlong, heedless, rash. ANT.—aware, calculated, discerning, perceiving, sensible.

obscene, SYN.—coarse, dirty, disgusting, filthy, gross, impure, indecent, lewd, offensive, pornographic, smutty. ANT.—decent, modest, pure, refined.

obscure, SYN.—abstruse, ambiguous, cloudy, cryptic, dark, dim, dusky, enigmatic, indistinct, mysterious, unintelligible, vague. ANT.—bright, clear, distinct, lucid.

observance, SYN.—ceremony, formality, parade, pomp, protocol, rite, ritual, solemnity.

observant, SYN.—alert, alive, attentive, awake, aware, careful, considerate, heedful, mindful, thoughtful, wary, watchful. ANT.—indifferent, oblivious, unaware.

observe, SYN.—behold, detect, discover, examine, eye, inspect, mark, note, notice, perceive, see,

view, watch; keep, cele-
brate, commemorate;
express, mention, re-
mark, utter. ANT.—disre-
gard, ignore, neglect,
overlook.

obsolete, SYN.—ancient,
antiquated, archaic,
obsolescent, old, out-
of-date, venerable.
ANT.—current, extant,
fashionable, modern, re-
cent.

obstacle, SYN.—bar, barrier, block, check, difficulty, hindrance, impedi-
ment, obstruction, snag.
ANT.—aid, assistance,
encouragement, help.

obstinate, SYN.—contumacious, determined, dog-
ged, firm, headstrong,
immovable, inflexible,
intractable, obdurate,
pertinacious, stubborn,
uncompromising, un-
yielding. ANT.—amen-
able, compliant, docile,
submissive, yielding.

obstruct, SYN.—bar, barricade, block, clog, close,
stop; delay, impede, hin-
der. ANT.—clear, open;
aid, further, promote.

obtain, SYN.—acquire, assimilate, attain, earn, get,
procure, secure, win.
ANT.—forego, forfeit,
lose, miss, surrender.

obtuse, SYN.—dense, dull,
slow, stupid; blunt.
ANT.—animated, lively,
sharp; clear, interesting.

obvious, SYN.—apparent,
clear, distinct, evident,
manifest, palpable, pat-
ent, plain, self-evident,
unmistakable. ANT.—

abstruse, concealed, hid-
den, obscure.

occupation, SYN.—art,
business, commerce,
employment, engage-
ment, enterprise, job,
profession, trade, trad-
ing, vocation, work.
ANT.—avocation, hobby,
pastime.

occupy, SYN.— absorb,
busy, dwell, fill, have,
hold, inhabit, keep, pos-
sess. ANT.—abandon, re-
lease, relinquish.

occur, SYN.—bechance,
befall, betide, chance,
happen, take place, tran-
spire.

occurence, SYN.—circumstance, episode, event,
happening, incident, is-
sue; consequence, end,
outcome, result.

odd, SYN.—bizarre, curious, eccentric, peculiar,
quaint, queer, singular,
strange, unique, unusual;
remaining, single, un-
even, unmatched.
ANT.—common, famil-
iar, normal, regular, typical; even, matched.

odious, SYN.—base, debased, depraved, foul,
loathsome, obscene, re-
volting, sordid, vicious,
vile, vulgar, wicked; ab-
ject, despicable, innoble,
low, mean, worthless,
wretched. ANT.—attrac-
tive, decent, laudable;
honorable, upright.

odor, SYN.—aroma, fetidness, fragrance, fume,
incense, perfume, redo-
lence, scent, smell,
stench, stink.

offense, SYN.—affront, atrocity, indignity, insult, outrage; aggression, crime, injustice, misdeed, sin, transgression, trespass, vice, wrong. ANT.—gentleness, innocence, morality, right.

offer, SYN.—overture, proposal, proposition, suggestion, tender. ANT.—acceptance, denial, rejection, withdrawal.

offer, SYN.—advance, exhibit, extend, present, proffer, propose, sacrifice, tender, volunteer. ANT.—accept, receive, reject, retain, spurn.

office, SYN.—berth, incumbency, job, position, post, situation.

often, SYN.—commonly, frequently, generally, recurrently, repeatedly. ANT.—infrequently, occasionally, rarely, seldom, sporadically.

old, SYN.—aged, ancient, antiquated, antique, archaic, elderly, obsolete, old-fashioned, senile, superannuated, venerable. ANT.—modern, new, young, youthful.

omen, SYN.—emblem, gesture, indication, mark, note, portent, proof, sign, signal, symbol, symptom, token.

omission, SYN.—default, deletion, failure, neglect, oversight. ANT.—attention, inclusion, insertion, notice.

omit, SYN.—cancel, delete, disregard, drop, eliminate, exclude, ignore, miss, neglect, overlook, skip. ANT.—enter, include, insert, introduce, notice.

onerous, SYN.—arduous, burdensome, difficult, hard, tough; intricate, perplexing, puzzling. ANT.—easy, effortless, facile; simple.

onslaught, SYN.—aggression, assault, attack, criticism, denunciation, invasion, offense. ANT.—defense, opposition, resistance, surrender, vindication.

opaque, SYN.—dark, dim, gloomy, murky, obscure, shadowy, unilluminated. ANT.—light; bright, clear.

open, SYN.—agape, ajar, unclosed, uncovered, unlocked; clear, passable, unobstructed; available, disengaged, free, unoccupied; accessible, exposed, public, unrestricted; candid, frank, honest, overt, plain.

open, SYN.—exhibit, expand, spread, unbar, unfasten, unfold, unlock, unseal. ANT.—close, conceal, hide, shut.

opening, SYN.—abyss, aperture, cavity, chasm, gap, gulf, hole, pore, void.

operate, SYN.—act, behave, comport, conduct, demean, deport, interact, manage.

operation, SYN.—action, agency, effort, enterprise, execution, instrumentality, maneuver, performance, proceeding, working. ANT.—cessation, inaction, inactivity, rest.

operative, SYN.—active, working; busy, industrious. ANT.—dormant, inactive.

opinion, SYN.—belief, conviction, decision, feeling, idea, impression, judgment, notion, persuasion, sentiment, view. ANT.—fact, skepticism, misgiving, knowledge.

opinionated, SYN.—arrogant, authoritarian, dictatorial, doctrinaire, dogmatic, domineering, magisterial, overbearing, positive. ANT.—fluctuating, indecisive, openminded, questioning, skeptical.

opponent, SYN.—adversary, antagonist, competitor, contestant, enemy, foe, rival. ANT.—ally, comrade, confederate, team.

opportunity, SYN.—chance, contingency, occasion, opening, possibility. ANT.—disadvantage, hindrance, obstacle.

oppose, SYN.—bar, combat, confront, contradict, counteract, defy, hinder, obstruct, resist, thwart, withstand. ANT.—agree, cooperate, submit, succumb, support.

opposed, SYN.—adverse, antagonistic, contrary, hostile, opposite; counteractive, disastrous, unfavorable, unlucky.

ANT.—benign, favorable, fortunate, lucky, propitious.

opposition, SYN.—battle, collision, combat, conflict, encounter, fight, struggle; contention, controversy, discord, inconsistency, interference, variance. ANT.—amity, concord, consonance, harmony.

oppress, SYN.—afflict, annoy, badger, harass, harry, hound, persecute, pester, plague, torment, torture, vex, worry. ANT.—aid, assist, comfort, encourage, support.

optimism, SYN.—confidence, faith, hope, trust. ANT.—despair, despondency, pessimism.

option, SYN.—alternative, choice, election, preference, selection.

opulence, SYN.—abundance, affluence, fortune, luxury, money, plenty, possessions, riches, wealth. ANT.—indigence, need, poverty, want.

oral, SYN.—spoken, verbal, vocal. ANT.—documentary, recorded, written.

ordain, SYN.—appoint, create, constitute. ANT.—disband, terminate.

ordeal, SYN.—examination, proof, test; affliction, hardship, misery, misfortune, suffering, trial, tribulation, trouble. ANT.—alleviation, consolation.

order, SYN.—arrangement,

class, method, plan, rank, regularity, sequence, series, succession, system; bidding, command, decree, dictate, injunction, instruction, mandate, requirement. ANT.—confusion, disarray, disorder, irregularity; consent, license, permission.

order, SYN.—conduct, direct, govern, guide, manage, regulate, rule; bid, command, instruct. ANT.—deceive, distract, misdirect, misguide.

ordinary, SYN.—accustomed, common, conventional, customary, familiar, habitual, normal, plain, regular, typical, usual, vulgar. ANT.—extraordinary, marvelous, remarkable, strange, uncommon.

organization, SYN.—arrangement, method, mode, order, plan, process, regularity, rule, scheme, system. ANT.—chance, chaos, confusion, disarrangement, disorder, irregularity.

organize, SYN.—adjust, arrange, assort, classify, dispose, regulate; devise, plan, prepare. ANT.—confuse, disorder, disturb, jumble, scatter.

origin, SYN.—beginning, birth, commencement, cradle, derivation, foundation, inception, source, spring, start. ANT.—end, harvest, issue, outcome, product.

original, SYN.—first, initial;

primary, primeval, primordial, pristine; creative, fresh, inventive, new, novel. ANT.—derivative, later, modern, subsequent, terminal; banal, plagiarized, trite.

originate, SYN.—cause, create, engender, fashion, form, formulate, generate, invent, make, produce. ANT.—annihilate, demolish, destroy; disband, terminate.

ornament, SYN.—adornment, decoration, embellishment, garnish, ornamentation.

oscillate, SYN.—change, fluctuate, hesitate, undulate, vacillate, vary, waver. ANT.—adhere, decide, persist, resolve, stick.

ostentation, SYN.—boasting, display, flourish, pageantry, parade, pomp, show, vaunting. ANT.—humility, modesty, reserve, unobtrusiveness.

ostracize, SYN.—bar, blackball, except, exclude, expel, hinder, omit, prevent, prohibit, restrain, shut out. ANT.—accept, admit, include, welcome.

oust, SYN.—banish, deport, dismiss, dispel, eject, exclude, exile, expatriate, expel, ostracize. ANT.—accept, admit, harbor, receive, shelter.

outcome, SYN.—consequence, doom, fate, fortune, lot, portion; destiny, issue, necessity, result.

outline, SYN.—brief, contour, delineation, draft, figure, form, plan, profile, silhouette, sketch.

outrage, SYN.—affront, atrocity, indignity, insult, offense; aggression, crime, injustice, misdeed, sin, transgression, trespass, vice, wrong. ANT.—gentleness, innocence, morality, right.

outset, SYN.—beginning, commencement, inception, opening, origin, source, start. ANT.—close, completion, consummation, end, termination.

outsider, SYN.—alien, foreigner, immigrant, newcomer, stranger. ANT.—acquaintance, associate, countryman, friend, neighbor.

outspoken, SYN.—bluff, blunt, brusque, impolite, plain, rough, rude, unceremonious. ANT.—polished, polite, suave, subtle, tactful.

overcast, SYN.—cloudy, dark, dim, indistinct, murky, shadowy. ANT.—bright, clear, distinct, limpid, sunny.

overcome, SYN.—beat, conquer, crush, defeat, humble, master, quell, rout, subdue, subjugate, surmount, vanquish. ANT.—capitulate, cede, lose, retreat, surrender.

overdue, SYN.—delayed, late, slow, tardy; advanced, new, recent.

ANT.—early, timely.

overflowing, SYN.—abundant, ample, bountiful, copious, plenteous, plentiful, profuse, teeming. ANT.—deficient, insufficient, scant, scarce.

overload, SYN.—afflict, burden, encumber, load, oppress, tax, trouble, weigh. ANT.—alleviate, console, ease, lighten, mitigate.

overlook, SYN.—disregard, drop, eliminate, exclude, ignore, miss, neglect, omit, skip. ANT.—enter, include, insert, introduce, notice.

overseer, SYN.—chief, commander, employer, head, leader, lord, manager, master, ruler, teacher. ANT.—servant, slave.

oversight, SYN.—error, inadvertence, inattention, mistake, neglect, omission; charge, control, inspection, management, superintendence, supervision, surveilance. ANT.—attention, care, observation, scrutiny.

overt, SYN.—candid, frank, honest, open, plain.

overturn, SYN.—demolish, destroy, overcome, overthrow, rout, ruin, supplant, upset, vanquish. ANT.—build, construct, preserve, uphold.

overthrow, SYN.—demolish, destroy, overcome, overturn, rout, ruin, supplant, upset, vanquish. ANT.—build, conserve, construct, preserve, uphold.

P

pacific, SYN.—calm, composed, dispassionate, imperturbable, peaceful, placid, quiet, serene, still, tranquil, undisturbed, unruffled. ANT.—excited, frantic, stormy, turbulent, wild.

pacify, SYN.—allay, alleviate, appease, assuage, calm, compose, lull, placate, quell, quiet, relieve, satisfy, soothe, still, tranquilize. ANT.—arouse, excite, incense, inflame.

packed, SYN.—crammed, filled, fall, gorged, replete, satiated, soaked; ample, complete, copious, entire, extensive, perfect, plentiful, sufficient. ANT.—depleted, devoid, empty, vacant; insufficient, lacking, partial.

pact, SYN.—agreement, bargain, compact, contract, covenant, stipulation. ANT.—difference, disagreement, discord, dissension, variance.

pain, SYN.—ache, pang, paroxysm, throe; twinge; agony, anguish, distress, grief, suffering. ANT.—comfort, ease, relief; happiness, pleasure, solace.

painful, SYN.—bitter, galling, grievous, poignant. ANT.—pleasant, sweet.

painting, SYN.—drawing, illustration, image, likeness, panorama, picture, portrait, portrayal, print, representation, scene, sketch, view.

palpable, SYN.—apparent, clear, distinct, evident, manifest, obvious, patent, plain, self-evident, unmistakable. ANT.—abstruse, concealed, hidden, obscure.

palpable, SYN.—bodily, corporeal, material, physical, sensible, tangible. ANT.—mental, metaphysical, spiritual.

paltry, SYN.—abject, contemptible, despicable, low, mean, miserable, worthless. ANT.—noble, significant.

panic, SYN.—alarm, apprehension, dread, fear, fright, horror, terror, trembling. ANT.—calmness, composure, serenity, tranquility.

parable, SYN.—allegory, chronicle, fable, fiction, legend, myth, saga. ANT.—fact, history.

parade, SYN.—cavalcade, cortege, file, procession, retinue, sequence, succession, train.

paradoxical, SYN.—contradictory, contrary, discrepant, illogical, incompatible, incongruous, inconsistent, irreconcilable, unsteady, vacillating, wavering. ANT.—compatible, congruous, consistent, correspondent.

parallel, SYN.—akin, alike, allied, analogous, comparable, correlative, correspondent, corresponding, like, similar. ANT.—different, incongruous, opposed.

parched, SYN.—arid, dehydrated, desiccated, drained, dry, thirsty. ANT.—damp, moist.

pardon, SYN.—absolution, acquittal, amnesty, forgiveness, remission. ANT.—conviction, penalty, punishment, sentence.

pardon, SYN.—absolve, acquit, condone, excuse, forgive, overlook, release, remit. ANT.—accuse, chastise, condemn, convict, punish.

parley, SYN.—chat, colloquy, conference, conversation, dialogue, interview, talk.

paroxism, SYN.—ache, pain, pang, throe, twinge. ANT.—comfort, ease, relief.

parsimonious, SYN.—acquisitive, avaricious, greedy, miserly, niggardly, penurious, stingy, tight. ANT.—altruistic, bountiful, extravagant, generous, munificent.

part, SYN.—allotment, apportionment, division, fragment, moiety, piece, portion, scrap, section, segment, share; component, element, ingredient, member, organ; concern, faction, interest, party, side; character, lines, role. ANT.—entirety, whole.

part, SYN.—divide, sepa-

rate, sever, sunder. ANT.—combine, convene, gather, join, unite.

partake, SYN.—allot, apportion, appropriate, assign, dispense, distribute, divide, parcel, partition, portion, share. ANT.—aggregate, amass, combine, condense.

partiality, SYN.—bias, bigotry, preconception, predisposition, prejudice. ANT.—fairness, impartiality, proof, reason.

participation, SYN.—association, communion, fellowship, intercourse, sacrament, union. ANT.—alienation, nonparticipation.

particle, SYN.—atom, bit, corpuscle, crumb, grain, iota, jot, mite, scrap, shred, smidgen, speck. ANT.—aggregate, bulk, mass, quantity.

particular, SYN.—characteristic, distinctive, individual, peculiar, specific; singular, unusual; circumstantial, detailed, exact, minute, specific; careful, fastidious, squeamish. ANT.—comprehensive, general, universal; ordinary; general, rough; undiscriminating.

particular, SYN.—circumstance, detail, item, minutia, part. ANT.—generality.

partisan, SYN.—adherent, attendant, devotee, disciple, follower, henchman, successor, supporter, votary. ANT.—chief, head, leader, master.

partner, SYN.—associate, attendant, colleague, companion, comrade, consort, crony, friend, mate. ANT.—adversary, enemy, stranger.

pass by, SYN.—avert, avoid, dodge, escape, eschew, elude, forbear, forestall, free, shun, ward. ANT.—confront, encounter, meet, oppose.

passable, SYN.—average, fair, mediocre. ANT.—excellent, first-rate, worst.

passion, SYN.—affection, agitation, emotion, feeling, perturbation, sentiment, trepidation, turmoil. ANT.—calm, dispassion, indifference, restraint, tranquility.

passionate, SYN.—ardent, burning, excitable, fervent, fervid, fiery, glowing, hot, impetuous, irascible, vehement. ANT.—apathetic, calm, cool, deliberate, quiet.

passive, SYN.—idle, inactive, inert, quiet, relaxed; enduring, patient, stoical, submissive. ANT.—active, aggressive, dynamic.

pastime, SYN.—amusement, contest, diversion, fun, game, match, merriment, play, recreation, sport. ANT.—business, cold; apathy, quiescence.

patch, SYN.—fix, mend, refit, repair, restore, sew; ameliorate, better, correct, improve, rectify, reform, remedy.

ANT.—deface, destroy, hurt, injure, rend.

patent, SYN.—apparent, clear, conspicuous, evident, indubitable, manifest, obvious, open, overt, unmistakable. ANT.—concealed, covert, hidden, obscure.

path, SYN.—avenue, channel, course, passage, road, route, street, thoroughfare, track, trail, walk, way.

pathetic, SYN.—affecting, moving, piteous, pitiable, poignant, sad, touching. ANT.—comical, funny, ludicrous.

patience, SYN.—composure, endurance, forbearance, fortitude, long-suffering, perseverance, resignation. ANT.—impatience, nervousness, restlessness, unquiet.

patient, SYN.—assiduous, composed, forbearing, indulgent, long-suffering, passive, resigned, stoical, uncomplaining. ANT.—chafing, clamorous, high-strung, hysterical, turbulent.

paunchy, SYN.—chubby, corpulent, fat, obese, plump, portly, pudgy, rotund, stocky, stout, thickset. ANT.—gaunt, lean, slender, slim, thin.

pause, SYN.—delay, demur, doubt, falter, hesitate, scruple, vacillate, waver. ANT.—continue, decide, persevere, proceed, resolve.

pay, SYN.—allowance,

compensation, earnings, fee, payment, recompense, salary, stipend, wages. ANT.—gift, gratuity, present.

peace, SYN.—calm, calmness, hush, quiescence, quiet, quietude, repose, rest, serenity, silence, stillness, tranquility. ANT.—agitation, disturbance, excitement, noise, tumult.

peaceful, SYN.—calm, gentle, mild, pacific, placid, quiet, serene, still, tranquil, undisturbed. ANT.—agitated, disturbed, noisy, turbulent, violent.

peak, SYN.—acme, apex, climax, consummation, culmination, height, summit, zenith. ANT.—anticlimax, base, depth, floor.

peculiar, SYN.—eccentric, exceptional, extraordinary, odd, rare, singular, strange, striking, unusual; characteristic, distinctive, individual, particular, special. ANT.—common, general, normal, ordinary.

peculiarity, SYN.—attribute, characteristic, feature, mark, property, quality, trait.

pedantic, SYN.—academic, bookish, erudite, formal, learned, scholarly, scholastic, theoretical. ANT.— common-sense, ignorant, practical, simple.

peevish, SYN.—fractious, fretful, ill-natured, ill-tempered, irritable, petulant, snappish, testy, touchy, waspish. ANT.—affable, genial, good-natured, good-tempered, pleasant.

penalty, ANT.—chastisement, fine, forfeiture, punishment, retribution; disadvantage, handicap. ANT.— compensation, pardon, remuneration, reward.

penchant, SYN.—bias, bent, disposition, inclination, leaning. partiality, predilection, predisposition, proclivity, propensity, slant, tendency, turn. ANT.—equity, fairness, impartiality, justice.

penetrating, SYN.—abstruse, deep, profound, recondite, solemn. ANT.—shallow, slight, superficial, trivial.

penitent, SYN.—contrite, regretful, remorseful, repentant, sorrowful, sorry. ANT.—objurate, remorseless.

penniless, SYN.—destitute, impecunious, indigent, needy, poor, poverty-stricken. ANT.—affluent, opulent, rich, wealthy.

pensive, SYN.—comtemplative, dreamy, introspective, meditative, reflective, thoughtful. ANT.—heedless, inconsiderate, precipitous, rash, thoughtless.

penurious, SYN.—acquisitive, avaricious, greedy, miserly, niggardly, parsimonious, stingy, tight. ANT.—altruistic, bountiful, extravagant, generous, munificent.

penury, SYN.—destitution, indigence, necessity, need, poverty, privation, want. ANT.—abundance, affluence, plenty, riches, wealth.

perceive, SYN.—conceive, discern, note, notice, observe, recognize, see; apprehend, comprehend, understand. ANT.—ignore, miss, overlook.

perceptible, SYN.—appreciable, apprehensible, sensible. ANT.—absurd, impalpable, imperceptible.

perception, SYN.—apprehension, cognizance, comprehension, conception, discernment, insight, understanding. ANT.—ignorance, insensibility, misapprehension, misconception.

perceptive, SYN.—apprised, aware, cognizant, conscious, informed, mindful, observant, sensible. ANT.—ignorant, insensible, oblivious, unaware.

perfect, SYN.—complete, entire, finished, full, utter, whole; blameless faultless, holy, immaculate, pure, sinless; complete, consummate, excellent, ideal, superlative, supreme; absolute, downright, unqualified, utter. ANT.—deficient, incomplete, lacking; blemished, defective, faulty, imperfect.

perform, SYN.—act, imper-

sonate, play, pretend.

performance, SYN.—demonstration, flourish, ostentation, parade, spectacle, entertainment, movie, production, show.

perfunctory, SYN.—affected, ceremonious, correct, decorous, exact, methodical, precise, proper, regular, solemn, stiff; external, formal, outward. ANT.—easy, natural, unconstrained, unconventional; heartfelt.

peril, SYN.—danger, hazard, jeopardy, risk. ANT.—defense, immunity, protection, safety.

perilous, SYN.—critical, dangerous, hazardous, insecure, menacing, precarious, risky, threatening, unsafe. ANT.—firm, protected, safe, secure.

period, SYN.—age, date, duration, epoch, era, interim, season, span, spell, tempo, term, time.

periodical, SYN.—customary, methodical, orderly, regular, steady, systematic, uniform, unvaried. ANT.—abnormal, erratic, exceptional, rare, unusual.

perish, SYN.—cease, decay, decease, decline, depart, die, expire, fade, languish, sink, wane, wither. ANT.—begin, flourish, grow, live, survive.

permanent, SYN.—abiding, changeless, constant, durable, enduring, fixed, indestructible, lasting, stable, unchangeable. ANT.—ephemeral, temporary, transient, transitory, unstable.

permeate, SYN.—diffuse, fill, infiltrate, penetrate, pervade, run through, saturate.

permissible, SYN.—admissible, allowable, fair, justifiable, probable, tolerable, warranted. ANT.—inadmissible, irrelevant, unsuitable.

permission, SYN.—authority, authorization, consent, leave, liberty, license, permit. ANT.—denial, opposition, prohibition, refusal.

permit, SYN.—allow, let, sanction, suffer, tolerate; authorize, give, grant, yield. ANT.—forbid, object, protest, refuse, resist.

perpetrate, SYN.—do, commit, perform. ANT.—fail, miscarry, neglect.

perpetual, SYN.—ceaseless, deathless, endless, eternal, everlasting, immortal, infinite, timeless, undying. ANT.—ephemeral, finite, mortal, temporal, transient.

perpetually, SYN.—always, constantly, continually, eternally, ever, evermore, forever, incessantly, unceasingly. ANT.—fitfully, never, occasionally, rarely, sometimes.

perplex, SYN.—bewilder, confound, confuse, dumfound, mystify, nonplus,

puzzle. ANT.—clarify, explain, illumine, instruct, solve.

perplexed, SYN.—bewildered, confused, deranged, disconcerted, disordered, disorganized, indistinct, mixed, muddled. ANT.—clear, lucid, obvious, organized, plain.

perplexing, SYN.—complex, complicated, compound, intricate, involved, vex, worry. ANT.—plain, simple, uncompounded.

persecute, SYN.—afflict, annoy, badger, harass, harry, hound, oppress, pester, plague, torment, torture, vex, worry. ANT.—aid, assist, comfort, encourage, support.

persevere, SYN.—abide, continue, endure, last, persist, remain. ANT.—cease, desist, discontinue, vacillate, waver.

perseverance, SYN.—constancy, industry, persistence, persistency; pertinacity, steadfastness, tenacity. ANT.—cessation, idleness, laziness, rest, sloth.

persist, SYN.—abide, continue, endure, last, persevere, remain. ANT.—cease, desist, discontinue, vacillate, waver.

persistence, SYN.—constancy, industry, perseverance, persistency, pertinacity, steadfastness, tenacity. ANT.—cessation, idleness, laziness, rest, sloth.

persistent, SYN.—constant,

enduring, fixed, immovable, indefatigable, lasting, persevering, steady; dogged, obstinate, perverse, stubborn. ANT.—hesitant, unsure, vacillating, wavering.

perspicacity, SYN.—discernment, discrimination, intelligence, judgment, sagacity, understanding, wisdom. ANT.— arbitrariness, senselessness, stupidity, thoughtlessness.

persuade, SYN.—allure, coax, convince, entice, exhort, incite, induce, influence, prevail upon, urge, win over. ANT.—coerce, compel, deter, dissuade, restrain.

persuasion, SYN.—belief, conviction, decision, feeling, idea, impression, judgment, notion, opinion, sentiment, view. ANT.—fact, skepticism, misgiving, knowledge.

pertain, SYN.—apply, refer, relate.

pertinacious, SYN.—contumacious, determined, dogged, firm, headstrong, immovable, inflexible, intractable, obdurate, obstinate, stubborn, uncompromising, unyielding. ANT.—amenable, compliant, docile, submissive, yielding.

pertinent, SYN.—applicable, apposite, appropriate, apropos, apt, fit, germane, material, related, relating, relevant, to the point. ANT.—alien, extraneous, foreign, unrelated.

pervade, SYN.—diffuse, fill, infiltrate, penetrate, permeate, run through, saturate.

perverse, SYN.—contrary, disobedient, fractious, peevish, petulant; forward, intractable, obstinate, stubborn, ungovernable, untoward; perverted, sinful, wicked. ANT.—aggreeable, obliging; docile, tractable.

perversion, SYN.—abuse, desecration, maltreatment, misuse, outrage, profanation, reviling. ANT.—respect.

pervert, SYN.—abase, corrupt, defile, debase, degrade, deprave, humiliate, impair, lower vitiate. ANT.—enhance, improve, raise.

perverted, SYN.—perverse, sinful, wicked.

pester, SYN.—annoy, bother, chafe, disturb, inconvenience, irk, irritate, molest, tease, trouble, vex. ANT.—accommodate, console, gratify, soothe.

petition, SYN.—appeal, entreaty, invocation, plea, prayer, request, suit, supplication.

petty, SYN.—frivolous, insignificant, paltry, small, trifling, trivial, unimportant. ANT.—important, momentous, serious, weighty.

petulant, SYN.—fracious, fretful, ill-natured, ill-tempered, irritable, peevish, snappish, testy, touchy, waspish. ANT.—affable, genial, good-natured, good-tempered, pleasant.

philanthropy, SYN.—altruism, beneficence, benevolence, charity, generosity, humanity, kindness, liberality, magnanimity, tenderness. ANT.—cruelty, inhumanity, malevolence, selfishness, unkindness.

phlegmatic, SYN.—cold, passionless, stoical, unfeeling. ANT.—ardent, passionate.

phony, SYN.—affected, assumed, artificial, bogus, counterfeit, ersatz, fake, feigned, fictitious, sham, spurious, synthetic, unreal. ANT.—genuine, natural, real, true.

phrase, SYN.—expression, name, term, word.

physical, SYN.—bodily, carnal, corporal, corporeal, somatic; material, natural. ANT.—mental, spiritual.

pick, SYN.—choose, cull, elect, opt, select. ANT.—refuse, reject.

picture, SYN.—appearance, cinema, drawing, effigy, engraving, etching, film, illustration, image, likeness, painting, panorama, photograph, portrait, portrayal, print, representation, resemblance, scene, sketch, view.

piece, SYN.—amount, bit, fraction, fragment, morsel, part, portion, scrap. ANT.—all, entirety, sum,

total, whole.

pigment, SYN.—color, complexion, dye, hue, paint, shade, stain, tincture, tinge, tint. ANT.—achromatism, paleness, transparency.

pinnacle, SYN.—apex, chief, crest, crown, head, summit, top, zenith. ANT.—base, bottom, foot, foundation.

pious, SYN.—blessed, consecrated, devout, divine, hallowed, holy, religious, sacred, saintly, spiritual. ANT.—evil, profane, sacrilegious, secular, worldly.

pitch, SYN.—cast, fling, hurl, propel, throw, thrust, toss. ANT.—draw, haul, hold, pull, retain.

piteous, SYN.—affecting, moving, pathetic, pitiable, poignant, sad, touching. ANT.—comical, funny, ludicrous.

pitfall, SYN.—ambush, artifice, bait, intrigue, lure, net, ruse, snare, stratagem, trap, trick, wile.

pitiable, SYN.—affecting, moving, piteous, poignant, sad, touching. ANT.—comical, funny, ludicrous.

pity, SYN.—commiseration, compassion, condolence, mercy, sympathy. ANT.—brutality, cruelty, hardness, inhumanity, ruthlessness.

place, SYN.—arrange, deposit, dispose, lay, put, set. ANT.—disarrange, disturb, mislay, misplace, remove.

placid, SYN.—calm, composed, dispassionate, imperturbable, pacific, peaceful, quiet, serene, still, tranquil, undisturbed, unruffled. ANT.—excited, frantic, stormy, turbulent, wild.

plagiarize, SYN.—adduce, cite, extract, paraphrase, quote, recite, repeat. ANT.—contradict, misquote, refute, retort.

plague, SYN.—afflict, annoy, badger, harass, harry, hound, oppress, persecute, pester, torment, torture, vex, worry. ANT.—aid, assist, comfort, encourage, support.

plain, SYN.—even, flat, level, smooth; apparent, clear, distinct, evident, manifest, obvious, palpable, visible; candid, frank, open, simple, sincere, unpretentious; absolute, unqualified. ANT.—abrupt, broken, rough, undulatory, uneven; abstruse, ambiguous, enigmatical, obscure; adorned, embellished, feigned, insincere.

plan, SYN.—contrive, create, design, devise, invent, scheme; intend, mean, purpose; draw, sketch.

plausible, SYN.—credible, feasible, likely, possible, practicable, practical, probable. ANT.—impossible, impracticable, visionary.

play, SYN.—amusement, diversion, entertainment, fun, game, pastime, recreation, sport. ANT.—boredom, labor, toil, work.

play, SYN.—caper, frolic, gamble, gambol, revel, romp, sport, stake, toy, wager; execute, perform; act, impersonate, pretend.

plea, SYN.—appeal, entreaty, invocation, petition, prayer, request, suit, supplication.

plead, SYN.—appeal, ask, beg, beseech, entreat, implore, petition, supplicate; argue, defend, discuss, rejoin. ANT.—deny, deprecate, refuse.

pleasant, SYN.—acceptable, agreeable, amiable, charming, gratifying, pleasing, pleasurable, suitable, welcome. ANT.—disagreeable, obnoxious, offensive, unpleasant.

please, SYN.—appease, compensate, content, fulfill, gratify, remunerate, satiate, satisfy, suffice. ANT.—annoy, displease, dissatisfy, frustrate, tantalize.

pleasing, SYN.—agreeable, delightful, engaging, gentle, honeyed, luscious, mellifluous, melodious, saccharine, sugary, winning. ANT.—acrid, bitter, offensive, repulsive, sour.

pleasure, SYN.—amusement, comfort, delight, enjoyment, felicity, gladness, gratification, happiness, joy. ANT.—affliction, pain, suffering, trouble, vexation.

pledge, SYN.—assurance, promise, word; assertion, declaration, statement.

pledge, SYN.—bind, commit, obligate. ANT.—neglect; mistrust, release, renounce.

plentiful, SYN.—abundant, ample, bounteous, bountiful, copious, luxurious, plenteous, profuse, replete. ANT.—deficient, insufficient, rare, scanty, scarce.

pliable, SYN.—compliant, ductile, elastic, flexible, pliant, resilient, supple, tractable. ANT.—brittle, hard, rigid, stiff, unbending.

plight, SYN.—condition, difficulty, dilemma, fix, predicament, scrape, situation, strait. ANT.—calmness, comfort, ease, satisfaction.

plot, SYN.—cabal, conspiracy, design, intrigue, machination, plan, scheme, stratagem; chart, diagram, graph, sketch.

plotting, SYN.—artfulness, contrivance, cunning, design, scheming; intent, intention, objective, purpose. ANT.—result; candor, sincerity; accident, chance.

ploy, SYN.—antic, artifice, cheat, deception, device, fraud, guile, hoax, imposture, ruse, stratagem, stunt, subterfuge, trick, wile. ANT.—candor, ex-

posure, honesty, openness, sincerity.

plump, SYN.—chubby, corpulent, fat, obese, paunchy, portly, pudgy, rotund, stocky, stout, thickset. ANT.—gaunt, lean, slender, slim, thin.

pogrom, SYN.—butchery, carnage, massacre, slaughter.

poignant, SYN.—affecting, heart-rending, impressive, moving, pitiable, sad, tender, touching.

point, SYN.—aim, direct, level, train. ANT.—deceive, distract, misdirect, misguide.

pointed, SYN.—acute, cutting, keen; sharp; penetrating, piercing, severe; astute, clever, cunning, quick, shrewd, wily, witty. ANT.—bland, blunt, gentle, shallow, stupid.

poise, SYN.—balance, calmness, carriage, composure, equanimity, equilibrium, self-possession. ANT.—agitation, anger, excitement, rage, turbulence.

poise, SYN.—adjourn, defer, delay, discontinue, interrupt, postpone, stay; balance, dangle, hang, suspend, swing. ANT.—continue, maintain, persist, proceed, prolong.

poison, SYN.—befoul, contaminate, corrupt, defile, infect, pollute, sully, taint. ANT.—disinfect, purify.

polished, SYN.—refined, sleek, slick; glib, diplo-

matic, suave, urbane.
ANT.—bluff, blunt,
harsh, rough, rugged.

polite, SYN.—accomplished, civil, considerate, courteous, cultivated, genteel, refined, urbane, well-bred, well-mannered. ANT.—boorish, impertinent, rude, uncivil, uncouth.

pollute, SYN.—befoul, contaminate, corrupt, defile, infect, poison, sully, taint. ANT.—disinfect, purify.

pomp, SYN.—boasting, display, flourish, ostentation, pageantry, parade, show, vaunting. ANT.—humility, modesty, reserve, unobstrusiveness.

pompous, SYN.—august, dignified, grand, grandiose, high, imposing, lofty, magnificent, majestic, noble, stately, sublime. ANT.—common, humble, lowly, ordinary, undignified.

ponder, SYN.—contemplate, examine, investigate, scrutinize, study, weigh; cogitate, meditate, muse, reflect.

ponderous, SYN.—heavy, massive, weighty; burdensome, cumbersome, grievous, trying; gloomy, grave, serious; dull, sluggish. ANT.—animated, brisk, light.

poor, SYN.—destitute, impecunious, indigent, needy, penniless, poverty-stricken; bad, deficient, inferior,

scanty, shabby, unfavorable, wrong. ANT.—affluent, opulent, rich, wealthy; ample, good, right, sufficient.

popular, SYN.—common, familiar, favorite, general, prevailing, prevalent. ANT.—esoteric, exclusive, restricted, unpopular.

pornographic, SYN.—coarse, dirty, disgusting, filthy, gross, impure, indecent, lewd, obscene, offensive, smutty. ANT.—decent, modest, pure, refined.

portal, SYN.—doorway, entrance, entry, inlet, opening. ANT.—departure, exit.

portion, SYN.—bit, division, fragment, parcel, part, piece, section, segment, share. ANT.—bulk, whole.

portray, SYN.—delineate, depict, describe, draw, paint, picture, represent, sketch. ANT.—caricature, misrepresent, suggest.

position, SYN.—locality, place, site, situation, station; caste, condition, place, rank, standing, status; berth, incumbency, job, office, post, situation; attitude, bearing, pose, posture.

positive, SYN.—assured, certain, definite, fixed, indubitable, inevitable, secure, sure, undeniable, unquestionable. ANT.—doubtful, probably, questionable, uncertain.

possess, SYN.—control, have, hold, occupy, own, affect, obtain, seize. ANT.—abandon, lose, renounce, surrender.

possessions, SYN.—belongings, commodities, effects, estate, goods, merchandise, property, stock, wares, wealth.

possible, SYN.—credible, feasible, likely, plausible, practicable, practical, probable. ANT.—impossible, impracticable, visionary.

possibility, SYN.—chance, contingency, occasion, opening, opportunity. ANT.— disadvantage, hindrance, obstacle.

post, SYN.—berth, incumbency, job, office, position, situation.

postpone, SYN.—adjourn, defer, delay, discontinue, interrupt, stay, suspend. ANT.—continue, maintain, persist, proceed, prolong.

postulate, SYN.—adage, aphorism, apothegm, axiom, byword, fundamental, maxim, principle, proverb, saw, saying, theorem, truism.

potency, SYN.—ability, capability, competency, effectiveness, efficacy, efficiency, skillfullness. ANT.—inability, ineptitude, wastefulness.

pound, SYN.—beat, belabor, buffet, dash, hit, knock, pummel, punch, smite, strike, thrash, thump; conquer, defeat, overpower, overthrow, rout, subdue, vanquish; palpitate, pulsate, pulse, throb. ANT.—defend, shield, stroke; fail, surrender.

poverty, SYN.—destitution, indigence, necessity, need, penury, privation, want. ANT.—abundance, affluence, plenty, riches, wealth.

power, SYN.—ability, capability, competency, faculty, potency, talent, validity; cogency, energy, force, might, strength, vigor; authority, command, control, dominion, influence, predominance, sovereignty, sway. ANT.—disablement, impotence, incapacity, ineptitude; debility, fatigue, weakness.

powerful, SYN.—athletic, cogent, concentrated, enduring, firm, forceful, forcible, fortified, hale, hardy, impregnable, mighty, potent, robust, sinewy, strong, sturdy, tough. ANT.—brittle, delicate, feeble, fragile, insipid.

practical, SYN.—prudent, reasonable, sagacious, sage, sensible, sober, sound, wise. ANT.—absurd, impalpable, imperceptible, stupid, unaware.

practice, SYN.—custom, drill, exercise, habit, manner, training, usage, use, wont. ANT.—disuse, idleness, inexperience, speculation, theory.

praise, SYN.—acclaim, applaud, commend, compliment, eulogize, extol, flatter, glorify, laud. ANT.—censure, condemn, criticize, disparage, reprove.

prayer, SYN.—appeal, entreaty, invocation, petition, plea, request, suit, supplication.

preamble, SYN.—beginning, foreword, introduction, overture, preface, prelude, prologue, start. ANT.—completion, conclusion, end, epilogue, finale.

precarious, SYN.—critical, dangerous, hazardous, insecure, menacing, perilous, risky, threatening, unsafe. ANT.—firm, protected, safe, secure.

precept, SYN.—belief, creed, doctrine, dogma, teaching, tenet. ANT.—conduct, deed, performance, practice.

precious, SYN.—costly, expensive, dear, esteemed; profitable, useful, valuable. ANT.—cheap, mean, poor; trashy, worthless.

precipitous, SYN.—abrupt, hasty, precipitate, sudden, unannounced, unexpected, rough, rugged, sharp, steep. ANT.—anticipated, expected, gradual, smooth.

precise, SYN.—accurate, correct, definite, distinct, exact, strict, unequivocal; ceremonious, formal, prim, rigid, stiff. ANT.—erroneous, loose,

rough, vague; careless, easy, informal.

preclude, SYN.—forstall, hinder, impede, obstruct, obviate, prevent, thwart. ANT.—aid, encourage, expedite, permit, promote.

preclusion, SYN.—exception, exclusion, omission, stant. ANT.—inclusion, rule, standard.

predicament, SYN.—condition, difficulty, dilemma, fix, plight, scrape, situation, strait. ANT.—calmness, comfort, ease, satisfaction.

predilection, SYN.—affection, attachment, bent, bias, desire, disposition, inclination, penchant, preference. ANT.—apathy, aversion, distaste, nonchalance, repugnance.

predominant, SYN.—cardinal, chief, essential, first, foremost, highest, leading, main, paramount, principal, supreme. ANT.—auxiliary, minor, subordinate, subsidiary, supplemental.

preference, SYN.—alternative, choice, election, option, selection.

prejudiced, SYN.—bigoted, dogmatic, fanatical, illiberal, intolerant, narrowminded. ANT.—liberal, progressive, radical, tolerant.

premeditated, SYN.—contemplated, deliberate, designed, intended, intentional, studied, voluntary, wilful. ANT.—accidental, fortuitous.

premeditation, SYN.—deliberation, forecast, forethought, intention. ANT.—accident, extemporization, hazard, impromptu.

premise, SYN.—assumption, basis, postulate, presumption, presupposition, principle. ANT.—derivation, implication, superstructure, trimming.

preoccupied, SYN.—absent, absent-minded, abstracted, distracted, inattentive. ANT.—attending, present; attentive, watchful.

prepare, SYN.—concoct, condition, contrive, equip, fit, furnish, get ready, make ready, predispose, provide, qualify, ready.

preposterous, SYN.—absurd, foolish, inconsistent, irrational, nonsensical, ridiculous, self-contradictory, silly, unreasonable. ANT.—consistent, rational, reasonable, sensible, sound.

prerogative, SYN.—authority, grant, liberty, license, privilege, right. ANT.— encroachment, injustice, violation, wrong.

present, SYN.—boon, donation, gift, grant, gratuity, largess; now, today.

present, SYN.—advance, exhibit, extend, offer, proffer, propose, sacrifice, tender. ANT.—accept, receive, reject, re-

tain, spurn.

preserve, SYN.—conserve, defend, guard, keep, maintain, protect, rescue, safeguard, save, secure, spare, uphold. ANT.—abandon, abolish, destroy, impair, injure.

press, SYN.—crowd, drive, force, impel, jostle, propel, push, shove; hasten, promote, urge. ANT.—drag, falter, halt, pull, retreat; ignore, oppose.

pressing, SYN.—cogent, compelling, critical, crucial, exigent, impelling, imperative, important, importunate, insistent, instant, necessary, serious, urgent. ANT.—insignificant, petty, trifling, trivial, unimportant.

pressure, SYN.—compression, force; constraint, influence; compulsion, exigency, hurry, press, stress, urgency. ANT.—ease, leniency, recreation, relaxation.

presume, SYN.—apprehend, assume, believe, conjecture, deduce, guess, imagine, speculate, suppose, surmise, think. ANT.—ascertain, conclude, demonstrate, know, prove.

presumption, SYN.—assurance, audacity, boldness, effrontery, impertinence, impudence, insolence, rudeness, sauciness. ANT.—diffidence, politeness, subserviency, truckling.

presupposition, SYN.—assumption, basis, postulate, premise, presumption, principle. ANT.—derivative, implication, superstructure.

pretend, SYN.—act, affect, assume, feign, profess, sham, stimulate. ANT.—display, exhibit, expose, reveal.

pretense, SYN.—affection, cloak, disguise, excuse, garb, mask, pretension, pretext, semblance, show, simulation, subterfuge. ANT.—actuality, fact, reality, sincerity, truth.

pretty, SYN.—beauteous, beautiful, charming, comely, elegant, fair, fine, handsome, lovely. ANT.—foul, hideous, homely, repulsive, unsightly.

prevalent, SYN.—common, familiar, frequent, general, ordinary, popular, universal, usual. ANT.—exceptional, extraordinary, odd, scarce.

prevent, SYN.—forstall, hinder, impede, obstruct, obviate, preclude, thwart. ANT.—aid, encourage, expedite, permit, promote.

previous, SYN.—aforesaid, antecedent, anterior, foregoing, former, preceeding, prior. ANT.—consequent, following, later, subsequent, succeeding.

price, SYN.—charge, cost, expense, value, worth.

pride, SYN.—arrogance, conceit, haughtiness, self-esteem, self-respect, superciliousness, vainglory, vanity. ANT.—humility, lowliness, meekness, modesty, shame.

primary, SYN.—beginning, earliest, first, initial, original, prime, primeval, primitive, pristine; chief, foremost. ANT.—hindmost, last, latest; least, subordinate.

primeval, SYN.—first, initial, original, primary, primordial, pristine; creative, fresh, inventive, new, novel. ANT.—derivative, later, modern, subsequent, terminal; banal, plagiarized, trite.

primitive, SYN.—aboriginal, ancient, antiquated, early, old, primary, primeval, primordial, pristine. ANT.—civilized, late, modern, modish, sophisticated.

primordial, SYN.—first, initial, original, primary, primeval, pristine; creative, fresh, inventive, new, novel. ANT.—derivative, later, modern, subsequent, terminal; banal, plagiarized, trite.

principal, SYN.—cardinal, chief, essential, first, foremost, highest, leading, main, paramount, predominant, supreme. ANT.—auxiliary, minor, subordinate, subsidiary, supplemental.

principal, SYN.—chief, commander, director, head, leader, master. ANT.—follower, subordinate, underling.

principle, SYN.—axiom,

canon, formula, guide, law, maxim, method, order, precept, propriety, regulation, rule, statute, system. ANT.—chance, deviation, exception, hazard.

prior, SYN.—aforesaid, antecedent, anterior, foregoing, former, preceding, previous. ANT.—consequent, following, later, subsequent, succeeding.

pristine, SYN.—first, initial, original, primary, primeval, primordial, creative, fresh, inventive, new, novel. ANT.—derivative, later, modern, subsequent, terminal; banal, plagiarized, trite.

private, SYN.—clandestine, concealed, covert, hidden, latent, secret, surreptitious, unknown. ANT.—conspicuous, disclosed, exposed, known, obvious.

privation, SYN.—destitution, indigence, necessity, need, penury, poverty, want. ANT.—abundance, affluence, plenty, riches, wealth.

privilege, SYN.—advantage, exemption, favor, immunity, liberty, license, prerogative, right, sanction. ANT.—disallowance, inhibition, prohibition, restriction.

prize, SYN.—award, bonus, bounty, compensation, premium, recompense, remuneration, requital, reward. ANT.—assessment, charge, earnings, punishment, wages.

probe, SYN.—extend, reach, stretch. ANT.—short, miss.

procedure, SYN.—fashion, form, habit, manner, method, mode, plan, practice, process, style, system, way.

proceed, SYN.—advance, improve, progress, rise, thrive. ANT.—hinder, oppose, retard, retreat, withhold.

proceeding, SYN.—affair, business, deal, deed, negotiation, occurrence, transaction.

proceeds, SYN.—crop, fruit, harvest, produce, product, reaping, result, store, yield.

procession, SYN.—cavalcade, cortege, file, parade, retinue, sequence, succession, train.

proclaim, SYN.—affirm, announce, assert, aver, broadcast, declare, express, make known, profess, promulgate, protest, state, tell. ANT.—conceal, repress, suppress, withhold.

procreate, SYN.—beget, breed, create, engender, father, generate, originate, produce, propagate, sire. ANT.—abort, destroy, extinguish, kill, murder.

procure, SYN.—acquire, attain, earn, gain, get, obtain, secure, win. ANT.—lose.

prodigious, SYN.—amazing, astonishing, astounding, enormous, huge, immense, marvelous, monstrous, monumental, remarkable, stupendous, vast. ANT.—commonplace, insignificant, small.

produce, SYN.—crop, fruit, harvest, proceeds, product, reaping, result, store, yield.

produce, SYN.—bear, breed, conceive, generate, hatch, procreate, yield; fabricate, fashion, make, manufacture, supply; bring forward, exhibit, show; accomplish, cause, effect, occasion, originate. ANT.—consume, destroy, reduce, waste; conceal, hide.

productive, SYN.—bountiful, fecund, fertile, fruitful, luxuriant, plenteous, prolific, rich, teeming. ANT.—barren, impotent, sterile, unproductive.

profanation, SYN.—abuse, aspersion, defamation, desecration, dishonor, disparagement, insult, invective, maltreatment, misuse, outrage, perversion, reproach, reviling, upbraiding. ANT.—approval, commendation, laudation, plaudit, respect.

profane, SYN.—desecrate, dishonor, pollute, debauch, deflower, ravish, violate.

profess, SYN.—affirm, announce, assert, aver, broadcast, declare, express, make known, proclaim, promulgate, protest, state, tell.

ANT.—conceal, repress, suppress, withhold.

proffer, SYN.—advance, extend, present, propose, tender, volunteer. ANT.—accept, receive, reject, retain, spurn.

proficient, SYN.—able, accomplished, adept, clever, competent, cunning, expert, ingenious, practiced, skillful, skilled, versed. ANT.—awkward, bungling, clumsy, inexpert, untrained.

profit, SYN.—advantage, avail, benefit, emolument, gain, improvement, service, use. ANT.—damage, detriment, loss, ruin, waste.

profitable, SYN.—advantageous, beneficial, good, helpful, salutary, serviceable, useful, wholesome. ANT.—deleterious, destructive, detrimental, harmful, injurious.

profligate, SYN.—contaminated, corrupt, corrupted, crooked, debased, depraved, dishonest, impure, tainted, unsound, venal, vitiated.

profound, SYN.—abstruse, deep, penetrating, recondite, solemn. ANT.—shallow, slight, superficial, trivial.

profuse, SYN.—abundant, copious, excessive, extravagant, exuberant, immoderate, improvident, lavish, luxuriant, overflowing, plentiful, prodigal, wasteful. ANT.—economical, meager, poor, skimpy, sparse.

profusion, SYN.—extravagance, immoderation, intemperance, superabundance, superfluity, surplus. ANT.—dearth, deficiency, lack, paucity, want.

progress, SYN.—advance, advancement, betterment, development, growth, improvement, progression. ANT.—decline, delay, regression, relapse, retrogression.

progress, SYN.—advance, improve, proceed, rise, thrive. ANT.—hinder, oppose, retard, retreat, withhold.

progression, SYN.—arrangement, chain, following, gradation, order, sequence, series, string, succession, train.

prohibit, SYN.—ban, debar, forbid, hinder, inhibit, interdict, prevent. ANT.—allow, permit, sanction, tolerate.

project, SYN.—contrivance, design, device, plan, scheme. ANT.—accomplishment, performance, production.

prolific, SYN.—bountiful, fecund, fertile, fruitful, luxuriant, plenteous, productive, rich, teeming. ANT.—barren, impotent, sterile, unproductive.

prolong, SYN.—draw, extend, lengthen, protract, stretch. ANT.—shorten.

prominent, SYN.—celebrated, conspicuous, distinguished, eminent, famous, illustrious, influential, noteworthy, outstanding, remarkable, renowned. ANT.—common, humble, low, ordinary, vulgar.

promise, SYN.—agreement, assurance, bestowal, contract, engagement, fulfillment, guarantee, oath, pledge, undertaking, vox.

promote, SYN.—advance, aid, assist, encourage, facilitate, forward, foster, ANT.—demote, discourage, hinder, impede, obstruct.

prompt, SYN.—exact, precise, punctual, ready, timely. ANT.—dilatory, late, slow, tardy.

prompt, SYN.—cause, effect, evoke, incite, induce, make, occasion, originate.

promptly, SYN.—directly, forthwith, immediately, instantaneously, instantly, now, presently, straightaway. ANT.—distantly, hereafter, later, shortly, sometime.

promulgate, SYN.—affirm, announce, assert, aver, broadcast, declare, express, make known, proclaim, profess, protest, state, tell. ANT.—conceal, repress, suppress, withhold.

proof, SYN.—confirmation, corroboration, demonstration, evidence, experiment, test, testimony, trial, verification. ANT.—failure, fallacy, invalidity.

propagate, SYN.—beget, breed, create, engender, father, generate, originate, procreate, produce, sire. ANT.—abort, destroy, extinguish, kill, murder.

propel, SYN.—actuate, agitate, drive, impel, induce, instigate, move, persuade, push, shift, stir, transfer. ANT.—deter, halt, rest, stay, stop.

propensity, SYN.—aim, bent, bias, drift, inclination, leaning, predisposition, proclivity, proneness, tendency, trend. ANT.—aversion, deviation, disinclination.

proper, SYN.—appropriate, befitting, correct, fit, legitimate, meet, right, seemly, suitable; conventional, correct, decent, formal, respectable; individual, peculiar, special.

property, SYN.—belongings, commodities, effects, estate, goods, merchandise, possessions, stock, wares, wealth; attribute, characteristic, peculiarity, quality, trait. ANT.—deprvation, destitution, poverty, privation, want.

propitious, SYN.—fortunate, happy, lucky, opportune.

proportion, SYN.—balance, composure, equilibrium, poise, stability, steadiness; symmetry. ANT.—fall, imbalance, instability, unsteadiness.

proposal, SYN.—offer, overture, proposition, suggestion, tender. ANT.—acceptance, denial, rejection, withdrawal.

propose, SYN.—design, intend, move, offer, present, proffer, propound, purpose, suggest. ANT.—effect, fulfill, perform.

proposition, SYN.—motion, proposal.

propound, SYN.—advance, allege, assign, bring forward, offer, propose. ANT.—hinder, oppose, retard, retreat, withhold.

proprietor, SYN.—master, owner. ANT.—servant, slave.

prosper, SYN.—achieve, flourish, gain, prevail, succeed, thrive, win. ANT.—fail, miscarry, miss.

prosperous, SYN.—affluent, luxurious, opulent, rich, sumptuous, wealthy, well-to-do. ANT.—beggarly, destitute, indigent, needy, poor.

protect, SYN.—conserve, defend, guard, keep, maintain, preserve, safeguard, save, secure. ANT.—abandon, abolish, destroy, impair, injure.

protection, SYN.—bulwark, fence, refuge, safeguard, shelter, shield; defense, guard, security.

protest, SYN.—challenge, difference, disagreement, dissent, dissentience, noncompliance, nonconformity, objection, recusancy, rejection, remonstrance, variance. ANT.—acceptance, agreement, assent, compliance.

protest, SYN.—abominate, disagree, disapprove, object, oppose, reject, remonstrate. ANT.—acquiesce, approve, assent, comply, concur.

prototype, SYN.—archetype, example, illustration, instance, model, pattern, sample, specimen. ANT.—concept, precept, principle, rule.

protract, SYN.—distend, distort, elongate, expand, extend, lengthen, spread, strain, stretch. ANT.—contract, loosen, shrink, slacken, tighten.

proud, SYN.—arrogant, disdainful, haughty, overbearing, stately, supercilious, vain, vainglorious. ANT.—ashamed, humble, lowly, meek.

prove, SYN.—confirm, corroborate, demonstrate, establish, manifest, test, try, verify. ANT.—contradict, disprove, refute.

proverb, SYN.—adage, aphorism, apothegm, byword, maxim, motto, saw, saying.

provide, SYN.—endow, equip, fit, fit out, supply; afford, give, produce, yield. ANT.—denude, despoil, divest, strip.

provident, SYN.—economical, frugal, niggardly, saving, sparing, thrifty. ANT.—extravagant, improvident, lavish, prodigal, wasteful.

provision, SYN.—accumulation, fund, hoard, reserve, stock, store, supply.

provoke, SYN.—agitate, arouse, awaken, disquiet, disturb, excite, incite, irritate, rouse, stimulate, stir up. ANT.—allay, calm, pacify, quell, quiet.

prowess, SYN.—boldness, bravery, chivalry, courage, fearlessness, fortitude, intrepidity, mettle, resolution. ANT.—cowardice, fear, pusillanimity, timidity.

proximate, SYN.—adjacent, bordering, close, near, neighboring, nigh; approaching, imminent, impending. ANT.—distant, far, removed.

proxy, SYN.—agent, alternate, deputy, lieutenant, representative, substitute, understudy; equivalent, expedient, makeshift. ANT.—head, master, principal, sovereign.

prudence, SYN.—care, caution, heed, vigilance, wariness, watchfulness. ANT.—abandon, carelessness, recklessness.

prudent, SYN.—discreet, intelligent, judicious, practical, reasonable, sagacious, sage, sensible, sober, sound, wise. ANT.—absurd, stupid, unaware.

prying, SYN.—curious, inquiring, inquisitive, interrogative, meddling, nosy, peeping, peering, searching, snoopy. ANT.—incurious, indifferent, unconcerned, uninterested.

psyche, SYN.—brain, faculties, intellect, intelligence, judgment, mentality, mind, reason, soul, spirit, understanding, wit. ANT.—body, corporeality, materiality, matter.

psychosis, SYN.—aberration, craziness, delirium, dementia, derangement, frenzy, insanity, lunacy, madness, mania. ANT.—rationality, sanity, stability.

public, SYN.—open, unrestricted.

pulchritude, SYN.—attractiveness, beauty, charm, comeliness, elegance, fairness, grace, handsomeness, loveliness. ANT.—deformity, disfigurement, eyesore, homeliness, ugliness.

pull, SYN.—drag, draw, haul, tow, tug; extract, remove, take out, unsheathe; allure, attract, entice, induce, lure, persuade; lengthen, prolong, protract, stretch. ANT.—alienate, contract, drive, propel, shorten.

pulsate, SYN.—beat, palpitate, pulse, throb.

pummel, SYN.—castigate, chastise, correct, discipline, punish, strike. ANT.—acquit, exonerate, free, pardon, release.

pump, SYN.—ask, examine, inquire, interrogate, query, question, quiz. ANT.—answer, reply, respond, state.

punctual, SYN.—exact, nice, precise, prompt, ready, timely. ANT.—dilatory, late, slow, tardy.

punish, SYN.—castigate, chastise, correct, discipline, pummel, strike. ANT.—acquit, exonerate, free, pardon, release.

punishment, SYN.—correction, discipline. ANT.—chaos, confusion, turbulence.

puny, SYN.—decrepit, delicate, enervated, exhausted, faint, feeble, forceless, impaired, infirm, languid, powerless, weak. ANT.—forceful, lusty, stout, strong, vigorous.

purchase, SYN.—acquire, buy, get, obtain, procure. ANT.—dispose of, sell, vend.

pure, SYN.—clean, clear, genuine, immaculate, spotless, unadulterated, untainted; chaste, guiltless, innocent, modest, sincere, undefiled, virgin; absolute, bare, sheer. ANT.—foul, polluted, sullied, tainted, tarnished; corrupt, defiled.

purify, SYN.—clean, cleanse, mop, scrub, sweep, wash. ANT.—dirty, pollute, soil, stain, sully.

purloin, SYN.—burglarize, embezzle, loot, pilfer, pillage, plagiarize, plunder, rob, snitch, steal,

swipe. ANT.—buy, re-
fund, repay, restore, re-
turn.

purport, SYN.—acceptation, connotation, drift,
explanation, gist, impli-
cation, import, intent, interpretation, meaning,
purpose, sense, signifi-
cance, signification.

purpose, SYN.—aim, design, drift, end, goal, intent, intention, object,
objective. ANT.—acci-
dent, fate, hazard.

pursue, SYN.—chase, follow, hunt, persist, track,
trail. ANT.—abandon,
elude, escape, evade,
flee.

push, SYN.—crowd, drive,
force, impel, jostle,
press, propel, shove;
hasten, promote, urge.
ANT.—drag, falter, halt,
pull, retreat; ignore, oppose.

pushy, SYN.—bold, brazen,
forward, impudent, inso-
lent, rude; abrupt, con-
spicuous, prominent,
striking. ANT.—coward-
ly, flinching, timid; bashful, retiring.

putrefy, SYN.—decay, decompose, disintegrate,
rot, spoil, waste.
ANT.—flourish, grow, in-
crease, luxuriate.

puzzle, SYN.—conundrum,
enigma, mystery, prob-
lem, riddle. ANT.—an-
swer, clue, key, resolu-
tion, solution.

puzzle, SYN.—bewilder,
confound, confuse, dum-
found, mystify, nonplus,
perplex. ANT.—clarify,

explain, illumine, in-
struct, solve.

Q

quaint, SYN.—curious,
droll, eccentric, odd, peculiar, queer, singular,
strange, unusual, whim-
sical. ANT.—common,
familiar, normal, ordi-
nary, usual.

qualification, SYN.—ability,
aptitude, aptness, capa-
bility, capacity, dexterity, efficiency, faculty,
power, skill, talent.
ANT.—disability, inca-
pacity, incompetency,
unreadiness.

qualified, SYN.—able, clever, competent, efficient,
fitted, skillful. ANT.—inadequate, incapable, in-
competent, unfitted.

quality, SYN.—attribute,
characteristic, distinc-
tion, feature, peculiarity,
property, trait; caliber,
grade, value. ANT.—be-
ing, essence, nature, substance.

quantity, SYN.—content,
extent, measure, portion;
aggregate, amount, num-
ber, sum, volume.
ANT.—nothing, nothing-
ness, zero.

quarrel, SYN.—affray, altercation, argument,
bickering, contention,
disagreement, dispute,
feud, spat, squabble,
wrangle. ANT.—agree-
ment, friendliness, har-
mony, peace, reconcilia-
tion.

queer, SYN.—curious,

droll, eccentric, odd, peculiar, quaint, singular, strange, unusual, whimsical. ANT.—common, familiar, normal, ordinary, usual.

quest, SYN.—examination, exploration, interrogation, investigation, query, question, research, scrutiny. ANT.—disregard, inactivity, inattention, negligence.

question, SYN.—ask, examine, inquire, interrogate, pump, query, quiz; challenge, dispute, doubt. ANT.—answer, reply, respond, state; accept.

quick, SYN.—active, brisk, fast, hasty, lively, nimble, precipitate, rapid, speedy, swift; excitable, impatient, irascible, sharp, testy, touchy; acute, clever, discerning, keen, sensitive, shrewd. ANT.—slow, sluggish; dull, inattentive, unaware.

quicken, SYN.—accelerate, dispatch, expedite, facilitate, forward, hasten, hurry, push, rush, speed. ANT.—block, hinder, impede, retard, slow.

quickness, SYN.—action, activity, agility, briskness, energy, enterprise, exercise, intensity, liveliness, motion, movement, rapidity, vigor. ANT.—dullness, idleness, inactivity, inertia, sloth.

quiescent, SYN.—concealed, dormant, hidden, inactive, latent, potential, secret, undeveloped,

unseen. ANT.—conspicuous, evident, explicit, manifest, visible.

quiet, SYN.—hushed, motionless, peaceful, placid, quiescent, still, tranquil, undisturbed; calm, gentle, meek, mild, modest, passive, patient, silent. ANT.—loud, strident; agitated, disturbed, perturbed.

quiet, SYN.—calm, calmness, hush, peace, quiescence, quietude, repose, rest, serenity, silence, stillness, tranquility. ANT.—agitation, disturbance, excitement, noise, tumult.

quiet, SYN.—allay, alleviate, appease, assuage, calm, compose, lull, pacify, placate, quell, relieve, satisfy, soothe, still, tranquilize. ANT.—arouse, excite, incense, inflame.

quit, SYN.— abandon, cease, desist, discontinue, stop; give up, relinquish, resign, surrender; abandon, depart, leave, withdraw. ANT.—continue, endure, occupy, persist, stay.

quiz, SYN.—ask, examine, inquire, interrogate, pump, query, question, challenge, dispute, doubt. ANT.—answer, reply, respond, state; accept.

quote, SYN.—adduce, cite, extract, paraphrase, plagiarize, recite, repeat. ANT.—contradict, misquote, refute, retort.

R

race, SYN.—ancestry, clan, folk, lineage, nation, people, stock, strain, tribe.

racket, SYN.—babel, clamor, cry, din, noise, outcry, row, sound, tumult, uproar. ANT.—hush, quiet, silence, stillness.

radiance, SYN.—brightness, brilliance, brilliancy, effulgence, luster, splendor. ANT.—darkness, dullness, gloom, obscurity.

radiant, SYN.—brilliant, bright, dazzling, effulgent, glorious, gorgeous, grand, illustrious, magnificent, resplendent, shining, showy, splendid, sumptuous, superb. ANT.—dull, mediocre, modest, ordinary, unimpressive.

radical, SYN.—complete, extreme, insurgent, total, thorough, ultra, uncompromising; basic, constitutional, fundamental, inherent, innate, intrinsic, natural, organic, original. ANT.—conservative, moderate, superficial; extraneous.

ragamuffin, SYN.—beggar, mendicant, pauper, scrub, starveling, tatterdemalion, vagabond, wretch.

rage, SYN.—anger, animosity, choler, exasperation, fury, indignation, ire, irritation, passion, petulance, resentment, temper, wrath. ANT.—concil-iation, forbearance, patience, peace, self-control.

raging, SYN.—boisterous, fierce, forceful, furious, impetuous, passionate, powerful, raving, turbulent, vehement, violent, wild; acute, extreme, intense, severe. ANT.—calm, feeble, gentle, quiet, soft.

raise, SYN.—elevate, erect, exalt, heave, heighten, hoist, lift, uplift; breed, cultivate, grow, produce; gather, levy, muster. ANT.—abase, depreciate, depress, destroy, lower.

ramble, SYN.—deviate, digress, err, range, roam, rove, saunter, stray, stroll, traipse, wander. ANT.—halt, linger, settle, stay, stop.

rancor, SYN.—animosity, enmity, grudge, ill will, malevolence, malice, malignity, spite. ANT.—affection, kindness, love, toleration.

rank, SYN.—hue, range, row, series; blood, class, degree, estate, grade, quality, standing, station, status; dignity, distinction, eminence. ANT.—disrepute, humiliation, shame, stigma.

rapid, SYN.—fast, quick, speedy, swift. ANT.—slow, sluggish.

rapidity, SYN.—action, activity, agility, briskness, energy, enterprise, exercise, intensity, liveliness, motion, movement, quickness, vigor.

ANT.—dullness, idleness, inactivity, inertia, sloth.

rapture, SYN.—bliss, ecstasy, exaltation, gladness, happiness, joy, transport. ANT.—depression, grief, melancholy, misery, sorrow, woe, wretch.

rare, SYN.—infrequent, occasional, strange, unusual; choice, exceptional, incomparable, precious, scarce, singular, uncommon, unique. ANT.—customary, frequent, ordinary, usual; abundant, commonplace, numerous, worthless.

rash, SYN.—careless, hasty, heedless, impetuous, passionate, quick. ANT.—calculating, cautious, reasoning.

rate, SYN.—decide, decree, determine; adjudicate, arbitrate, condemn, judge, try, umpire; appreciate, consider, estimate, evaluate, measure, think.

rational, SYN.—intelligent, judicious, reasonable, sensible, wise; sane, sober, sound. ANT.—absurd, foolish; irrational, insane.

rationality, SYN.—argument, basis, cause, ground, motive; aim, design, purpose, intelligence, mind, reason, sense, understanding.

ravage, SYN.—despoil, destroy, devastate, pillage, plunder, ruin, sack, strip, waste. ANT.—accumulate, conserve, econo-mize, preserve, save.

ravenous, SYN.—craving, famished, hungry, starved, thirsting, voracious; ANT.—full, gorged, sated, satiated.

ravish, SYN.—debauch, deflower, violate.

raw, SYN.—coarse, crude, green, harsh, ill-prepared, rough, unfinished, unpolished, unrefined. ANT.—finished, well-prepared.

raze, SYN.—annihilate, demolish, destroy, devastate, eradicate, exterminate, extinguish, obliterate, ravage, ruin, wreck. ANT.—construct, establish, make, preserve, save.

reach, SYN.—extend, stretch; arrive at, attain, come to, overtake. ANT.—fail, fall short, miss.

react, SYN.—answer, rejoin, reply, respond. ANT.—disregard, ignore, overlook.

ready, SYN.—complete, consummate, finished, full-grown, mature, matured, mellow, ripe, seasonable. ANT.—crude, green, immature, raw, undeveloped.

ready, SYN.—concoct, condition, contrive, equip, fit, furnish, get ready, make ready, predispose, prepare, provide, qualify.

real, SYN.—actual, authentic, certain, genuine, positive, substantial, true, veritable. ANT.—apparent, fictitious, imaginary, supposed, unreal.

realization, SYN.—accomplishment, achievement, attainment, completion, performance. ANT.—defeat, failure.

realize, SYN.—appreciate, apprehend, comprehend, conceive, discern, grasp, know, learn, perceive, see, understand. ANT.—ignore, misapprehend, mistake, misunderstand.

realm, SYN.—domain, estate, farm, land.

reap, SYN.—acquire, gain, garner, gather, glean, harvest. ANT.—lose, plant, sow, squander.

reaping, SYN.—crop, fruit, harvest, proceeds, produce, product, result, store, yield.

rear, SYN.—foster, nurture, raise, train.

reason, SYN.—argument, basis, cause, ground, motive, sake; aim, design, purpose, intelligence, mind, rationality, sense, understanding.

reason, SYN.—argue, conclude, deduce, deliberate, discuss, infer, judge, reflect. ANT.—bewilder, confuse, guess.

reasonable, SYN.—discreet, intelligent, judicious, practical, prudent, sagacious, sage, sensible, sober, sound, wise. ANT.—absurd, impalpable, imperceptible, stupid, unaware.

rebel, SYN.—mutiny, revolt, strike.

rebellion, SYN.—coup, insurrection, mutiny, overthrow, revolt, revolution, uprising.

rebellious, SYN.—defiant, disobedient, forward, insubordinate, refractory, undutiful, unruly. ANT.—compliant, dutiful, obedient, submissive.

rebuild, SYN.—reconstruct, reestablish, refresh, rehabilitate, renew, renovate, repair, restore.

rebuke, SYN.—accuse, censure, condemn, implicate, reproach, upbraid. ANT.—absolve, acquit, exonerate.

rebuttal, SYN.—answer, defense. ANT.—argument.

recall, SYN.—mind, recollect, remember, remind, reminisce. ANT.—disregard, forget, ignore, overlook.

receive, SYN.—accept, gain, get, take; admit, shelter; entertain, welcome. ANT.—bestow, give, impart, reject; discharge, turn away.

recent, SYN.—fresh, late, modern, newfangled, novel, original. ANT.—ancient, antiquated, archaic, obsolete, old.

recital, SYN.—account, chronicle, description, detail, history, narration, narrative, relation. ANT.—caricature, confusion, distortion, misrepresentation.

recite, SYN.—declaim, deliver, describe, detail,

mention, narrate, recapitulate, rehearse, relate, repeat, tell.

reckless, SYN.—careless, heedless, imprudent, inattentive, inconsiderate, indiscreet, thoughtless, unconcerned. ANT.—accurate, careful, meticulous, nice.

recognize, SYN.—apprehend, identify, perceive, recollect, remember; acknowledge, avow, concede, confess, own. ANT.—forget, ignore, overlook; disown, renounce, repudiate.

recollection, SYN.—memory, remembrance, reminiscence, retrospection.ANT.— forgetfulness, oblivion.

recommend, SYN.—advise, allude, counsel, hint, imply, insinuate, intimate, offer, propose, refer, suggest. ANT.—declare, demand, dictate, insist.

recommendation, SYN.— admonition, advice, caution, counsel, exhortation, instruction, honesty, integrity, justice, openness, responsibility, sincerity, trustworthiness,uprightness.ANT.— cheating, deceit, dishonesty, fraud, trickery.

recuperate, SYN.—cure, rally, recover, restore, revive, recapture, recoup, redeem, regain, repossess, retrieve. ANT.—regress, relapse, revert, weaken; forfeit, lose.

reduce, SYN.—abate,

assuage, decrease, diminish, lessen, lower, moderate, suppress. ANT.—amplify, enlarge, increase, intensify, revive.

reduction, SYN.—abbreviation, abridgement, contraction, shortening. ANT.—amplification, enlargement, expansion, extension.

refined, SYN.—courtly, cultivated, cultured, genteel, polished, polite, well-bred; clarified, purified. ANT.—boorish, coarse, crude, rude, vulgar.

refinement, SYN.—breeding, civilization, cultivation, culture, education, enlightenment. ANT.— boorishness, ignorance, illiteracy, vulgarity.

reflect, SYN.—cogitate, contemplate, deliberate, meditate, muse, ponder, reason, speculate, think.

reflection, SYN.—cogitation, conception, suggestion, warning; information, intelligence, notification.

reckon, SYN.—account, believe, consider, deem, esteem, estimate, hold, judge,rate,regard, think, view.

reckoning, SYN.—account, computation, record.

reconsider, SYN.—consider, examine, inspect, review, revise, survey. ANT.—ignore, reject.

record, SYN.—account, archive, chronicle, document, memorandum, minute, note, report, register; mark, memorial, trace, vestige; achievement, career, history.

recount, SYN.—describe, narrate, recite, rehearse, relate, report, tell.

recover, SYN.—cure, rally, recuperate, restore, revive, recapture, recoup, redeem, regain, repossess, retrieve. ANT.—regress, relapse, revert, weaken; forfeit, lose.

recreation, SYN.—amusement, diversion, entertainment, fun, game, pastime, play, sport. ANT.—boredom, labor, toil, work.

rectify, SYN.—amend, correct, mend, reform, right. ANT.—aggravate, ignore, spoil.

rectitude, SYN.—candor, fairness, frankness, consideration, contemplation, deliberation, fancy, idea, imagination, impression, judgment, meditation, memory, notion, opinion, recollection, regard, retrospection, sentiment, thought, view.

reform, SYN.—amend, correct, improve, rectify, right. ANT.—aggravate, corrupt, damage, debase, impair, spoil, vitiate.

refrain, SYN.—abstain, desist, forbear, withhold. ANT.—continue, indulge, persist.

refreshing, SYN.—brisk, cool, fresh.

refuge, SYN.—asylum, harbor, haven, retreat, sanc-

tuary, shelter. ANT.—danger, exposure, hazard, jeopardy, peril.

refuse, SYN.—decline, deny, rebuff, reject, repudiate, spurn, withhold. ANT.—accept, grant, welcome.

refute, SYN.—confute, controvert, disprove, falsify, rebut. ANT.—accept, affirm, confirm, establish, prove.

regain, SYN.—recapture, recoup, recover, redeem, repossess, retrieve. ANT.—forfeit, lose.

regal, SYN.—courtly, dignified, grand, imperial, kingly, lordly, majestic, monarchial, noble, princely, royal, ruling, sovereign, stately, supreme. ANT.—common, humble, low, plebian, proletarian, servile, vulgar.

regalement, SYN.—celebration, dinner, entertainment, feast, festival.

regard, SYN.—attention, care, concern, consideration, notice, observation; affection, esteem, liking. ANT.—antipathy, disgust, disaffection, neglect.

regard, SYN.—esteem, honor, respect, value; behold, contemplate, look, mark, notice, observe, see, view, watch; account, believe, deem, hold, imagine, reckon, suppose, think. ANT.—insult, mock; ignore, neglect, overlook.

region, SYN.—area, belt,

climate, locale, locality, location, place, sector, site, situation, spot, station, vicinity, zone.

regressive, SYN.—backward, retrograde, revisionary. ANT.—advanced, civilized, progressive.

regret, SYN.—compunction, contrition, grief, penitence, qualm, remorse, repentance, self-reproach, sorrow. ANT.—complacency, impenitence, obduracy, self-satisfaction.

regular, SYN.—customary, methodical, natural, normal, orderly, ordinary, periodical, steady, systematic, uniform, unvaried. ANT.—abnormal, erratic, exceptional, rare, unusual.

regulation, SYN.—axiom, canon, control, discipline, formula, guide, law, maxim, method, order, precept, principle, propriety, restraint, rule, self-control, standard, statute, system. ANT.—chance, chaos, confusion, deviation, exception, hazard, irregularity, turbulence.

rehabilitate, SYN.—rebuild, reconstruct, reestablish, refresh, renew, renovate, repair, restore.

reiterate, SYN.—duplicate, iterate, recapitulate, repeat, reproduce.

reject, SYN.—decline, deny, rebuff, refuse, repudiate, spurn, withhold. ANT.—accept, grant,

welcome.

rejection, SYN.—challenge, difference, disagreement, dissent, dissentience, noncompliance, nonconformity, objection, protest, recusancy, remonstrance, variance. ANT.— acceptance, agreement, assent, compliance.

relate, SYN.—describe, narrate, recite, recount, rehearse, report, tell; apply, beat, connect, correlate, pertain, refer.

relation, SYN.—alliance, association, coalition, combination, confederacy, entente, federation, league, partnership, union; compact, covenant, marriage, treaty. ANT.—divorce, schism, separation.

relationship, SYN.—affinity, alliance, association, bond, conjunction, connection, link, relationship, tie, union. ANT.—disunion, isolation, separation.

relatives, SYN.—affinity, consanguinity, family, kindred, kinsfolk, relations, relationship. ANT.— disconnection, foreigners, strangers.

relaxed, SYN.—acceptable, agreeable, casual, comfortable, convenient, cozy, gratifying, incidental, informal, nonchalant, offhand, pleasing, pleasurable, restful, unconcerned, unpremeditated, welcome. ANT.—distressing, formal, miserable, planned, pretentious, troubling, uncomfortable, wretched.

release, SYN.—deliver, discharge, emancipate, free, let go, liberate, set free. ANT.—confine, imprison, oppress, restrict, subjugate.

relent, SYN.—abdicate, accede, acquiesce, capitulate, cede, quit, relinquish, resign, submit, succumb, surrender, waive, yield. ANT.—assert, resist, strive, struggle.

relevant, SYN.—applicable, apposite, appropriate, apropos, apt, fit, germane, material, pertinent, related, relating, to the point. ANT.—alien, extraneous, foreign, unrelated.

reliable, SYN.—certain, dependable, safe, secure, sure, tried, trustworthy, trusty. ANT.—dubious, fallible, questionable, uncertain, unreliable.

reliance, SYN.—confidence, credence, dependence, faith, trust. ANT.—doubt, incredulity, mistrust, skepticism.

relief, SYN.—aid, alms, assistance, backing, furtherance, help, patronage, succor, support. ANT.—antagonism, counteraction, defiance, hostility, resistance.

relieve, SYN.—abate, allay, alleviate, assuage, calm, comfort, diminish, ease, extenuate, facilitate, lighten, mitigate, pacify, soften, solace, soothe. ANT.—aggravate, agitate, augment, confound, distress, disturb, increase, irritate, trouble, worry.

religion, SYN.—belief, creed, doctrine, dogma, persuasion, tenet. ANT.—infidelity.

religious, SYN.—devout, divine, godly, holy, pietistic, pious, reverent, sacred, santimonious, spiritual, theological. ANT.—atheistic, impious, profane, secular, skeptical.

religiousness, SYN.—affection, ardor, attachment, consecration, dedication, devotion, devoutness, fidelity, love, loyalty, piety, zeal. ANT.—alienation, apathy, aversion, indifference, unfaithfulness.

relinquish, SYN.—abandon, acquiesce, capitulate, cede, renounce, resign, sacrifice, submit, surrender, yield. ANT.—conquer, overcome, resist, rout.

reluctance, SYN.—abhorrence, antipathy, aversion, disgust, disinclination, dislike, distaste, dread, hatred, loathing, repugnance, repulsion. ANT.—affection, attachment, devotion, enthusiasm.

reluctant, SYN.—averse, disinclined, hesitant, loath, slow, unwilling. ANT.—disposed, eager, inclined, ready, willing.

rely, SYN.—depend, lean, trust.

remain, SYN.—abide, dwell, halt, rest, stay, tarry, wait; continue, endure, last, survive. ANT.—depart, go, leave; dissipate, finish, terminate.

remains, SYN.—balance, remainder, residue, rest, surplus.

remark, SYN.—annotation, assertion, comment, declaration, observation, statement, utterance,

remark, SYN.—express, mention, observe, utter.

remarkable, SYN.—affecting, arresting, august, commanding, exciting, forcible, grandiose, imposing, impressive, majestic, moving, overpowering, splendid, stirring, striking, thrilling, touching. ANT.—commonplace, ordinary, regular, unimpressive.

remedy, SYN.—antidote, cure, help, medicant, restorative; redress, relief, reparation.

remedy, SYN.—ameliorate, better, correct, improve, mend, rectify, reform.

remember, SYN.—mind, recall, recollect, remind, reminisce. ANT.—disregard, forget, ignore, overlook.

remembrance, SYN.—commemoration, memento, memorial, monument, souvenir.

remonstrate, SYN.—complain, grouch, grumble, lament, murmur, protest, regret, repine, whine. ANT.—applaud, approve, praise, rejoice.

remorse, SYN.—compunction, contrition, grief, penitence, qualm, regret, repentance, self-reproach, sorrow. ANT.—complacency, impenitence, obduracy, self-satisfaction.

remorseless, SYN.—barbarian, barbaric, barbarous, brutal, crude, cruel, inhuman, merciless, rude, ruthless, savage, uncivilized, uncultured, unrelenting. ANT.—civilized, humane, kind, polite, refined.

remote, SYN.—distant, far, faraway, removed. ANT.—close, near, nigh.

remove, SYN.—dislodge, displace, move, shift, transfer, transport; discharge, dismiss, eject, oust, vacate; extract, withdraw. ANT.—leave, remain, stay; retain.

renounce, SYN.—abandon, forego, forsake, quit, relinquish, resign, sacrifice; deny, disavow, disclaim, disown, reject, retract, revoke. ANT.—defend, maintain, uphold; acknowledge, assert, recognize.

renovate, SYN.—rebuild, reconstruct, reestablish, refresh, rehabilitate, renew, repair, restore.

renown, SYN.—acclaim, distinction, eminence, fame, honor, luster, notability, reputation. ANT.—disgrace, disrepute, obscurity.

renowned, SYN.—celebrated, distinguished, eminent, famous, glorious, illustrious, noted, wellknown. ANT.—hidden, ignominious, infamous, obscure, unknown.

repair, SYN.—correct, darn, fix, mend, patch, refit, renew, renovate, restore, tinker with; amend, redress, remedy, retrieve. ANT.—break, destroy, harm.

repeal, SYN.—abolish, abrogate, annul, cancel, invalidate, nullify, quash, rescind, revoke.

repeat, SYN.—quote, recite, rehearse, relate; duplicate, iterate, recapitulate, reiterate, reproduce.

repentance, SYN.—compunction, contrition, grief, penitence, qualm, regret, remorse, selfreproach, sorrow. ANT.—complacency, impenitence, obduracy, self-satisfaction.

repentant, SYN.—contrite, penitent, regretful, remorseful, sorrowful, sorry. ANT.—obdurate, remorseless.

repine, SYN.—complain, grouch, grumble, lament, murmur, protest, regret, remonstrate, whine. ANT.—applaud, approve, praise, rejoice.

replace, SYN.—reinstate, restore, return.

replenish, SYN.—fill, fill up, occupy, pervade; furnish, stock, store, sup-

ply. ANT.—deplete, drain, empty, exhaust, void.

replica, SYN.—copy, duplicate, exemplar, facsimile, imitation, reproduction, transcript. ANT.—original, prototype.

reply, SYN.—answer, rejoinder, response, retort. ANT.—inquiry, questioning, summoning.

reply, SYN.—answer, react, rejoin, respond. ANT.—disregard, ignore, overlook.

report, SYN.—advertise, announce, declare, give out, herald, make known, notify, proclaim, promulgate, publish. ANT.—bury, conceal, stifle, suppress, withhold.

repose, SYN.—calm, calmness, hush, peace, quiescence, quiet, quietude, rest, serenity, silence, stillness, tranquility. ANT.—agitation, disturbance, excitement, noise, tumult.

represent, SYN.—delineate, depict, describe, draw, paint, picture, portray, sketch. ANT.—caricature, misrepresent, suggest.

representation, SYN.—appearance, cinema, drawing, effigy, engraving, etching, film, illustration, image, likeness, painting, panorama, photograph, picture, portrait, portrayal, print, resemblance, scene, sketch, view.

repress, SYN.—bridle,

check, constrain, curb, hinder, hold back, inhibit, limit, restrain, stop, suppress. ANT.—aid, encourage, incite, loosen.

reprimand, SYN.—admonish, berate, blame, censure, lecture, rate, rebuke, reprehend, scold, upbraid, vituperate. ANT.—approve, commend, praise.

reproach, SYN.—abuse, aspersion, defamation, desecration, dishonor, disparagement, insult, invective, maltreatment, misuse, outrage, perversion, profanation, reviling, upbraiding. ANT.—approval, commendation, laudation, plaudit, respect.

reproduction, SYN.—copy, duplicate, exemplar, facsimile, imitation, replica, transcript. ANT.—original, prototype.

repugnance, SYN.—abhorrence, antipathy, aversion, disgust, disinclination, dislike, distaste, dread, hatred, loathing, repulsion, reluctance. ANT.—affection, attachment, devotion, enthusiasm.

repulsive, SYN.—deformed, hideous, homely, plain, repellent, ugly, uncomely. ANT.—attractive, beautiful, fair, handsome, pretty.

reputation, SYN.—character, class, description, disposition, individuality, kind, nature, repute, sort, standing.

repute, SYN.—character, class, description, disposition, individuality, kind, nature, reputation, sort, standing.

request, SYN.—appeal, ask, beg, beseech, desire, entreat, implore, importune, petition, pray, seek, sue, supplicate. ANT.—demand, require.

require, SYN.—call for, claim, command, demand, exact, order, prescribe; lack, necessitate, need, want.

requisite, SYN.—basic, essential, fundamental, important, indispensable, intrinsic, necessary, needed, vital. ANT.—accidental, casual, contingent, expendable, extrinsic, nonessential, optional, peripheral.

rescind, SYN.—abolish, abrogate, annul, invalidate, nullify, quash, repeal, revoke.

research, SYN.—examination, exploration, inquiry, interrogation, investigation, query, quest, question, scrutiny. ANT.—disregard, inactivity, inattention, negligence.

resemblance, SYN.—analogy, correspondence, likeness, parity, similarity, similitude. ANT.—difference, distinction, variance.

resentfulness, SYN.—covetousness, envy, invidiousness, jealousy, suspicion. ANT.—geniality, indifference, liberality, tolerance.

reserve, SYN.—accumulation, fund, hoard, provision, stock, store, supply.

reserved, SYN.—aloof, bashful, cautious, chary, demure, diffident, distant, fearful, modest, retiring, sheepish, shrinking, stiff, timorous, unfriendly, wary. ANT.—audacious, bold, brazen, cordial, forward, friendly, immodest.

residence, SYN.—abode, domicile, dwelling, habitat, hearth, home, quarters, seat.

resign, SYN.—give up, quit, relinquish, surrender.

resignation, SYN.—composure, endurance, forbearance, fortitude, long-suffering, perseverance. ANT.—impatience, nervousness, restlessness, unquiet.

resigned, SYN.—assiduous, composed, forbearing, indulgent, long-suffering, passive, patient, stoical, uncomplaining. ANT.—chafing, clamorous, high-strung, hysterical, turbulent.

resist, SYN.—attack, confront, defy, hinder, impede, obstruct, oppose, thwart, withstand. ANT.—accede, allow, cooperate, relent, yield.

resolution, SYN.—courage, decision, determination, firmness, fortitude, persistence, resolve, steadfastness. ANT.—inconstancy, indecision, vacillation.

resolve, SYN.—courage, decision, determination, firmness, fortitude, persistence, resolution, steadfastness. ANT.—inconstancy, indecision, vacillation.

resolve, SYN.—adjudicate, close, conclude, decide, determine, end, fix, settle, terminate. ANT.—doubt, hesitate, suspend, vacillate, waver.

respect, SYN.—admire, consider, heed, honor, regard, revere, reverence, value, venerate. ANT.—abuse, despise, disdain, neglect, scorn.

respectable, SYN.—adequate, becoming, befitting, comely, decorous, fit, proper, seemly, suitable, tolerable. ANT.—coarse, gross, indecent, reprehensible, vulgar.

respond, SYN.—answer, react, rejoin, reply. ANT.—disregard, ignore, overlook.

response, SYN.—answer, rejoinder, reply, retort. ANT.—inquiry, questioning, summoning.

responsibility, SYN.—accountability, amenability, liability, obligation, trustworthiness; duty, trust.

responsbile, SYN.—accountable, amenable, liable; reliable, trustworthy. ANT.—exempt, free, immune; careless, negligent.

rest, SYN.—sleep, slumber; calm, ease, leisure,

peace, quiet, relaxation, repose, tranquillity; cessation, intermission, pause, respite; balance, remainder, surplus. ANT.—agitation, commotion, disturbance, motion, tumult.

restless, SYN.—agitated, disquieted, disturbed, irresolute, sleepless, uneasy, unquiet; active, roving, transient, wandering. ANT.—at ease, peaceable, quiet, tractable.

restore, SYN.—rebuild, reconstruct, reestablish, refresh, rehabilitate, renew, renovate, repair; cure, heal, recover, rejuvenate, revive; reinstate, replace, return.

restrain, SYN.—bridle, check, constrain, curb, hinder, hold back, inhibit, limit, repress, stop, suppress. ANT.—aid, encourage, incite, loosen.

restraint, SYN.—control, discipline, order, regulation, self-control. ANT.—chaos, confusion, turbulence.

restrict, SYN.—attach, bind, connect, engage, fasten, fetter, join, link, oblige, restrain, tie. ANT.—free, loose, unfasten, untie.

result, SYN.—conclusion, consequence, determination, effect, end, eventuality, issue, resolution, resolve.

retaliation, SYN.—reparation, reprisal, requital, retribution, revenge,

vengeance, vindictiveness. ANT.—mercy, pardon, reconciliation, remission, forgiveness.

retard, SYN.—arrest, detain, hinder, impede, stay.

retire, SYN.—abandon, depart, forsake, give up, go, leave, quit, relinquish, renounce, withdraw. ANT.—abide, remain, stay, tarry.

retort, SYN.—answer, rejoinder, reply, response. ANT.—inquiry, questioning, summoning.

retrograde, SYN.—backward, regressive, revisionary. ANT.—advanced, civilized, progressive.

retribution, SYN.—reparation, reprisal, requital, retaliation, revenge, vengeance, vindictiveness. ANT.—mercy, pardon, reconciliation, remission, forgiveness.

return, SYN.—go back, recur, retreat, revert; repay, replace, requite, restore. ANT.—appropriate, keep, retain, take.

reveal, SYN.—betray, disclose, discover, divulge, expose, impart, show, uncover. ANT.—cloak, conceal, cover, hide, obscure.

revelation, SYN.—apparition, daydream, dream, ghost, hallucination, mirage, phantoms, prophecy, specter, vision. ANT.—reality, substance, verity.

revenge, SYN.—reparation,

reprisal, requital, retaliation, retribution, vengeance, vindictiveness. ANT.—mercy, pardon, reconciliation, remission, forgiveness.

revenge, SYN.—avenge, requite, retaliate, vindicate. ANT.—forgive, pardon, pity, reconcile.

revere, SYN.—adore, esteem, honor, venerate, worship. ANT.—despise, hate, ignore.

reverence, SYN.—admiration, adoration, deference, dignity, esteem, fame, glory, homage, honor, praise, renown, respect, worship. ANT.—contempt, derision, disgrace, dishonor, reproach.

reverse, SYN.—invert, transpose, turn about; overthrow, overturn, subvert, unmake, upset; annual, countermand, repeal, rescind, revoke. ANT.—endorse, maintain, stabilize; affirm, confirm, vouch.

revert, SYN.—go back, recur, retreat, return. ANT—appropriate, keep, retain, take.

review, SYN.—commentary, criticism, critique, examination, inspection, reconsideration, retrospect, retrospection, revision, survey, synopsis; digest, journal, periodical.

review, SYN.—consider, examine, inspect, reconsider, revise, survey; analyze, criticize, discuss,

edit. ANT.—ignore, reject.

revile, SYN.—abuse, asperse, defame, disparage, ill-use, malign, scandalize, traduce, vilify. ANT.—cherish, honor, praise, protect, respect.

revision, SYN.—commentary, criticism, critique, examination, inspection, reconsideration, retrospect, retrospection, review, survey, synopsis.

revive, SYN.—abate, assuage, decrease, diminish, lessen, lower, moderate, reduce, suppress. ANT.—amplify, enlarge, increase, intensify.

revoke, SYN.—abolish, abrogate, annul, cancel, invalidate, nullify, quash, repeal, rescind.

revolting, SYN.—abominable, detestable, execrable, foul, hateful, loathsome, odious, vile. ANT.—agreeable, commendable, delightful, pleasant.

revolution, SYN.—coup, insurrection, mutiny, overthrow, rebellion, revolt, uprising.

revolve, SYN.—circle, gyrate, rotate, spin, turn, twirl, wheel, whirl. ANT.—proceed, stop, stray, travel, wander.

reward, SYN.—award, bonus, bounty, compensation, premium, prize, recompense, remuneration, requital. ANT.—assessment, charge, earnings, punishment, wages.

rich, SYN.—abundant, affluent, ample, bountiful, copious, costly, exorbitant, luxurious, opulent, plentiful, prosperous, sumptuous, wealthy, well-to-do; fecund, fertile, fruitful, luxuriant, prolific. ANT.—beggarly, destitute, indigent, needy, poor; barren, sterile, unfruitful, unproductive.

riddle, SYN.—conundrum, enigma, mystery, problem, puzzle. ANT.—answer, clue, key, resolution, solution.

ridicule, SYN.—banter, derision, gibe, irony, jeering, mockery, raillery, sarcasm, satire, sneering.

ridiculous, SYN.—absurd, foolish, inconsistent, irrational, nonsensical, preposterous, self-contradictory, silly, unreasonable. ANT.—consistent, rational, reasonable, sensible, sound.

right, SYN.—ethical, fair, just, lawful, legitimate; accurate, correct, real, true; appropriate, fit, proper, seemly, suitable; direct, erect, straight, upright. ANT.—bad, false, improper, wrong.

right, SYN.—authority, grant, liberty, license, prerogative, privilege; equity, honor, justice, propriety, virtue ANT.— encroachment, injustice, violation, wrong.

righteous, SYN.—chaste, decent, ethical, good, honorable, just, pure, right, scrupulous, virtuous. ANT.—amoral, libertine, licentious, sinful, unethical.

rigid, SYN.—austere, harsh, rigorous, severe, stern, strict, stringent, unyielding; inflexible, stiff, unbending. ANT.— compassionate, lax, lenient, mild, yielding; elastic, flexible, resilient, supple.

rigorous, SYN.—blunt, coarse, cruel, grating, gruff, hard, harsh, jarring, rough, severe, stern, strict, stringent, unfeeling. ANT.—gentle, lenient, melodious, mild, smooth, soft, tender.

rim, SYN.—border, boundary, brim, brink, edge, fringe, frontier, limit, margin, outskirts, termination, verge. ANT.—center, core, interior, mainland.

rip, SYN.—cleave, disunite, lacerate, rend, rive, sever, shred, slit, split, sunder, tear, wound. ANT.—join, mend, repair, sew, unite.

ripe, SYN.—complete, consummate, finished, full-grown, mature, matured, mellow, ready, seasonable. ANT.—crude, green, immature, raw, undeveloped.

rise, SYN.—climb, mount, proceed, progress, scale, soar, thrive, tower. ANT.—descend, fall, sink.

risk, SYN.—danger, hazard,

jeopardy, peril.
ANT.—defense, immunity, protection, safety.

risk, SYN.—endanger, expose, hazard, jeopardize, peril, speculate, venture. ANT.—insure, protect, secure.

risky, SYN.—critical, dangerous, hazardous, insecure, menacing, perilous, precarious, threatening, unsafe. ANT.—firm, protected, safe, secure.

rite, SYN.—ceremony, formality, observance, parade, pomp, protocol, ritual, solemnity.

ritual, SYN.—ceremony, formality, observance, parade, pomp, protocol, rite, solemnity.

rival, SYN.—adversary, antagonist, competitor, contestant, enemy, foe, opponent. ANT.—allay, comrade, confederate, teammate.

roam, SYN.—deviate, digress, err, ramble, range, rove, saunter, stray, stroll, traipse, wander. ANT.—halt, linger, settle, stay, stop.

rob, SYN.—despoil, fleece, loot, pilfer, pillage, plunder, sack, steal, strip.

robbery, SYN.—burglary, depredation, larceny, pillage, plunder, theft.

robust, SYN.—hale, healthy, hearty, sound, strong, well. ANT.—delicate, diseased, frail, infirm.

rock, SYN.—boulder, gravel, jewel, pebble, stone.

role, SYN.—character, lines, part.

romantic, SYN.—dreamy, extravagant, fanciful, fantastic, fictitious, ideal, idealistic, imaginative, maudlin, mawkish, picturesque, poetic, sentimental. ANT.—factual, literal, matter-of-fact, practical, prosaic.

roomy, SYN.—ample, broad, capacious, extensive, large, spacious, vast, wide. ANT.—confined, cramped, limited, narrow.

root, SYN.—base, basis, bottom, foundation, ground, groundwork, substructure, support, underpinning. ANT.—building, cover, superstructure, top.

rot, SYN.—decay, decline, decompose, decrease, disintegrate, dwindle, ebb, putrefy, spoil, wane, waste. ANT.—flourish, grow, increase, luxuriate, rise.

rotate, SYN.—circle, circulate, invert, revolve, spin, twirl, twist, wheel, whirl. ANT.—arrest, fix, stand, stop.

rotund, SYN.—bulbous, chubby, circular, complete, curved, cylindrical, entire, globular, plump, round, spherical.

rough, SYN.—craggy, irregular, jagged, rugged, scabrous, scratchy, uneven; approximate, coarse, crude, cursory, imperfect, incomplete, unfinished, unpolished; harsh, severe, stormy, tempestuous, turbulent, violent; blunt, brusque, churlish, gruff, rude, uncivil. ANT.—even, level, sleek, slippery, smooth; fine, finished, polished, refined; calm, placid, tranquil, unruffled; civil, courteous, gentle, mild.

round, SYN.—bulbous, chubby, circular, complete, curved, cylindrical, entire, globular, plump, rotund, spherical.

roundabout, SYN.—circuitous, crooked, distorted, erratic, indirect, swerving, tortuous, wandering, winding. ANT.—direct, straight.

rout, SYN.—beat. conquer, crush, defeat, humble, master, overcome, quell, subdue, subjugate, surmount, vanquish. ANT.—capitulate, cede, lose, retreat, surrender.

route, SYN.—avenue, channel, course, passage, road, street, thoroughfare, track, trail, walk, way.

routine, SYN.—custom, fashion, habit, practice, usage, use, wont.

royal, SYN.—courtly, dignified, grand, imperial, kingly, lordly, majestic, monarchial, noble, princely, regal, ruling, sovereign, stately, supreme. ANT.—common, humble, low, plebian, proletarian, servile, vulgar.

rude, SYN.—blunt, boorish, discourteous, gruff, impolite, impudent, inso-

lent, rough, saucy, surly,

uncivil, vulgar; coarse, crude, ignorant, illiterate, primitive, raw, rough, savage, unpolished, untaught; fierce, harsh, inclement, tumultuous, violent. ANT.—civil, genteel, polished; courtly, dignified, noble, stately; calm, mild, peaceful.

rugged, SYN.—craggy, irregular, jagged, rough, scabrous, scratchy, uneven. ANT.—even, level, sleek, slippery, smooth.

ruin, SYN.—annihilate, demolish, devastate, eradicate, exterminate, extinguish, obliterate, ravage, raze, wreck. ANT.—construct, establish, make, preserve, save.

ruinous, SYN.—baneful, deadly, deleterious, destructive, detrimental, devastating, fatal, injurious, noxious, pernicious. ANT.—beneficial, constructive, creative, profitable, salutary.

rule, SYN.—axiom, canon, formula, guide, law, maxim, method, order, precept, principle, propriety, regulation, standard, statute, system; authority, control, direction, dominion, government, jurisdiction, mastery, reign, sovereignty, sway. ANT.—chance, deviation, exception, hazard, irregularity; anarchy, chaos, misrule.

rule, SYN.—command,

control, direct, dominate, govern, manage, regulate, superintend. ANT.—abandon, follow, forsake, ignore, submit.

rupture, SYN.—break, burst, crack, crush, demolish, destroy, fracture, infringe, pound, rack, rend, shatter, smash, squeeze. ANT.—join, mend, renovate, repair, restore.

rural, SYN.—country, pastoral, rustic. ANT.—cultured, elegant, polished, refined, urbane.

ruse, SYN.—antic, artifice, cheat, deception, device, fraud, guile, hoax, imposture, ploy, stratagem, stunt, subterfuge, trick, wile. ANT.—candor, exposure, honesty, openness, sincerity.

rush, SYN.—accelerate, expedite, hasten, hurry, precipitate, quicken, speed. ANT.—delay, detain, hinder, retard, tarry.

rustic, SYN.—country, pastoral, rural; coarse, homely, plain, simple; boorish, bucolic, uncouth, unsophisticated. ANT.—cultured, elegant, polished, refined, urbane.

ruthless, SYN.—barbarous, bestial, brutal, brute, brutish, carnal, coarse, cruel, ferocious, gross, inhuman, merciless, remorseless, rough, rude, savage, sensual. ANT.—civilized, courteous, gentle, humane, kind.

S

sacrament, SYN.—association, communion, fellowship, intercourse, participation, union. ANT.—alienation, nonparticipation.

sacred, SYN.—blessed, consecrated, devout, divine, hallowed, holy, pious, religious, saintly, spiritual. ANT.—evil, profane, sacrilegious, secular, worldly.

sad, SYN.—cheerless, dejected, depressed, despondent, disconsolate, dismal, doleful, downcast, gloomy, lugubrious, melancholy, mournful, somber, sorrowful. ANT.—cheerful, glad, happy, joyous, merry.

safe, SYN.—certain, dependable, harmless, protected, reliable, secure, snug, trustworthy. ANT.—dangerous, hazardous, insecure, perilous, unsafe.

safeguard, SYN.—bulwark, fence, protection, refuge, shelter, shield; defense, guard, security.

sag, SYN.—bend, incline, lean, slant, slope, tend; depend, rely, trust. ANT.—erect, raise, rise, straighten.

sagacity, SYN.—discretion, erudition, foresight, information, insight, intelligence, judgment, knowledge, learning, prudence, reason, sageness, sense, wisdom.

ANT.—foolishness, ignorance, imprudence, nonsense, stupidity.

sage, SYN.—disciple, intellectual, learner, pupil, savant, scholar, student. ANT.—dolt, dunce, fool, idiot, ignoramus.

salary, SYN.—allowance, compensation, earnings, fee, pay, payment, recompense, stipend, wages. ANT.—gift, gratuity, present.

salient, SYN.—clear, distinguished, manifest, noticeable, obvious, prominent, striking, visible. ANT.—common, hidden, inconspicuous, obscure.

salubrious, SYN.—hale, healthy, robust, sound, strong, well; hygienic, salutary, wholesome. ANT.—delicate, diseased, frail, infirm; injurious, noxious.

salutary, SYN.—advantageous, beneficial, good, helpful, profitable, serviceable, useful, wholesome. ANT.—deleterious, destructive, detrimental, harmful, injurious.

same, SYN.—coincident, equal, equivalent, indistinguishable, like. ANT.—contrary, disparate, dissimilar, distinct, opposed.

sample, SYN.—case, example, illustration, instance, model, pattern, prototype, specimen.

sanction, SYN.—approbation, approval, assent, commendation, consent, endorsement, praise, support. ANT.—censure, reprimand, reproach, stricture.

sanction, SYN.—allow, let, permit, suffer, tolerate. ANT.—forbid, object, protest, refuse, resist.

sanctuary, SYN.—asylum, harbor, haven, refuge, retreat, shelter. ANT.—danger, exposure, hazard, jeopardy, peril.

sarcastic, SYN.—acrimonious, biting, caustic, cutting, derisive, ironic, sardonic, satirical, sneering, taunting. ANT.—affable, agreeable, amiable, pleasant.

sardonic, SYN.—acrimonious, bitter, caustic, harsh, severe. ANT.—delicious, mellow, pleasant, sweet.

sate, SYN.—fill, fill up, occupy, pervade; furnish, replenish, stock, store, supply; content, glut, gorge, satiate, satisfy, stuff. ANT.—deplete, drain, empty, exhaust, void.

satiate, SYN.—appease, compensate, content, fulfill, gratify, please, remunerate, satisfy, suffice. ANT.—annoy, displease, dissatisfy, frustrate, tantalize.

satire, SYN.—banter, cleverness, fun, humor, irony, pleasantry, raillery, sarcasm, wit, witticism. ANT.— commonplace, platitude, sobriety, solemnity, stupidity.

satirical, SYN.—acrimonious, biting, caustic, cutting, derisive, ironic, sarcastic, sardonic, sneering, taunting. ANT.—affable, agreeable, amiable, pleasant.

satisfaction, SYN.—beatitude, blessedness, bliss, contentment, delight, felicity, gladness, pleasure, well-being. ANT.—despair, grief, misery, sadness, sorrow.

satisfactory, SYN.—adequate, ample, capable, commensurate, enough, fitting, sufficient, suitable. ANT.—deficient, lacking, scant.

satisfy, SYN.—appease, compensate, content, fulfill, gratify, please, remunerate, satiate, suffice. ANT.—annoy, displease, dissatisfy, frustrate, tantalize.

saturate, SYN.—diffuse, fill, infiltrate, penetrate, permeate, pervade, run through.

savage, SYN.—barbarous, brutal, cruel, ferocious, inhuman, malignant, merciless, ruthless. ANT.—benevolent, compassionate, forbearing, gentle, humane, kind, merciful.

save, SYN.—conserve, defend, guard, keep, maintain, protect, preserve, rescue, safeguard, secure, spare, uphold. ANT.—abandon, abolish, destroy, impair, injure. ·

savory, SYN.—delectable, delicious, delightful, luscious, palatable, sweet, tasty. ANT.—acrid, distasteful, nauseous, unpalatable, unsavory.

say, SYN.—articulate, converse, declare, discourse, express, harangue, speak, talk, tell, utter. ANT.—be silent, hush, refrain.

saying, SYN.—adage, aphorism, apothegm, byword, maxim, motto, proverb, saw.

scalding, SYN.—burning, hot, scorching, torrid, warm; ardent, fervent, fiery, hot-blooded, impetuous, intense, passionate; peppery, pungent. ANT.—cold, cool, freezing, frigid; passionless, phlegmatic; bland.

scandal, SYN.—abashment, chagrin, humiliation, mortification; disgrace, dishonor, disrepute, ignominy, odium, opprobrium, shame. ANT.—dignity, glory, honor, praise, renown.

scandalize, SYN.—abuse, asperse, defame, disparage, ill-use, malign, revile, traduce, vilify. ANT.—cherish, honor, praise, respect.

scandalous, SYN.—discreditable, disgraceful, dishonorable, disreputable, ignominious, shameful. ANT.—esteemed, honorable, renowned, respectable.

scant, SYN.—concise, succinct, summary, terse;

deficient, inadequate, insufficient, lacking, limited. ANT.—abundant, ample, big, extended, protracted.

scarce, SYN.—infrequent, occasional; choice, exceptional, incomparable, precious, rare, singular, uncommon, unique. ANT.—customary, frequent, ordinary, usual; abundant, commonplace, numerous, worthless.

scare, SYN.—affright, alarm, appal, astound, daunt, dismay, frighten, horrify, intimidate, startle, terrify, terrorize. ANT.—allay, compose, embolden, reassure, soothe.

scared, SYN.—afraid, apprehensive, fainthearted, fearful, frightened, timid, timorous. ANT.—assured, bold, composed, courageous, sanguine.

scatter, SYN.—diffuse, dispel, disperse, disseminate, dissipate, separate. ANT.—accumulate, amass, assemble, collect, gather.

scent, SYN.—aroma, fetidness, fragrance, fume, incense, odor, perfume, redolence, smell, stench, stink.

scheme, SYN.—cabal, conspiracy, design, intrigue, machination, plan, plot, stratagem; chart, diagram, graph, sketch.

scheme, SYN.—contrive, delineate, design, devise, intend, outline, plan, plot, prepare, project, sketch.

scheming, SYN.—contrive, create, design, devise, invent, plan, intend, mean, purpose; draw, sketch.

scholar, SYN.—disciple, intellectual, learner, pupil, sage, savant, student. ANT.—dolt, dunce, fool, idiot, ignoramus.

scholarly, SYN.—academic, bookish, erudite, formal, learned, pedantic, scholastic, theoretical. ANT.— common-sense, ignorant, practical, simple.

scholarship, SYN.—apprehension, cognizance, erudition, information, knowledge, learning, lore, science, understanding, wisdom. ANT.—ignorance, illiteracy, misunderstanding, stupidity.

science, SYN.—discipline, enlightenment, knowledge, learning, scholarship. ANT.—ignorance, nescience, superstition.

scold, SYN.—admonish, berate, blame, censure, lecture, rate, rebuke, reprehend, reprimand, upbraid, vituperate. ANT.—approve, commend, praise.

scope, SYN.—amount, area, compass, degree, expanse, extent, length, magnitude, measure, range, reach, size, stretch.

scorch, SYN.—blaze, burn, char, consume, inciner-

ate, scald, sear, singe.
ANT.—extinguish, put
out, quench.

scorn, SYN.—contempt,
contumely, derision, de-
testation, disdain, ha-
tred. ANT.—awe, esteem,
regard, respect, rever-
ence.

scrap, SYN.—apportionment, fragment, moiety,
part, piece, portion, section, segment, share.
ANT.—entirety, whole.

scrape, SYN.—condition,
difficulty, dilemma, fix,
plight, predicament, situation, strait. ANT.—
calmness, comfort, ease,
satisfaction.

scrub, SYN.—clean,
cleanse, mop, purify,
sweep, wash.
ANT.—dirty, pollute,
soil, stain, sully.

scrupulous, SYN.—candid,
conscientious, fair, hon-
est, honorable, just, sincere, trustworthy, truth-
ful, upright. ANT.—de-
ceitful, dishonest, fraudulent, lying, tricky.

scrutinize, SYN.—analyze,
appraise, criticize, evaluate, examine, inspect.
ANT.—approve, neglect,
overlook.

search, SYN.—examina-
tion, exploration, in-
quiry, investigation, pursuit, quest. ANT.—aban-
donment, cession, resig-
nation.

search, SYN.—examine, explore, ferret (out), hunt,
investigate, look, probe,
ransack, rummage,
scour, scrutinize, seek.

searching, SYN.—curious,
inquiring, inquisitive, interrogative, meddling,
nosy, peeping, peering,
prying, snoopy.
ANT.—incurious, indif-
ferent, unconcerned, un-
interested.

season, SYN.—age, develop, mature, perfect, rip-
en.

secluded, SYN.—alone, deserted, desolate, isolat-
ed, lonely, unaided; lone,
only, single, sole, soli-
tary. ANT.—accompa-
nied, attended, sur-
rounded.

seclusion, SYN.—alienation,
insulation, isolation,
loneliness, quarantine,
retirement, segregation,
separation, solitude,
withdrawal. ANT.—asso-
ciation, communion,
connection, fellowship,
union.

secondary, SYN.—inferior,
lower, minor, poorer,
subordinate, ANT.—bet-
ter, greater, higher, su-
perior.

secret, SYN.—clandestine,
concealed, covert, hid-
den, latent, private, surreptitious, unknown.
ANT.—conspicuous, dis-
closed, exposed, known,
obvious.

secrete, SYN.—cloak,
clothe, conceal, cover,
curtain, disguise, envel-
op, guard, hide, mask,
protect, screen, shield,
shroud, veil. ANT.—bare,
divulge, expose, reveal,
unveil.

section, SYN.—country,

district, division, domain, dominion, land, place, province, quarter, region, territory.

secular, SYN.—earthly, laic, lay, mundane, profane, temporal, worldly. ANT.—ecclesiastical, religious, spiritual, unworldly.

secure, SYN.—assured, certain, definite, fixed, indubitable, inevitable, positive, sure, undeniable, unquestionable. ANT.—doubtful, probable, questionable, uncertain.

secure, SYN.—achieve, acquire, attain, earn, gain, get, obtain, procure, receive. ANT.—forfeit, leave, lose, renounce, surrender.

security, SYN.—bail, bond, earnest, guaranty, pawn, pledge, surety, token, warrant.

see, SYN.—behold, contemplate, descry, discern, distinguish, espy, glimpse, inspect, look at, notice, observe, perceive, scan, scrutinize, view, watch, witness.

seek, SYN.—examine, explore, ferret (out), hunt, investigate, look, probe, ransack, rummage, search, scour, scrutinize.

seem, SYN.—appeal, look. ANT.—be, exist; disappear, vanish, withdraw.

segment, SYN.—allotment, apportionment, division, fragment, moiety, part, piece, portion, scrap, section, share; element, ingredient, faction, inter-

est, side. ANT.—entirely, whole.

seize, SYN.—apprehend, arrest, check, detain, hinder, interrupt, obstruct, restrain, stop, withhold. ANT.—activate, discharge, free, liberate, release.

select, SYN.—choose, cull, elect, opt, pick. ANT.—refuse, reject.

selection, SYN.—alternative, choice, election, option, preference.

self-contradictory, SYN.—absurd, foolish, inconsistent, irrational, nonsensical, preposterous, ridiculous, silly, unreasonable. ANT.—consistent, rational, reasonable, sensible, sound.

self-denial, SYN.—abstention, abstinence, continence, fasting, forbearance, moderation, sobriety, temperance. ANT.—excess, gluttony, greed, intoxication, self-indulgence.

self-indulgence, SYN.—egotism, illiberality, mercenariness, narrowness, parsimoniousness, self-centeredness, self-seeking, selfishness, stinginess, ungenerousness. ANT.—altruism, charity, liberality, magnanimity.

selfish, SYN.—egoistic, illiberal, mercenary, narrow, parsimonious, self-centered, self-seeking, stingy, ungenerous. ANT.—altruistic, charitable, liberal, magnanimous.

send, SYN.—cast, discharge, dispatch, emit, impel, propel, throw, transmit. ANT.—bring, get, hold, receive, retain.

senescence, SYN.—age, dotage, senility, seniority. ANT.—childhood, infancy, youth.

senile, SYN.—aged, ancient, antiquated, antique, archaic, elderly, obsolete, old, old-fashioned, superannuated, venerable. ANT.—modern, new, young, youthful.

sensation, SYN.—apprehension, feeling, image, impression, perception, sense, sensibility. ANT.—apathy, insensibility, stupor, torpor.

sense, SYN.—acceptation, connotation, drift, explanation, gist, implication, import, intent, interpretation, meaning, purport, purpose, significance, signification.

senseless, SYN.—brainless, crass, dense, dull, dumb, foolish, obtuse, stupid, witless. ANT.—alert, bright, clever, discerning, intelligent.

sensibility, SYN.—feeling, sensation; emotion, passion, sentiment, tenderness. ANT.—anesthesia; coldness, imperturbability, insensibility; fact.

sensible, SYN.—appreciable, apprehensible, perceptible; alive, awake, aware, cognizant, comprehending, conscious, perceiving, sentient; discreet, intelligent, judicious, practical, prudent, reasonable, sagacious, sage, sober, sound, wise. ANT.—absurd, impalpable, imperceptible, stupid, unaware.

sensitive, SYN.—impressionable, perceptive, prone, responsive, sentient, susceptible, tender. ANT.—callous, dull, hard, indifferent, insensitive.

sensual, SYN.—carnal, earthy, lascivious, lecherous, lewd, licentious, sensory, voluptuous, wanton. ANT.—abstemious, ascetic, chaste, continent, virtuous.

sentence, SYN.—condemn, convict. ANT.—absolve, acquit, exonerate, pardon.

sentiment, SYN.—sensation; affection, emotion, feeling, passion, sensibility, tenderness; impression, opinion. ANT.—anesthesia; coldness, imperturbability, insensibility; fact.

sentimental, SYN.—dreamy, extravagant, fanciful, fantastic, fictitious, ideal, idealistic, imaginative, maudlin, mawkish, picturesque, poetic, romantic. ANT.—factual, literal, matter-of-fact, practical, prosaic.

separate, SYN.—divide, part, sever, sunder; allot, deal out, dispense, distribute, share. ANT.—combine, convene, gather, join, unite.

separation, SYN.—alienation, insulation, isolation, loneliness, quarantine, retirement, seclusion, segregation, solitude, withdrawal. ANT.—association, communion, connection, fellowship, union.

sequence, SYN.—arrangement, chain, following, graduation, order, progression, series, string, succession, train.

serene, SYN.—calm, composed, dispassionate, imperturbable, pacific, peaceful, placid, quiet, still, tranquil, undisturbed, unruffled. ANT.—excited, frantic, stormy, turbulent, wild.

serenity, SYN.—calm, calmness, hush, peace, quiescence, quiet, quietude, repose, rest, silence, stillness, tranquility. ANT.—agitation, disturbance, excitement, noise, tumult.

series, SYN.—arrangement, chain, following, graduation, order, progression, sequence, string, succession, train.

serious, SYN.—great, important, momentous, weighty, earnest, grave, sedate, sober, solemn, staid; alarming, critical, dangerous, risky. ANT.—small, trifling, trivial; informal, relaxed.

serve, SYN.—aid, assist, attend, help, oblige, succor; advance, benefit, forward, promote; answer, content, satisfy, suffice; distribute, supply, wait on. ANT.—command, dictate, direct, rule.

service, SYN.—account, advantage, avail, behalf, benefit, favor, gain, good, interest, profit. ANT.—calamity, distress, handicap, trouble.

serviceable, SYN.—advantageous, beneficial, good, helpful, profitable, salutary, useful, wholesome. ANT.—deleterious, destructive, detrimental, harmful, injurious.

servile, SYN.—abject, base, contemptible, despicable, dishonorable, groveling, ignoble, ignominious, low, lowly, mean, menial, sordid, vile, vulgar. ANT.—esteemed, exalted, honored, lofty, noble, righteous.

servitude, SYN.—bondage, captivity, confinement, imprisonment, serfdom, slavery, thralldom, vassalage. ANT.—freedom, liberation.

set, SYN.—arrange, deposit, dispose, lay, place, put. ANT.—disarrange, disturb, mislay, misplace, remove.

settle, SYN.—adjudicate, close, conclude, decide, determine, end, resolve, terminate. ANT.—doubt, hesitate, suspend, vacillate, waver.

settlement, SYN.—close, completion, conclusion, end, finale, issue, termination; decision, deduction, inference, judgment. ANT.—beginning, commencement, inception, prelude, start.

sever, SYN.—divide, part, separate, sunder. ANT.—combine, convene, gather, join, unite.

severe, SYN.—acute, arduous, distressing, exacting, extreme, hard, harsh, intense, relentless, rigid, rigorous, sharp, stern, stringent, unmitigated, unyielding, violent. ANT.—considerate, genial, indulgent, merciful, yielding.

sew, SYN.—fix, mend, patch, refit, repair, restore. ANT.—deface, destroy, hurt, injure, rend.

shabby, SYN.—destitute, impecunious, indigent, needy, penniless, poor, poverty-stricken; deficient, inferior, scanty. ANT.—affluent, opulent, rich, wealthy; ample, good, right, sufficient.

shade, SYN.—color, complexion, dye, hue, paint, pigment, stain, tincture, tinge, tint. ANT.—achromatism, paleness, transparency.

shadowy, SYN.—black, dark, dim, gloomy, murky, obscure, unilluminated; dusky; dismal, gloomy; evil, sinister, wicked; hidden, mystic, occult, secret. ANT.—light; bright, clear; pleasant; lucid.

shake, SYN.—agitate, flutter, jar, jolt, quake, quiver, rock, shiver, shudder, sway, totter, tremble, vibrate, waver.

shallow, SYN.—cursory, exterior, flimsy, frivolous, imperfect, slight, superficial. ANT.—abstruse, complete, deep, profound, thorough.

sham, SYN.—act, affect, assume, feign, pretend, profess, simulate. ANT.—display, exhibit, expose, reveal.

shame, SYN.—abashment, chagrin, humiliation, mortification; disgrace, dishonor, disrepute, ignominy, odium, opprobrium, scandal. ANT.—dignity, glory, honor, praise, renown.

shameful, SYN.—discreditable, disgraceful, dishonorable, disreputable, ignominious, scandalous. ANT.—esteemed, honorable, renowned, respectable.

shape, SYN.—appearance, build, cast, configuration, contour, cut, figure, form, frame, guise, image, mould, outline, pattern. ANT.—contortion, deformity, distortion, mutilation.

shape, SYN.—construct, create, fashion, forge, form, make, mold, produce, compose, constitute, make up; arrange, combine, organize; devise, frame, invent. ANT.—destroy, disfigure, dismantle, misshape, wreck.

share, SYN.—bit, division, fragment, parcel, part,

piece, portion, section, segment. ANT.—bulk, whole.

share, SYN.—allot, apportion, appropriate, assign, dispense, distribute, divide, parcel, partake, partition, portion. ANT.—aggregate, amass, combine, condense.

shared, SYN.—common, correlative, interchangeable, joint, mutual, reciprocal. ANT.—dissociated, separate, unrequited, unshared.

sharp, SYN.—acute, cutting, keen, pointed; acrid, biting, bitter, pungent; penetrating, piercing, severe, shrill; astute, clever, cunning, quick, shrewd, wily, witty; blunt, brusque, curt, rude; craggy, harsh, precipitous, rough, rugged, steep. ANT.—bland, blunt, gentle, shallow, stupid; courteous, gradual, smooth.

shatter, SYN.—break, burst, crack, crush, demolish, destroy, fracture, infringe, pound, rack, rend, rupture, smash. ANT.—join, mend, renovate, repair, restore.

shattered, SYN.—broken, crushed, destroyed, flattened, fractured, interrupted, reduced, rent, ruptured, separated, smashed, wrecked. ANT.—integral, repaired, united, whole.

sheepish, SYN.—abashed, bashful, coy, diffident,

embarrassed, humble, modest, recoiling, shamefaced, shy, timid, timorous. ANT.—adventurous, daring, fearless, gregarious, outgoing.

shelter, SYN.—asylum, harbor, haven, refuge, retreat, sanctuary; cover, protection, safety, security. ANT.—danger, exposure, hazard, jeopardy, peril.

shelter, SYN.—cloak, clothe, conceal, cover, curtain, disguise, envelop, guard, hide, mask, protect, screen, shield, shroud, veil. SYN.—bare, divulge, expose, reveal, unveil.

shield, SYN.—cloak, clothe, conceal, cover, curtain, disguise, envelop, guard, hide, mask, protect, screen, shroud, veil. ANT.—bare, divulge, expose, reveal, unveil.

shift, SYN.—change, exchange, substitute; alter, convert, modify, transfigure, transform, vary, veer. ANT.—retoain, continue, establish, preserve, settle, stablize.

shifting, SYN.—changeable, fickle. fitful, inconstant, unstable, vacillating, variable, wavering. ANT.—constant, stable, steady, unchanging, uniform.

shine, SYN.—beam, blaze, flash, flicker, glare, gleam, glimmer, glisten, glitter, glow, radiate, scintillate, shimmer, sparkle, twinkle.

shining, SYN.—brilliant, bright, dazzling, effulgent, glorious, gorgeous, grand, illustrious, magnificent, radiant, resplendent, showy, splendid, sumptuous, superb. ANT.—dull, mediocre, modest, ordinary, unimpressive.

shock, SYN.—alarm, amaze, astonish, astound, disconcert, dumbfound, flabbergast, startle, stun, surprise, take aback. ANT.—admonish, caution, forewarn, prepare.

shocking, SYN.—appalling, awful, dire, dreadful, fearful, frightful, gruesome, hideous, horrible, horrid, severe, terrible. ANT.—happy, joyous, pleasing, safe, secure.

short, SYN.—dumpy, dwarfed, little, low, pudgy, small, squat, undersized; abrupt, brief, compendious, concise, curt, laconic, succinct, summary, terse; deficient, inadequate, insufficient, lacking, limited. ANT.—abundant, ample, big, extended, protracted.

shortcoming, SYN.—blemish, defect, error, failure, fault, flaw, imperfection, mistake, omission, vice. ANT.— completeness, correctness, perfection.

shorten, SYN.—abbreviate, abridge, condense, contract, curtail, diminish, lessen, limit, reduce, restrict. ANT.—elongate, extend, lengthen.

shortening, SYN.—abbreviation, abridgement, contraction, reduction. ANT.—amplification, enlargement, expansion, extension.

shout, SYN.—call out, cry, cry out, ejaculate, exclaim, vociferate. ANT.—intimate, whisper, write.

shove, SYN.—crowd, drive, force, impel, jostle, press, propel, push; hasten, promote, urge. ANT.—drag, falter, halt, pull, retreat; ignore, oppose.

show, SYN.—array, display, exhibition, exposition; demonstration, flourish, ostentation, parade, spectacle, splurge; entertainment, movie, performance, production.

show, SYN.—disclose, display, exhibit, expose, indicate, manifest, parade, present, reveal, unfold; demonstrate, evidence, manifest, prove, verify; conduct, direct, guide, usher; inform, instruct, teach. ANT.—conceal, confuse, hide.

showy, SYN.—affected, artificial, ceremonious, dramatic, histrionic, melodramatic, stagy, theatrical. ANT.—modest, subdued, unaffected, unemotional.

shred, SYN.—bit, iota, jot, mite, particle, scrap, smidgen, speck. ANT.—aggregate, bulk, mass, quantity.

shred, SYN.—cleave, disunite, lacerate, rend, rip, rive, sever, slit, split, sunder, tear, wound. ANT.—join, mend, repair, sew, unite.

shrewd, SYN.—artful, astute, clandestine, covert, crafty, cunning, foxy, furtive, guileful, insidious, shy, stealthy, subtle, surreptitious, tricky, underhand, wily. ANT.—candid, frank, ingenuous, open, sincere.

shrill, SYN.—acute, cutting, keen, pointed; penetrating, piercing, severe, sharp. ANT.—bland, blunt, gentle, shallow.

shrivel, SYN.—droop, dry, sear, shrink, waste, wilt, wither, wizen; decline, fail, languish, sink, weaken. ANT.—refresh, rejuvenate, renew, revive.

shun, SYN.—avert, avoid, dodge, escape, eschew, elude, forbear, forestall, free, ward. ANT.—confront, encounter, meet, oppose.

shut, SYN.—close, seal; clog, obstruct, stop; cease, complete, conclude, end, finish, terminate. ANT.—open, unbar, unlock; begin, commence, inaugurate, start.

shy, SYN.—bashful, cautious, chary, demure, diffident, fearful, modest, reserved, retiring, sheepish, shrinking, timorous, wary. ANT.—audacious, bold, brazen, forward, immodest.

sick, SYN.—ailing, diseased, ill, indisposed, infirm, morbid, unhealthy, unwell. ANT.—healthy, robust, sound, strong, well.

sickness, SYN.—ailment, complaint, disease, disorder, illness, infirmity, malady. ANT.—health, healthiness, soundness, vigor.

sightless, SYN.—blind, ignorant, oblivious, undiscerning, unmindful, unseeing; headlong, heedless, rash. ANT.—aware, calculated, discerning, perceiving, sensible.

sign, SYN.—emblem, gesture, indication, mark, note, omen, portent, proof, signal, symbol, symptom, token.

signal, SYN.—alarm, warning. ANT.—quiet, security, tranquility.

significance, SYN.—acceptation, connotation, drift, explanation, gist, implication, import, intent, interpretation, meaning, purport, purpose, sense, signification.

significant, SYN.—critical, grave, important, indicative, material, momentous, telling, weighty. ANT.—insignificant, irrelevant, meaningless, negligible, unimportant.

signify, SYN.—denote, designate, disclose, imply, intimate, indicate, manifest, reveal, show, specify. ANT.—conceal, distract, divert, falsify, mislead.

silence, SYN.—hushed, motionless, peaceful, placid, quiescent, quiet, still, tranquil, undisturbed. ANT.—loud, strident; agitated, disturbed, perturbed.

silent, SYN.—calm, dumb, hushed, mute, noiseless, peaceful, quiet, still, taciturn, tranquil. ANT.—clamorous, loud, noisy, raucous.

silhouette, SYN.—brief, contour, delineation, draft, figure, form, outline, plan, profile, sketch.

silly, SYN.—absurd, asinine, brainless, crazy, foolish, idiotic, irrational, nonsensical, preposterous, ridiculous, senseless, simple. ANT.—judicious, prudent, sagacious, sane, wise.

similar, SYN.—akin, alike, allied, analogous, comparable, correlative, correspondent, corresponding, like, parallel. ANT.—different, dissimilar, divergent, incongruous, opposed.

similarity, SYN.—analogy, correspondence, likeness, parity, resemblance, similtude. ANT.—difference, distinction, variance.

simple, SYN.—easy, effortless, elementary, facile, mere, pure, single, uncompounded, unmixed; homely, humble, plain; artless, frank, naive, natural, open, unsophisticated; asinine, credulous, foolish, silly.

ANT.— adorned, artful, complex, intricate, wise.

simulate, SYN.—ape, copy, counterfeit, duplicate, imitate, impersonate, mimic, mock. ANT.—alter, distort, diverge, invent.

sin, SYN.—crime, evil, guilt, iniquity, offense, transgression, ungodliness, vice, wickedness, wrong. ANT.—goodness, innocence, purity, righteousness, virtue.

sincere, SYN.—candid, earnest, frank, genuine, heartfelt, honest, open, straightforward, true, truthful, unfeigned, upright. ANT.—affected, dishonest, hypocritical, insincere, untruthful.

sincerity, SYN.—candor, fairness, frankness, honesty, integrity, justice, openness, rectitude, responsibility, trustworthiness, uprightness. ANT.—cheating, deceit, dishonesty, fraud, trickery.

sinful, SYN.—antisocial, bad, corrupt, dissolute, immoral, indecent, licentious, profligate, unprincipled, vicious, wicked. ANT.—chaste, highminded, noble, pure, virtuous.

sing, SYN.—carol, chant, croon, hum, intone, lilt, warble.

singe, SYN.—blaze, burn, char, consume, incinerate, scald, scorch, sear. ANT.— extinguish, put out, quench.

single, SYN.—distinctive, individual, marked, particular, separate, singular, special, specific, unique. ANT.—common, general, ordinary, universal.

singular, SYN.—eccentric, exceptional, extraordinary, odd, peculiar, rare, strange, striking, unusual; characteristic, distinctive, individual, particular, special. ANT.—common, general, normal, ordinary.

sinless, SYN.—blameless, faultless, holy, immaculate, perfect, pure; consummate, excellent, ideal, superlative, supreme. ANT.—blemished, defective, faulty, imperfect.

sink, SYN.—collapse, decline, decrease, descend, diminish, drop, fall, subside; droop, extend, downward, hang. ANT.—arise, ascend, climb, mount, soar; steady.

sire, SYN.—beget, breed, create, engender, father, generate, originate, procreate, produce, propagate. ANT.—abort, destroy, extinguish, kill, murder.

site, SYN.—locality, place, position, situation, station.

situation, SYN.—case, circumstance, condition, plight, predicament, state.

size, SYN.—amplitude, area, bigness, bulk, dimensions, expanse, extent, greatness, largeness, magnitude, mass, volume.

skeptic, SYN.—agnostic, deist, doubter, freethinker, infidel, questioner, unbeliever. ANT.—adorer, believer, follower, worshiper.

skepticism, SYN.—doubting, hesitation, questioning, wavering; distrust, mistrust, suspicion. ANT.—belief, confidence, decision, reliance, trust.

sketch, SYN.—contour, delineation, draft, figure, form, outline, plan, profile, silhouette.

sketch, SYN.—delineate, depict, draw, trace; compose, draft, formulate, write.

skill, SYN.—ability, adroitness, cleverness, cunning, deftness, dexterity, facility, ingenuity, knack, readiness, skillfulness. ANT.—awkwardness, clumsiness, inability, ineptitude.

skillful, SYN.—able, accomplished, adept, clever, competent, cunning, expert, ingenious, practiced, proficient, skilled, versed. ANT.—awkward, bungling, clumsy, inexpert, untrained.

skip, SYN.—cancel, delete, disregard, drop, eliminate, exclude, ignore, miss, neglect, omit, overlook. ANT.—enter, include, insert, introduce, notice.

skirmish, SYN.—battle,

brawl, combat, conflict, contend, dispute, encounter, fight, quarrel, scuffle, squabble, struggle, wrangle.

slack, SYN.—disengaged, free, indefinite, lax, limp, loose, unbound, unfastened, untied, vague; careless, dissolute, heedless, unrestrained, wanton. ANT.—fast, tied, right; inhibited, restrained.

slander, SYN.—aspersion, backbiting, calumny, defamation, libel, scandal, vilification. ANT.—applause, commendation, defense, flattery, praise.

slant, SYN.—bent, bias, disposition, inclination, leaning, partiality, penchant, predilection, predisposition, prejudice, proclivity, proneness, propensity, tendency, turn. ANT.—equity, fairness, impartiality, justice.

slavery, SYN.—bondage, captivity, confinement, imprisonment, serfdom, servitude, thralldom, vassalage. ANT.—freedom, liberation.

slaughter, SYN.—butchery, carnage, massacre, pogrom.

slaughter, SYN.—assassinate, butcher, execute, kill, massacre, murder, put to death, slay. ANT.—animate, protect, resuscitate, save, vivify.

sleek, SYN.—polished, slick, smooth. ANT.—

bluff, blunt, harsh, rough, rugged.

sleep, SYN.—catnap, doze, drowse, nap, nod, repose, rest, slumber, snooze.

slender, SYN.—emaciated, gaunt, lank, lean, meager, narrow, rare, scanty, scrawny, skinny, slight, slim, spare, tenuous, thin. ANT.—broad, bulky, fat, thick, wide.

slight, SYN.—emaciated, fine, gaunt, lank, lean, meager, narrow, rare, scanty, scrawny, skinny, slender, slim, spare, tenuous, thin. ANT.—broad, bulky, fat, thick, wide.

slight, SYN.—disregard, neglect, ignore, omit, overlook, skip. ANT.—include, notice, regard.

slip, SYN.—blunder, error, fallacy, fault, inaccuracy, mistake. ANT.—accuracy, precision, truth.

slope, SYN.—bending, incline, inclination, leaning.

sloth, SYN.—idleness, inactivity, indolence, inertia, sluggishness, supineness, torpidity. ANT.—activity, alertness, assiduousness, diligence.

slothful, SYN.—idle, inactive, indolent, inert, lazy, sluggish, supine, torpid. ANT.—active, alert, assiduous, diligent.

slow, SYN.—dawdling, delaying, deliberate, dull, gradual, laggard, leisurely, sluggish, tired. ANT.—fast, quick, rapid, speedy, swift.

sluggish, SYN.—dawdling, delaying, deliberate, dull, gradual, laggard, leisurely, slow, tired. ANT.—fast, quick, rapid, speedy, swift.

slumber, SYN.—catnap, doze, drowse, nap, nod, repose, rest, sleep, snooze.

sly, SYN.—artful, astute, clandestine, covert, crafty, cunning, foxy, furtive, guileful, insidious, shrewd, stealthy, subtle, surreptitious, tricky, underhand, wily. ANT.—candid, frank, ingenuous, open, sincere.

small, SYN.—diminutive, insignificant, little, miniature, minute, petty, puny, slight, tiny, trivial, wee. ANT.—big, enormous, huge, immense, large.

smart, SYN.—adroit, apt, clever, dexterous, quick, quick-witted, skillful, talented, witty; bright, ingenious, sharp. ANT.—awkward, bungling, clumsy, slow, unskilled; dull, foolish, stupid.

smash, SYN.—break, burst, crack, crush, demolish, destroy, fracture, infringe, pound, rack, rend, rupture, shatter. ANT.—join, mend, renovate, repair, restore.

smell, SYN.—aroma, fetidness, fragrance, fume, incense, odor, perfume, redolence, scent, stench, stink.

smidgen, SYN.—bit, crumb, grain, iota, jot, mite, particle, scrap, shred, speck. ANT.—aggregate, bulk, mass, quantity.

smite, SYN.—beat, belabor, buffet, dash, hit, knock, pound, pummel, punch, strike, thrash, thump; conquer, defeat, overpower, overthrow, rout, subdue, vanquish. ANT.—defend, shield, stroke; fail, surrender.

smooth, SYN.—flat, level, plain, polished, sleek, slick; glib, diplomatic, suave, urbane. ANT.—bluff, blunt, harsh, rough, rugged.

smutty, SYN.—coarse, dirty, disgusting, filthy, gross, impure, indecent, lewd, obscene, offensive, pornographic. ANT.—decent, modest, pure, refined.

snag, SYN.—bar, barrier, block, check, difficulty, hindrance, impediment, obstacle, obstruction. ANT.—aid, assistance, encouragement, help.

snappish, SYN.—fractious, fretful, ill-natured, ill-tempered, irritable, peevish, petulant, testy, touchy, waspish. ANT.—affable, genial, good-natured, good-tempered, pleasant.

snare, SYN.—apprehend, arrest, capture, catch, clutch, grasp, grip, lay hold of, seize, trap. ANT.—liberate, lose, release, throw.

sneer, SYN.—deride, fleer, flout, gibe, jeer, mock,

scoff, taunt. ANT.—compliment, flatter, laud, praise.

sneering, SYN.—banter, derision, gibe, irony, jeering, mockery, raillery, ridicule, sarcasm, satire.

snoopy, SYN.—curious, inquiring, inquisitive, interrogative, meddling, nosy, peeping, peering, prying, searching. ANT.—incurious, indifferent, unconcerned, uninterested.

snug, SYN.—close, compact, constricted, contracted, firm, narrow, stretched, taut, tense, tight. ANT.—lax, loose, open, relaxed, slack.

soar, SYN.—flit, float, flutter, fly, glide, hover, mount, sail. ANT.—descend, fall, plummet, sink.

sober, SYN.—earnest, grave, sedate, serious, solemn, staid. ANT.—boisterous, informal, joyful, ordinary.

sobriety, SYN.—abstinence, abstention, forbearance, moderation, self-denial, temperance. ANT.—excess, intoxication, self-indulgence.

social, SYN.—affable, civil, communicative, friendly, gregarious, hospitable, out-going, sociable. ANT.—antisocial, disagreeable, hermitic, inhospitable.

soft, SYN.—compassionate, flexible, gentle, lenient, malleable, meek, mellow, mild, subdued, supple, tender, yielding. ANT.—hard, rigid, rough, tough, unyielding.

soften, SYN.—abate, allay, alleviate, assuage, diminish, extenuate, mitigate, relieve, solace, soothe. ANT.—aggravate, agitate, augment, increase, irritate.

soil, SYN.—continent, country, earth, field, ground, island, land, plain, region, tract.

soil, SYN.—befoul, blemish, blight, defile, discolor, disgrace, spot, stain, sully, tarnish. ANT.—bleach, cleanse, decorate, honor, purify.

solace, SYN.—comfort, consolation, contentment, ease, enjoyment, relief, succor. ANT.—affliction, discomfort, misery, suffering, torment, torture.

sole, SYN.—alone, deserted, desolate, isolated, lonely, secluded, unaided; lone, only, single, solitary. ANT.—accompanied, attended, surrounded.

solemn, SYN.—august, awe-inspiring, ceremonious, formal, imposing, impressive, majestic, reverential, ritualistic; earnest, grave, sedate, serious, sober, staid. ANT.—boisterous, informal, joyful, ordinary.

solicitude, SYN.—anxiety, care, concern, worry; attention, caution, regard, vigilance, wariness. ANT.—disregard, indif-

solitary, SYN.—alone, deserted, desolate, isolated, lonely, secluded, unaided; lone, only, single, sole. ANT.—accompanied, attended, surrounded.

solitude, SYN.—alienation, asylum, concealment, isolation, loneliness, privacy, refuge, retirement, retreat, seclusion. ANT.—exposure, notoriety, publicity.

somatic, SYN.—bodily, carnal, corporal, corporeal, material, natural, physical. ANT.—mental, spiritual.

somber, SYN.—bleak, cheerless, dark, dismal, doleful, dreary, dull, funereal, gloomy, lonesome, melancholy, sad. ANT.—cheerful, gay, joyous, lively.

soon, SYN.—beforehand, betimes, early, shortly. ANT.—belated, late, overdue, tardy.

soothe, SYN.—cheer, comfort, console, encourage, gladden, solace, sympathize. ANT.—antagonize, aggravate, depress, dishearten.

soothing, SYN.—benign, calm, docile, gentle, mild, peaceful, placid, relaxed, serene, soft, tame, tractable. ANT.—fierce, harsh, rough, savage, violent.

sophisticated, ANT.—blase, cultivated, cultured, worldly, worldly-wise.

ANT.—crude, ingenuous, naive, simple, uncouth.

sorcery, SYN.—black art, charm, conjuring, enchantment, legerdemain, magic, necromancy, voodoo, witchcraft, wizardry.

sordid, SYN.—base, debased, depraved, foul, loathsome, obscene, odious, revolting, vicious, vile, vulgar, wicked; abject, despicable, ignoble, low, mean, worthless, wretched. ANT.—attractive, decent, laudable; honorable, upright.

sorrow, SYN.—affliction, anguish, distress, grief, heartache, lamentation, misery, mourning, sadness, trial, tribulation, woe. ANT.—comfort, consolation, happiness, joy, solace.

sorrowful, SYN.—dejected, depressed, despondent, disconsolate, dismal, dispirited, doleful, gloomy, glum, melancholy, moody, sad, somber; grave, pensive. ANT.—cheerful, happy, joyous, merry.

sorry, SYN.—afflicted, grieved, hurt, pained, sad, sorrowful, vexed; contrite, penitent, remorseful, repentant; beggarly, contemptible, mean, paltry, pitiable, pitiful, poor, shabby, vile, worthless, wretched. ANT.—cheerful, delighted, impenitent, splendid, unrepentant.

sort, SYN.—category, character, class, description, kind, nature, stamp, type. ANT.—deviation, eccentricity, monstrosity, peculiarity.

sound, SYN.—binding, cogent, conclusive, convincing, effective, efficacious, legal, logical, powerful, strong, telling, valid, weighty. ANT.—counterfeit, null, spurious, void, weak.

sound, SYN.—din, noise, note, tone. ANT.—hush, quiet, silence, stillness.

sour, SYN.—acid, acrimonious, bitter, glum, morose, peevish, rancid, sharp, sullen, tart. ANT.—genial, kindly, sweet, wholesome.

source, SYN.—agent, cause, determinant, incentive, inducement, motive, origin, principle, reason; beginning, birth, commencement, cradle, derivation, foundation, inception, origin, spring, start. ANT.—consequence, effect, end, result; end, harvest, issue, outcome, product.

souvenir, SYN.—commemoration, memento, memorial, monument, remembrance.

sovereignty, ANT.—authority, command, control, dominion, influence, predominance, sway. ANT.—disablement, impotence, incapacity, ineptitude; debility, fatigue, weakness.

spacious, SYN.—ample, broad, capacious, exten-

sive, large, roomy, vast, wide. ANT.—confined, cramped, limited, narrow.

spare, SYN.—conserve, defend, guard, keep, maintain, preserve, protect, rescue, safeguard, save, secure, uphold. ANT.—abandon, abolish, destroy, impair, injure.

sparkle, SYN.—beam, blaze, flash, flicker, glare, gleam, glimmer, glisten, glitter, glow, radiate, scintillate, shimmer, shine, twinkle.

spat, SYN.—affray, altercation, argument, bickering, contention, disagreement, dispute, feud, quarrel, squabble, wrangle. ANT.—agreement, friendliness, harmony, peace, reconciliation.

spawn, SYN.—bear, produce, yield.

speak, SYN.—articulate, converse, declare, discourse, express, harangue, say, talk, tell, utter. ANT.—be silent, hush, refrain.

special, SYN.—distinctive, exceptional, extraordinary, individual, particular, peculiar, uncommon, unusual. ANT.—broad, comprehensive, general, prevailing, widespread.

specific, SYN.—definite, explicit, limited, precise; categorical, characteristic, especial, peculiar. ANT.—general, generic, vague.

specify, SYN.—appoint,

call, denominate, entitle, mention, name. ANT.—hint, miscall, misname.

specimen, SYN.—example, instance, prototype, sample.

speck, SYN.—bit, crumb, grain, iota, jot, mite, particle, scrap, shred, smidgen. ANT.—aggregate, bulk, mass, quantity.

spectacle, SYN.—array, display, exhibition, exposition; demonstration, flourish, ostentation, parade, show, splurge; entertainment, movie, performance, production.

speculate, SYN.—apprehend, assume, believe, conjecture, deduce, guess, imagine, presume, suppose, surmise, think. ANT.—ascertain, conclude, demonstrate, know, prove.

speech, SYN.—chatter, conference, conversation, dialogue, discourse, discussion, gossip, lecture, report, rumor, talk. ANT. — correspondence, meditation, silence, writing.

speed, SYN.—accelerate, dispatch, expedite, facilitate, forward, hasten, hurry, push, quicken, rush. ANT.—block, hinder, impede, retard, slow.

spherical, SYN.—circular, curved, globular, round.

spirit, SYN.—apparition, ghost, phantom, soul, specter; courage, enthusiasm, fortitude, liveliness, temper, verve, vig-

or, vitality, zeal. ANT.—body, flesh, substance; languor, listlessness.

spiritless, SYN.—dead, deceased, defunct, departed, dull, gone, inanimate, insensible, lifeless, unconscious. ANT.—alive, animate, living, stirring.

spiritual, SYN.—divine, ethereal, ghostly, holy, immaterial, incorporeal, religious, sacred, supernatural, unearthly, unworldly. ANT.—carnal, corporeal, material, mundane, physical.

spite, SYN.—animosity, enmity, grudge, ill will, malevolence, malice, malignity, rancor. ANT.—affection, kindness, love, toleration.

spiteful, SYN.—disagreeable, ill-natured, surly, ugly, vicious. ANT.—attractive, beautiful, fair, handsome, pretty.

splendid, SYN.—brilliant, bright, dazzling, effulgent, glorious, gorgeous, grand, illustrious, magnificent, radiant, resplendent, shining, showy, sumptuous, superb. ANT.—dull, mediocre, modest, ordinary, unimpressive.

splendor, SYN.—brightness, brilliance, brilliancy, effulgence, luster, radiance. ANT.—darkness, dullness, gloom, obscurity.

split, SYN.—cleave, disunite, lacerate, rend, rip, rive, sever, shred, slit, tear, wound. ANT.—join, mend, repair, sew, unite.

spoil, SYN.—decay, decompose, disintegrate, putrefy, rot, waste. ANT.—flourish, grow, increase, luxuriate.

spoken, SYN.—oral, verbal, vocal. ANT.—documentary, recorded, written.

spontaneous, SYN.—automatic, extemporaneous, impulsive, instinctive, offhand, voluntary, willing. ANT.—compulsory, forced, planned, prepared, rehearsed.

sport, SYN.—amusement, contest, diversion, fun, game, match, merriment, pastime, play, recreation. ANT.—business.

sport, SYN.—caper, frolic, gamble, gambol, play, revel, romp, stake, toy, wager.

spread, SYN.—exhibit, expand, open, unfold, unseal. ANT.—close, conceal, hide, shut.

sprightly, SYN.—buoyant, effervescent, light, resilient; animated, blithe, cheerful, elated, hopeful, jocund, lively, spirited, vivacious. ANT.—dejected, depressed, despondent, hopeless, sullen.

spring, SYN.—beginning, birth, commencement, cradle, derivation, foundation, inception, origin, source, start. ANT.—end, harvest, issue, outcome, product.

spruce, SYN.—clear, neat, nice, orderly, precise, tidy, trim. ANT.—dirty,

disheveled, sloppy, slovenly, unkempt.

spry, SYN.—active, agile, alert, brisk, flexible, lively, nimble, quick, supple. ANT.—clumsy, heavy, inert, slow, sluggish.

spur, SYN.—cause, impulse, incentive, incitement, inducement, motive, principle, purpose, reason, stimulus. ANT.—action, attempt, deed, effort, result.

squabble, SYN.—altercate, argue, bicker, contend, contest, debate, discuss, dispute, quarrel, wrangle. ANT.—agree, allow, assent, concede.

squalid, SYN.—dirty, filthy, foul, grimy, muddy, soiled, indecent, nasty, obscene; base, contemptible, despicable, low, mean, pitiful, shabby. ANT.—clean, neat, presentable, pure, wholesome.

squander, SYN.—consume, corrode, dissipate, lavish, misuse, scatter, spend, waste. ANT.—accumulate, conserve, economize, preserve, save.

squeamish, SYN.—careful, fastidious, particular. ANT.—undiscriminating.

stability, SYN.—balance, composure, equilibrium, poise, steadiness; proportion, symmetry. ANT.—fall, imbalance, instability, unsteadiness.

stable, SYN.—constant, durable, enduring, established, firm, fixed, im-

staid, SYN.—earnest, grave, sedate, serious, sober, solemn. ANT.—boisterous, informal, joyful, ordinary.

stain, SYN.—befoul, blemish, blight, defile, discolor, disgrace, soil, spot, sully, tarnish; color, dye, tinge, tint. ANT.—bleach, cleanse, decorate, honor, purify.

stale, SYN.—dull, flat, insipid, tasteless, vapid. ANT.—savory, tasty.

stand, SYN.—abide, bear, continue, endure, suffer, sustain, tolerate; halt, pause, remain, rest, stay, stop. ANT.—advance, progress, run, submit, yield.

standard, SYN.—criterion, gauge, law, measure, principle, proof, rule, test, touchstone. ANT.—chance, fancy, guess, supposition.

start, SYN.—beginning, commencement, inception, opening, origin, outset, source. ANT.—close, completion, consummation, end, termination.

start, SYN.—arise, begin, commence, establish, found, inaugurate, initiate, institute, organize, originate. ANT.—complete, end, finish, terminate.

startle, SYN.—alarm, amaze, astonish, astound, disconcert, dumbfound, flabbergast, shock, stun, surprise, take aback. ANT.—admonish, caution, forewarn, prepare.

starved, SYN.—craving, famished, hungry, ravenous, voracious; avid, greedy, longing. ANT.—full, gorged, sated, satiated; satisfied.

state, SYN.—case, condition, circumstance, plight, predicament, situation.

state, SYN.—affirm, assert, avow, claim, declare, explain, express, propound, recite, recount, say, specify, tell, utter. ANT.—conceal, deny, imply, retract.

stately, SYN.—courtly, dignified, grand, imperial, kingly, lordly, majestic, monarchial, noble, princely, regal, royal, ruling, sovereign, supreme. ANT.—common, humble, low, plebian, proletarian, servile, vulgar.

statement, SYN.—allegation, announcement, declaration, mention, report; assertion, proposition, thesis.

status, SYN.—caste, condition, place, position, rank, standing, status.

statute, SYN.—act, decree, edict, law. ANT.—deliberation, inactivity, intention.

staunch, SYN.—constant, devoted, faithful, loyal, steadfast, true; reliable, trusty. ANT.—disloyal, false, fickle, treacherous, untrustworthy.

stay, SYN.—abide, arrest, check, delay, halt, hinder, linger, obstruct, remain, sojourn, stand, tarry, wait. ANT.—advance, expedite, hasten, leave, progress.

steadfast, SYN.—constant, fast, firm, inflexible, secure, solid, stable, steady, unswerving, unyielding. ANT.—insecure, loose, unstable, unsteady.

steadfastness, SYN.—constancy, industry, perseverance, persistence, persistency, pertinacity, tenacity. ANT.—cessation, idleness, laziness, rest, sloth.

steal, SYN.—burglarize, embezzle, loot, pilfer, pillage, plagiarize, plunder, purloin, rob, snitch, swipe. ANT.—buy, refund, repay, restore, return.

steep, SYN.—abrupt, hilly, precipitous, sharp, sheer, sudden. ANT.—flat, gradual, level.

steer, SYN.—conduct, direct, escort, guide, lead, control, manage, regulate, supervise.

stench, SYN.—aroma, fetidness, fume, odor, redolence, scent, smell, stink.

stern, SYN.—exacting, hard, harsh, intense, relentless, rigid, rigorous, severe, sharp, stringent, unmitigated, unyielding. ANT.—considerate, genial, indulgent, merciful, yielding.

stiff, SYN.—harsh, rigorous, severe, stern, strict, strigent, unyielding; inflexible, rigid, unbending. ANT.—compassionate, lax, lenient, mild, yielding; elastic, flexible, resilient, supple.

stigma, SYN.—brand, mark, scar, stain, trace, vestige.

still, SYN.—hushed, motionless, peaceful, placid, quiet, quiescent, tranquil, undisturbed; calm, gentle, meek, mild, modest, passive, patient, silent. ANT.—loud, strident; agitated, disturbed, perturbed.

stimulate, SYN.—arouse, awaken, disquiet, excite, incite, irritate, provoke, rouse, stir up. ANT.—allay, calm, pacify, quell, quiet.

stimulus, SYN.—arousal, encouragement, goad, incentive, motive, provocation, stimulant. ANT.—depressant, discouragement, discussion, response.

stingy, SYN.—acquisitive, avaricious, greedy, miserly, niggardly, parsimonious, penurious, tight. ANT.—altruistic, bountiful, extravagant, generous, munificent.

stipend, SYN.—allowance, compensation, earnings, fee, pay, payment, recompense, salary, wages.

ANT.—gift, gratuity, present.

stir, SYN.—agitate, impel, induce, instigate, move, persuade, propel, push, shift. ANT.—deter, halt, rest, stay, stop.

stock, SYN.—accumulation, fund, hoard, provision, reserve, store; breed, kind, sort, strain, subspecies. ANT.—homogeneity, likeness, monotony, sameness, uniformity.

stock, SYN.—fill, fill up, furnish, replenish, store, supply. ANT.—deplete, drain, empty, exhaust, void.

stoical, SYN.—assiduous, composed, forbearing, indulgent, long-suffering, passive, patient, resigned, uncomplaining. ANT.—chafing, clamorous, high-strung, hysterical, turbulent.

stolid, SYN.—blunt, dull, edgeless, obtuse, pointless, thick-witted, unsharpened. ANT.—polished, polite, suave, subtle, tactful.

stone, SYN.—boulder, gravel, jewel, pebble, rock.

stop, SYN.—abstain, arrest, bar, cease, check, close, cork, desist, discontinue, end, halt, hinder, impede, interrupt, obstruct, plug, seal, terminate. ANT.—begin, proceed, promote, speed, start.

store, SYN.—accrue, accumulate, amass, collect, gather, heap, hoard, increase. ANT.—diminish,

disperse, dissipate, scatter, waste.

stormy, SYN.—blustery, gusty, inclement, roaring, rough, tempestuous, turbulent, windy. ANT.—calm, clear, peaceful, quiet, tranquil.

story, SYN.—account, anecdote, chronicle, fable, fabrication, falsehood, fiction, history, narration, narrative, novel, report, tale, yarn.

stout, SYN.—chubby, corpulent, fat, obese, paunchy, plump, portly, pudgy, rotund, stocky, thickset. ANT.—gaunt, lean, slender, slim, thin.

straight, SYN.—direct, right, undeviating, unswerving, erect, unbent, upright, vertical, fair, honest, honorable, just, square. ANT.—circuitous, winding; bent, crooked; dishonest.

strain, SYN.—breed, kind, sort, stock, subspecies, variety.

strait, SYN.—condition, difficulty, dilemma, fix, plight, predicament, scrape, situation. ANT.—calmness, comfort, ease, satisfaction.

strange, SYN.—abnormal, bizarre, curious, eccentric, extraordinary, grotesque, irregular, odd, mysterious, peculiar, queer, singular, surprising, uncommon, unusual. ANT.—common, conventional, familiar, ordinary, regular.

stranger, SYN.—alien, foreigner, immigrant, new-comer, outsider. ANT.—acquaintance, associate, countryman, friend, neighbor.

stratagem, SYN.—cabal, conspiracy, design, intrigue, machination, plan, plot, scheme.

stray, SYN.—deviate, digress, err, ramble, range, roam, rove, saunter, stroll, traipse, wander. ANT.—halt, linger, settle, stay, stop.

stream, SYN.—flow, gush, run, spout, spurt; come, emanate, issue, originate, proceed, result; abound, be copious.

strength, SYN.—durability, force, fortitude, intensity, lustiness, might, potency, power, stamina, stoutness, sturdiness, toughness, vigor. ANT.—feebleness, frailty, infirmity, weakness.

strengthen, SYN.—confirm, corroborate, substantiate, verify; acknowledge, assure, establish, settle; approve, fix, ratify, sanction.

stress, SYN.—compulsion, exigency, press, pressure, urgency. ANT.—ease, lenience, recreation, relaxation.

stretch, SYN.—distend, distort, elongate, expand, extend, lengthen, protract, spread, strain. ANT.—contract, loosen, shrink, slacken, tighten.

strict, SYN.—harsh, rigorous, rough, rugged, severe, stringent. ANT.—

gentle, mild.

strike, SYN.—beat, hit, hurt, knock, pound, pummel, smite.

striking, SYN.—affecting, arresting, august, commanding, exciting, forcible, grandiose, imposing, impressive, majestic, moving, over-powering, remarkable, splendid, stirring, thrilling, touching. ANT.—commonplace, ordinary, regular, unimpressive.

stringent, SYN.—grating, gruff, harsh, jarring, rigorous, rough, rugged, severe, strict. ANT.—gentle, mild.

stripped, SYN.—bare, exposed, naked, nude, unclad, uncovered; bald, barren, unfurnished; mere, plain, simple; defenseless, open, unprotected. ANT.—clothed, covered, dressed; concealed; protected.

strive, SYN.—attempt, endeavor, struggle, try, undertake; aim, aspire, design, intend, mean. ANT.—abandon, decline, ignore, neglect, omit.

strong, SYN.—athletic, cogent, concentrated, enduring, firm, forceful, forcible, fortified, hale, hardy, impregnable, mighty, potent, powerful, robust, sinewy, sturdy, tough. ANT.—brittle, delicate, feeble, fragile, insipid.

struggle, SYN.—battle, combat, conflict, contest, fight, fray, skirmish,

strife. ANT.— agreement,
concord, peace, truce.

stubborn, SYN.—contumacious, determined, dog-
ged, firm, head-strong,
immovable, inflexible,
intractable, obdurate,
obstinate, pertinacious,
uncompromising, un-
yielding. ANT.—ame-
nable, compliant, docile,
submissive, yielding.

student, SYN.—disciple,
learner, observer, pupil,
scholar.

study, SYN.—contemplate,
examine, investigate,
scrutinize, weigh; cogi-
tate, meditate, muse,
ponder, reflect; learn,
master.

stuff, SYN.—material, matter, substance; subject,
theme, thing, topic.
ANT.— immateriality,
phantom, spirit.

stuff, SYN.—fill, fill up, furnish, replenish; content,
glut, gorge, sate, satiate,
satisfy. ANT.—deplete,
drain, empty, exhaust,
void.

stumble, SYN.—collapse,
drop, fall, sink, subside;
topple, tumble. ANT.—
arise, ascend, climb,
mount, soar; steady.

stun, SYN.—alarm, amaze,
astonish, astound, dis-
concert, dumbfound,
flabbergast, shock, star-
tle, surprise, take aback.
ANT.—admonish, cau-
tion, forewarn, prepare.

stupid, SYN.—brainless,
crass, dense, dull, dumb,
foolish, obtuse, sense-
less, witless. ANT.—

alert, bright, clever, discerning, intelligent.

stupor, SYN.—daze, drowsiness, insensibility, languor, lethargy, numb-
ness, stupefaction, tor-
por. ANT.—activity,
alertness, liveliness,
readiness, wakefulness.

sturdy, SYN.—enduring,
firm, fortified, hale, hardy, mighty, potent, pow-
erful, robust, strong,
tough. ANT.—brittle, del-
icate, feeble, fragile, insipid.

subdue, SYN.—beat, conquer, crush, defeat, hum-
ble, master, overcome,
quell, rout, subjugate,
surmount, vanquish.
ANT.—capitulate, cede,
lose, retreat, surrender.

subject, SYN.—citizen, dependent, inferior, liege-
man, subordinate, vas-
sal; argument, matter,
point, theme, thesis,
topic; case, object, pa-
tient.

sublime, SYN.—elevated,
exalted, glorious, grand,
high, lofty, majestic,
noble, raised, splendid,
supreme. ANT.—base, ig-
noble, low, ordinary, ri-
diculous.

submerge, SYN.—dip,
douse, dunk, immerse,
plunge, sink; absorb, en-
gage, engross.
ANT.—elevate, recover,
uplift.

submissive, SYN.—com-
pliant, deferential, dutiful, obedient, tractable,
yielding. ANT.—insubor-
dinate, intractable, obsti-

nate, rebellious.

submit SYN.—abdicate, accede, acquiesce, capitulate, cede, quit, relent, relinquish, resign, succumb, surrender, waive, yield. ANT.—deny, dissent, oppose, refuse; assert, resist, strive, struggle.

subordinate, SYN.—citizen, dependent, inferior, liegeman, subject, vasal.

subside, SYN.—collapse, decline, decrease, descend, diminish, drop, fall, sink; droop, extend downward, hang. ANT.—arise, ascend, climb, mount, soar; steady.

substance, SYN.—material, matter, stuff; consequence, importance, moment. ANT.—immateriality, phantom, spirit.

substantiate, SYN.—confirm, corroborate, verify; strengthen.

substitute, SYN.—agent, alternate, deputy, lieutenant, proxy; representative, understudy; equivalent, expedient, makeshift. ANT.—head, master, principal, sovereign.

substitution, SYN.—alteration, alternation, change, modification, mutation, variation, variety, vicissitude. ANT.—monotony, stability, uniformity.

subterfuge, SYN.—cloak, disguise, excuse, garb, mask, pretense, pretension, pretext, semblance, simulation. ANT.—actuality, fact, reality, sincer-

ity, truth.

subtract, SYN.—curtail, deduct, decrease, diminish, lessen, reduce, remove, shorten. ANT.—amplify, enlarge, expand, grow, increase.

succeed, SYN.—achieve, flourish, gain, prevail, prosper, thrive, win; ensue, follow; inherit, supersede, supplant. ANT.—fail, miscarry, miss; anticipate, precede.

succession, SYN.—arrangement, chain, following, gradation, order, progression, sequence, series, string, succession, train.

succinct, SYN.—brief, compendious, concise, curt, laconic, pithy, short, terse. ANT.—extended, lengthy, long, prolonged, protracted.

succor, SYN.—comfort, consolation, contentment, ease, enjoyment, relief, solace. ANT.—affliction, discomfort, misery, suffering, torment, torture.

sudden, SYN.—abrupt, hasty, immediate, instantaneous, rapid, unexpected. ANT.—anticipated, gradual, slowly.

suffer, SYN.—bear, endure, feel, stand, sustain; allow, indulge, let, permit, tolerate; feel, undergo. ANT.—banish, discard, exclude, overcome.

suffering, SYN.—ache, agony, anguish, distress,

misery, pain, throe, torment, torture, woe. ANT.—comfort, ease, mitigation, relief.

sufficient, SYN.—adequate, ample, commensurate, enough, fitting, satisfactory. ANT.—deficient, lacking, scant.

suggest, SYN.—advise, allude, counsel, hint, imply, insinuate, intimate, offer, propose, recommend, refer. ANT.—declare, demand, dictate, insist.

suggestion, SYN.—admonition, advice, caution, counsel, exhortation, instruction, recommendation, warning; information, intelligence, notification.

suit, SYN.—accommodate, adapt, conform, fit. ANT.—disturb, misapply, misfit.

suitable, SYN.—acceptable, agreeable, gratifying welcome. ANT.—disagreeable, offensive.

sulley, SYN.—crabbed, dour, fretful, gloomy, glum, moody, morose, surly. ANT.—amiable, gay, joyous, merry, pleasant.

sullen, SYN.—crabbed, dour, fretful, gloomy, glum, moody, morose, sulky, surly. ANT.—amiable, gay, joyous, merry, pleasant.

sum, SYN.—aggregate, entirety, total, whole. ANT.—fraction, ingredient, part, sample.

sum, SYN.—add, adjoin,

append, augment, increase, total. ANT.—deduct, detach, reduce, remove, subtract.

summarize, SYN.—abridge, abstract. ANT.—add, replace, restore, return, unite.

summit, SYN.—apex, crest, crown, head, pinnacle, top, zenith. ANT.—base, bottom, foot, foundation.

sundry, SYN.—different, divers, miscellaneous, various. ANT.—alike, congruous, identical, same, similar.

sunny, SYN.—clear, cloudless, fair. ANT.—cloudy, foul, overcast.

superannuated, SYN.—aged, ancient, antiquated, antique, archaic, elderly, obsolete, old, old-fashioned, senile, venerable. ANT.—modern, new, young, youthful.

supercilious, SYN.—arrogant, disdainful, haughty, overbearing, proud, stately, vain, vainglorious. ANT.—ashamed, humble, lowly, meek.

superficial, SYN.—cursory, exterior, flimsy, frivolous, imperfect, shallow, slight. ANT.—abstruse, complete, deep, profound, thorough.

superintend, SYN.—command, control, direct, dominate, govern, manage, regulate, rule. ANT.—abandon, follow, forsake, ignore, submit.

superintendence, SYN.—charge, control, inspection, management, oversight, supervision, surveillance.

superiority, SYN.—advantage, edge, mastery; benefit, good, profit, service, utility. ANT.—detriment, handicap, harm, impediment, obstruction.

superlative, SYN.—blameless, faultless, holy, immaculate, pure, sinless; complete, consummate, excellent, ideal, perfect, supreme; absolute, downright, unqualified, utter. ANT.—deficient, incomplete, lacking; blemished, defective, faulty, imperfect.

supernatural, SYN.—marvellous, metaphysical, miraculous, otherworldly, preternatural, spiritual, superhuman, unearthly. ANT.—common, human, natural, physical, plain.

supervise, SYN.—command, control, direct, dominate, govern, manage, regulate, rule, superintend. ANT.—abandon, follow, forsake, ignore, submit.

supervision, SYN.—charge, control, inspection, management, oversight, superintendence, surveillance.

supplant, SYN.—overcome, overthrow, overturn. ANT.—conserve, preserve, uphold.

supple, SYN.—elastic, flexible, lithe, pliable, pliant, resilient. ANT.—brittle, hard, rigid, stiff, unbend-

ing.

supplicate, SYN.—adjure, ask, beg, beseech, crave, entreat, implore, importune, petition, pray, request, solicit. ANT.—bestow, cede, favor, give, grant.

supplication, SYN.—appeal, entreaty, invocation, petition, plea, prayer, request, suit.

supply, SYN.—accumulation, fund, hoard, provision, reserve, stock, store.

supply, SYN.—endow, equip, fit, fit out, furnish, provide; give, produce, yield. ANT.—denude, despoil, divest, strip.

support, SYN.—base, basis, brace, buttress, foundation, groundwork, prop, stay; aid, assistance, backing, comfort, encouragement, favor, help, patronage, succor; livelihood, living, maintenance, subsistence; confirmation, evidence. ANT.—attack, enmity, opposition.

support, SYN.—advocate, assist, back, bear, brace, encourage, foster, further, help, keep, maintain, preserve, prop, sustain, uphold. ANT.—abandon, betray, destroy, discourage, oppose.

supporter, SYN.—adherent, attendant, devotee, disciple, follower, henchman, partisan, successor, votary. ANT.—chief, head, leader, master.

suppose, SYN.—apprehend, assume, believe, conjecture, deduce, guess, imagine, presume, speculate, surmise, think. ANT.—ascertain, conclude, demonstrate, know, prove.

supposition, SYN.—conjecture, hypothesis, theory. ANT.—certainty, fact, proof.

supress, SYN.—abate, decrease, diminish, lessen, lower, moderate, reduce. ANT.—amplify, enlarge, increase, intensify, revive.

supremacy, SYN.—ascendancy, domination, mastery, predominance, sovereignty, sway, transcendence. ANT.—inferiority.

supreme, SYN.—cardinal, chief, essential, first, foremost, highest, leading, main, paramount, predominant, principal. ANT.—auxiliary, minor, subordinate, subsidiary, supplemental.

sure, SYN.—assured, certain, definite, fixed, indubitable, inevitable, positive, secure, undeniable, unquestionable. ANT.—doubtful, probable, questionable, uncertain.

surly, ANT.—repellent; disagreeable, ill-natured, spiteful, ugly, vicious.

surname, SYN.—appellation, denomination, designation, epithet, name, style, title. ANT.—namelessness; anonymity.

surplus, SYN.—excess, extravagance, immoderation, intemperance, profusion, superabundance, superfluity. ANT.—dearth, deficiency, lack, paucity, want.

surprise, SYN.—curiosity, marvel, miracle, phenomenon, prodigy, rarity, spectacle; admiration, amazement, astonishment, awe, bewilderment, curiosity, wonder, wonderment. ANT.—familiarity, triviality; apathy, expectation, indifference.

surprise, SYN.—alarm, amaze, astonish, astound, disconcert, dumbfound, flabbergast, shock, startle, stun, take aback. ANT.—admonish, caution, forewarn, prepare.

surrender, SYN.—abandon, acquiesce, capitulate, cede, relinquish, renounce, resign, sacrifice, submit, yield. ANT.—conquer, overcome, resist, rout.

surround, SYN.—bound, circumscribe, confine, enclose, encompass, envelop, fence, limit. ANT.—distend, enlarge, expand, expose, open.

surveillance, SYN.—charge, control, inspection, management, oversight, superintendence, supervision.

suspect, SYN.—question, waver; distrust, doubt, mistrust. ANT.—believe, confide, decide, rely on, trust.

suspend, SYN.—adjourn, defer, delay, discontinue, interrupt, postpone, stay; balance, dangle, hang, poise, swing. ANT.—continue, maintain, persist, proceed, prolong.

suspicion, SYN.—distrust, doubt, incredulity, scruple, skepticism, suspense, unbelief, uncertainty. ANT.—belief, certainty, conviction, determination, faith.

sustain, SYN.—advocate, assist, back, bear, brace, encourage, foster, further, help, keep, maintain, preserve, prop, support, uphold. ANT.—abandon, betray, destroy, discourage, oppose.

sustenance, SYN.—diet, edibles, fare, feed, food, meal, nutriment, provisions, rations, repast, viands, victuals. ANT.—drink, hunger, starvation, want.

swallow up, SYN.—absorb, assimilate, consume, engulf, imbibe. ANT.—discharge, dispense, emit, expel, exude.

swarthy, SYN.—dark, dusky, sable. ANT.—light, bright.

sway, SYN.—actuate, affect, bias, control, impel, incite, influence, stir.

swear, SYN.—affirm, assert, aver, declare, maintain, protest, state. ANT.—contradict, demur, deny, dispute, oppose.

sweeping, SYN.—broad, expanded, extensive, large, vast, wide; liberal, tolerant. ANT.—confined, narrow, restricted.

sweet, SYN.—agreeable, delightful, engaging, gentle, honeyed, luscious, mellifluous, melodious, pleasing, saccharine, sugary, winning. ANT.—acrid, bitter, offensive, repulsive, sour.

swift, SYN.—expeditious, fast, fleet, quick, rapid, speedy. ANT.—slow, sluggish.

swindle, SYN.—artifice, cheat, chicanery, deceit, deception, duplicity, fraud, guile, imposition, imposture, trick. ANT.—fairness, honesty, integrity, sincerity.

swindle, SYN.—bilk, cheat, circumvent, deceive, defraud, dupe, fool, gull, hoax, hoodwink, outwit, trick, victimize.

symbol, SYN.—character, mark, sign.

symmetry, SYN.—balance, equilibrium; proportion. ANT.—imbalance, instability, unsteadiness.

sympathetic, SYN.—affable, benevolent, benign, compassionate, forbearing, gentle, good, humane, indulgent, kind, kindly, merciful, tender, thoughtful. ANT.—cruel, inhuman, merciless, severe, unkind.

sympathize, SYN.—cheer, comfort, console, encourage, gladden, solace, soothe. ANT.—antagonize, aggravate, depress, dishearten.

sympathy, SYN.—affinity, agreement, commiseration, compassion, concord, condolence, congeniality, empathy, harmony, pity, tenderness, warmth. ANT.—antipathy, harshness, indifference, malevolence, unconcern.

symptoms, SYN.—trace, vestige; characteristic, feature, indication, mark, property, trait.

synthetic, SYN.—artificial, bogus, counterfeit, ersatz, fake, feigned, fictitious, phony, sham, spurious, unreal. ANT.—genuine, natural, real, true.

system, SYN.—arrangement, method, mode, order, organization, plan, process, regularity, rule, scheme. ANT.—chance, chaos, confusion, disarrangement, disorder, irregularity.

T

tact, SYN.—address, adroitness, dexterity, diplomacy, finesse, knack, poise, savoir-faire, skill. ANT.—awkwardness, blunder, incompetence, rudeness, vulgarity.

tactful, SYN.—adroit, diplomatic, discreet, discriminating, judicious, politic. ANT.—boorish, churlish, coarse, gruff, rude.

tainted, SYN.—contaminated, corrupted, crooked, debased, depraved, dishonest, impure, profligate, putrid, spoiled, unsound, venal, vitiated.

take, SYN.—appropriate, capture, catch, confiscate, ensnare, gain, purloin, remove, steal; clasp, clutch, grasp, grip, seize; accept, get, obtain, receive; bear, endure, stand, tolerate; bring, carry, convey, escort; attract, captivate, charm, delight, interest; claim, demand, necessitate, require; adopt, assume, choose, espouse, select.

tale, SYN.—account, anecdote, chronicle, fable, fabrication, falsehood, fiction, history, narration, narrative, novel, report, story, yarn.

talent, SYN.—ability, aptitude, capability, cleverness, endowment, faculty, genius, gift, knack, skill. ANT.—incompetence, ineptitude, stupidity.

talented, SYN.—adroit, apt, clever, dexterous, quick, quick-witted, skillful, witty; bright, ingenious, sharp, smart. ANT.—awkward, bungling, clumsy, slow, unskilled; dull, foolish, stupid.

talk, SYN.—chatter, conference, conversation, dialogue, discourse, discussion, gossip, lecture, report, rumor, speech, ANT.— correspondence, meditation, silence, writing.

talk, SYN.—blab, chat, converse, gossip, jabber, mutter, prattle, speak, tattle; argue, comment, declaim, discourse, harangue, lecture, plead, preach, rant, spout; confer, consult, deliberate, discuss, reason.

talkative, SYN.—chattering, chatty, communicative, garrulous, glib, loquacious, verbose, voluble. ANT.—laconic, reticent, silent, taciturn, uncommunicative.

tall, SYN.—high, lofty, towering; elevated. ANT.—small, stunted, tiny.

tame, SYN.—docile, domestic, domesticated, gentle; meek, subdued, submissive; dull, flat, insipid, tedious. ANT.—fierce, savage, spirited, wild; animated, exciting, lively, spirited.

tamper, SYN.—interfere, interpose, interrupt, meddle, mix in, monkey.

tangible, SYN.—bodily, corporeal, material, palpable, physical, sensible. ANT.—mental, metaphysical, spiritual.

tardy, SYN.—delayed, late, overdue, slow. ANT.—early, timely.

tarnish, SYN.—befoul, blemish, blight, defile, discolor, disgrace, soil, spot, stain, sully. ANT.—bleach, cleanse, decorate, honor, purify.

tart, SYN.—acrid, biting, bitter, distasteful, pungent, sour. ANT.—delicious, mellow, pleasant, sweet.

task, SYN.—chore, job, labor, stint, toil, work, undertaking.

taste, SYN.—flavor, relish, savor, tang; discernment, disposition, inclination, judgment, liking, predilection, sensibility, zest. ANT.—antipathy, disinclination, indelicacy, insipidity.

taunt, SYN.—deride, fleer, flout, gibe, jeer, mock, scoff, sneer, tease. ANT.—compliment, flatter, laud, praise.

taunting, SYN.—acrimonious, biting, caustic, cutting, derisive, ironic, sarcastic, sardonic, satirical, sneering. ANT.—affable, agreeable, amiable, pleasant.

taut, SYN.—constricted, firm, snug, stretched, tight. ANT.—lax, loose, open, relaxed, slack.

tax, SYN.—assessment, custom, duty, exaction, excise, impost, levy, rate, toll, tribute; burden, strain. ANT.—gift, remuneration, reward, wages.

teach, SYN.—educate, inculcate, inform, instill, instruct, school, train, tutor. ANT.—misguide, misinform.

tear, SYN.—cleave, disunite, lacerate, rend, rip, rive, sever, shred, slit, split, sunder, wound. ANT.—join, mend, repair, sew, unite.

tease, SYN.—aggravate, annoy, badger, bother, disturb, harass, harry, irritate, molest, nag, pester, plague, provoke, tantalize, taunt, torment, vex, worry. ANT.—comfort, delight, gratify, please, soothe.

tedious, SYN.—boring, burdensome, dilatory, dreary, dull, humdrum, irksome, monotonous, slow, sluggish, tardy, tiresome, uninteresting, wearisome. ANT.—amusing, entertaining, exciting, interesting, quick.

teeming, SYN.—abundant, ample, bountiful, copious, overflowing, plenteous, plentiful, profuse, rich. ANT.—deficient, insufficient, scant, scarce.

tell, SYN.—describe, narrate, recount, rehearse, relate, report; communicate, express, mention, publish, speak, state, utter; announce, betray, confess, disclose, divulge, reveal; discern, discover, distinguish, recognize; acquaint, apprise, inform, instruct, notify; direct, order, request.

temerity, SYN.—audacity, boldness, foolhardiness, precipitancy, rashness, recklessness. ANT.—caution, hesitation, prudence, timidity, wariness.

temper, SYN.—anger, animosity, choler, exasperation, fury, indignation, ire, irritation, passion, petulance, rage, resentment, wrath. ANT.—con-

ciliation, forbearance, patience, peace, self-control.

temperament, SYN.—disposition, humor, mood, temper.

temperance, SYN.—abstention, abstinence, forbearance, moderation, self-denial, sobriety. ANT.—excess, gluttony, greed, intoxication, self-indulgence.

tempest, SYN.—blast, breeze, draft, gale, gust, hurricane, squall, storm, wind, zephyr.

temporal, SYN.—earthly, laic, lay, mundane, profane, worldly. ANT.—ecclesiastical, religious, spiritual, unworldly.

temporary, SYN.—brief, ephemeral, evanescent, fleeting, momentary, short-lived, transient. ANT.—abiding, immortal, lasting, permanent, timeless.

tenacity, SYN.—constancy, industry, perseverance, persistence, persistency, pertinacity, steadfastness. ANT.—cessation, idleness, laziness, rest, sloth.

tend, SYN.—accompany, attend, escort, follow, guard, lackey, protect, serve, watch.

tendency, SYN.—aim, bent, bias, drift, inclination, leaning, predisposition, proclivity, proneness, propensity, trend. ANT.—aversion, deviation, disinclination.

tender, SYN.—bland, gentle, kind, meek, mild, moderate, soft, soothing. ANT.—bitter, fierce, harsh, rough, severe.

tender, SYN.—advance, extend, offer, present, proffer, propose, volunteer. ANT.—accept, receive, reject, retain, spurn.

tenderness, SYN.—affection, attachment, endearment, fondness, kindness, love. ANT.—aversion, hatred, indifference, repugnance, repulsion.

tenet, SYN.—belief, creed, doctrine, dogma, precept, teaching. ANT.—conduct, deed, performance, practice.

term, SYN.—boundary, duration, limit, period, time; condition, expression, name, phrase, word.

terminal, SYN.—concluding, conclusive, decisive, ending, eventual, final, last, latest, ultimate. ANT.—first, inaugural, incipient, original, rudimentary.

terminate, SYN.—abolish, cease, close, complete, conclude, end, expire, finish, stop. ANT.—begin, commence, establish, initiate, start.

terrible, SYN.—appalling, awful, dire, dreadful, fearful, frightful, gruesome, hideous, horrible, horrid, severe, shocking. ANT.—happy, joyous, pleasing, safe, secure.

terrify, SYN.—affright,

alarm, appall, astound, daunt, dismay, frighten, horrify, intimidate, scare, startle, terrorize. ANT.—allay, compose, embolden, reassure, soothe.

territory, SYN.—country, district, division, domain, dominion, land, place, province, quarter, region, section.

terror, SYN.—alarm, consternation, dismay, dread, fear, fright, horror, panic. ANT.—assurance, calm, peace, security.

terse, SYN.—brief, compact, concise, condensed, incisive, neat, pithy, succinct, summary. ANT.—lengthy, prolix, verbose, wordy.

testimony, SYN.—attestation, confirmation, declaration, evidence, proof, witness. ANT.—argument, contradiction, disproof, refutation.

testy, SYN.—fractious, fretful, ill-natured, illtempered, irritable, peevish, petulant, snappish, touchy, waspish. ANT.—affable, genial, good-natured, goodtempered, pleasant.

theatrical, SYN.—affected, artificial, ceremonious, dramatic, histrionic, melodramatic, showy, stagy. ANT.—modest, subdued, unaffected, unemotional.

theft, SYN.—burglary, depredation, larceny, pillage, plunder, robbery.

theme, SYN.—composition,

essay, motive, subject, text, thesis, topic.

theoretical, SYN.—academic, bookish, erudite, formal, learned, pedantic, scholarly, scholastic. ANT.— common-sense, ignorant, practical, simple.

theory, SYN.—conjecture, doctrine, hypothesis, opinion, postulate, presupposition, speculation. ANT.—fact, practice, proof, verity.

therefore, SYN.—accordingly, consequently, hence, so, then, thence.

thick, SYN.—close, compact, compressed, concentrated, crowded, dense. ANT.—dispersed, dissipated, sparse.

thin, SYN.—attenuated, diaphanous, diluted, emaciated, fine, flimsy, gaunt, gauzy, gossamer, lank, lean, meager, narrow, rare, scanty, scrawny, skinny, slender, slight, slim, spare, tenuous. ANT.—broad, bulky, fat, thick, wide.

think, SYN.—conceive, imagine, picture, recall, recollect, remember; cogitate, contemplate, deliberate, meditate, muse, ponder, reason, reflect, speculate; apprehend, believe, consider, deem, esteem, judge, opine, reckon, regard, suppose; devise, intend, mean, plan, purpose. ANT.—conjecture, forget, guess.

thorough, SYN.—complete, consummate, entire, finished, full, perfect, total, unbroken, undivided. ANT.—imperfect, lacking, unfinished.

thought, SYN.—cogitation, conception, consideration, contemplation, deliberation, fancy, idea, imagination, impression, judgment, meditation, memory, notion, opinion, recollection, reflection, regard, retrospection, sentiment, view.

thoughtful, SYN.—attentive, careful, cautious, concerned, considerate, heedful, provident, prudent, contemplative, dreamy, introspective, meditative, pensive, reflective. ANT.—heedless, inconsiderate, precipitous, rash, thoughtless.

thoughtless, SYN.—careless, heedless, imprudent, inattentive, inconsiderate, indiscreet, reckless, unconcerned; desultory, inaccurate, lax, neglectful, negligent, remiss. ANT.—accurate, careful, meticulous, nice.

threatening, SYN.—approaching, imminent, impending, menacing, nigh, overhanging, ANT.—afar, distant, improbable, remote, retreating.

thrifty, SYN.—economical, frugal, parsimonious, provident, saving, sparing, stingy, temperate. ANT.—extravagant, intemperate, self-indulgent, wasteful.

throb, SYN.—beat, palpi-

tate, pulsate, pulse. ANT.—fail.

throe, SYN.—ache, pain, pang, paroxysm, twinge; agony, anguish, distress, grief, suffering. ANT.—comfort, ease, relief; happiness, pleasure, solace.

throng, SYN.—bevy, crowd, crush, horde, host, masses, mob, multitude, populace, press, rabble, swarm.

throw, SYN.—cast, fling, hurl, pitch, propel, thrust, toss. ANT.—draw, haul, hold, pull, retain.

thrust, SYN.—crowd, drive, force, impel, jostle, press, propel, push, shove; hasten, promote, urge. ANT.—drag, falter, halt, pull, retreat; ignore, oppose.

thwart, SYN.—baffle, balk, circumvent, defeat, disappoint, foil, frustrate, hinder, outwit, prevent. ANT.—accomplish, fulfill, further, promote.

tidings, SYN.—information, intelligence, message, news, report.

tidy, SYN.—clear, neat, nice, orderly, precise, spruce, trim. ANT.—dirty, disheveled, sloppy, slovenly, unkempt.

tie, SYN.—affinity, alliance, association, bond, conjunction, connection, link, relationship, union. ANT.—disunion, isolation, separation.

tie, SYN.—attach, bind, connect, engage, fasten, fetter, join, link, oblige,

restrain, restrict. ANT.—free, loose, unfasten, untie.

tight, SYN.—close, compact, constricted, contracted, firm, narrow, snug, stretched, taut, tense; close-fisted, niggardly, parsimonious, penny-pinching, stingy. ANT.—lax, loose, open, relaxed, slack.

time, SYN.—age, date, duration, epoch, era, interim, period, season, span, spell, tempo, term.

timely, SYN.—exact, precise, prompt, punctual, ready. ANT.—dilatory, late, slow, tardy.

timid, SYN.—abashed, bashful, coy, diffident, embarrassed, humble, modest, recoiling, shamefaced, sheepish, shy, timorous. ANT.—adventurous, daring, fearless, gregarious, outgoing.

tiny, SYN.—diminutive, insignificant, little, miniature, minute, petty, puny, slight, small, trivial, wee. ANT.—big, enormous, huge, immense.

tire, SYN.—bore, exhaust, fatigue, jade, tucker, wear out, weary. ANT.—amuse, invigorate, refresh, restore, revive.

tired, SYN.—exhausted, faint, fatigued, jaded, spent, weary, wearied, worn. ANT.—fresh, hearty, invigorated, rested.

title, SYN.—appellation, denomination, designation, epithet, name; claim, due, privilege, right.

toil, SYN.—achievement, business, drudgery, effort, employment, labor, occupation, opus, performance, production, task, travail, work. ANT.—ease, leisure, play, recreation, vacation.

tolerant, SYN.—broad, expanded, extensive, large, sweeping, vast, wide; liberal. ANT.—confined, narrow, restricted.

tolerate, SYN.—allow, permit; abide, bear, brook, endure, stand. ANT.—forbid, prohibit; protest.

toll, SYN.—assessment, custom, duty, exaction, excise, impost, levy, rate, tax, tribute; burden, strain. ANT.—gift, remuneration, reward, wages.

tongue, SYN.—cant, dialect, diction, idiom, jargon, language, lingo, phraseology, slang, speech, vernacular. ANT.—babble, drivel, gibberish, nonsense.

too, SYN.—also, besides, furthermore, in addition, likewise, moreover, similarly.

tool, SYN.—agent, apparatus, devise, instrument, means, medium, utensil, vehicle. ANT.—hindrance, impediment, obstruction, preventive.

top, SYN.—apex, chief, crest, crown, head, pinnacle, summit, zenith. ANT.—base, bottom, foot, foundation.

topic, SYN.—argument, matter, point, subject, theme, thesis.

torment, SYN.—ache, agony, anguish, distress, misery, pain, suffering, throe, torture, woe. ANT.—comfort, ease, mitigation, relief.

torment, SYN.—aggravate, annoy, badger, bother, disturb, harass, harry, irritate, molest, nag, pester, plague, provoke, tantalize, taunt, tease, vex, worry. ANT.—comfort, delight, gratify, please, soothe.

torpid, SYN.—idle, inactive, indolent, inert, lazy, slothful, sluggish, supine. ANT.—active, alert, assiduous, diligent.

torpor, SYN.—daze, drowsiness, insensibility, languor, lethargy, numbness, stupefaction, stupor. ANT.—activity, alertness, liveliness, readiness, wakefulness.

torrid, SYN.—burning, hot, scalding, scorching, warm; ardent, fervent, fiery, hotblooded, impetuous, intense, passionate. ANT.—cold, cool, freezing, frigid; apathetic, impassive, indifferent, passionless, phlegmatic.

torso, SYN.—body, form, frame. ANT.—intellect, mind, soul, spirit.

torture, SYN.—ache, agony, anguish, distress,

torture

misery, pain, suffering, throe, torment, woe. ANT.—comfort, ease, mitigation, relief.

torture, SYN.—afflict, annoy, badger, harass, harry, hound, oppress, pester, plague, persecute, torment, vex, worry. ANT.—aid, assist, comfort, encourage, support.

toss, SYN.—cast, fling, hurl, pitch, propel, throw, thrust. ANT.—draw, haul, hold, pull, retain.

total, SYN.—complete, concluded, consummate, ended, entire, finished, full, perfect, thorough, unbroken, undivided. ANT.—imperfect, lacking, unfinished.

total, SYN.—aggregate, amount, collection, conglomeration, entirety, sum, whole. ANT.—element, ingredient, part, particular, unit.

total, SYN.—add, sum. ANT.—deduct, detach, reduce, remove, subtract.

touching, SYN.—affecting, heart-rending, impressive, moving, pitiable, poignant, sad, tender; adjacent, adjunct, bordering, tangent. ANT.—animated, enlivening, exhilarating, removed.

touchy, SYN.—choleric, excitable, fiery, hasty, hot, irascible, irritable, peevish, petulant, snappish, testy. ANT.—agreeable, calm, composed, tranquil.

tough, SYN.—cohesive, firm, hardy, stout, strong, sturdy, tenacious; difficult, formidable, hard, laborious, troublesome, trying; callous, incorrigible, obdurate, stubborn, vicious. ANT.—brittle, fragile, frail; easy, facile; compliant, forbearing, submissive.

toughness, SYN.—durability, force, fortitude, intensity, lustiness, might, potency, power, stamina, stoutness, strength, sturdiness, vigor. ANT.—feebleness, frailty, infirmity, weakness.

tour, SYN.—go, journey, ramble, roam, rove, travel. ANT.—stay, stop.

tow, SYN.—drag, draw, haul, pull, tug; extract, remove, take out, unsheathe. ANT.—drive, propel.

towering, SYN.—high, lofty, tall, towering; elevated, eminent, exalted, proud. ANT.—small, stunted, tiny; base, low, mean.

toy, SYN.—caper, frolic, gamble, gambol, play, revel, romp, sport, stake, wager.

trace, SYN.—mark, scar, stain, stigma, vestige; characteristic, feature, indication, property, symptoms, trait.

track, SYN.—chase, follow, hunt, persist, pursue, trail. ANT.—abandon, elude, escape, evade, flee.

tractable, SYN.—compliant, deferential, dutiful, obedient, submissive, yielding. ANT.—insubordinate, intractable, obstinate, rebellious.

traduce, SYN.—abuse, asperse, defame, disparage, ill-use, malign, revile, scandalize, vilify. ANT.—cherish, honor, praise, protect, respect.

trail, SYN.—chase, follow, hunt, persist, pursue, track. ANT.—abandon, elude, escape, evade, flee.

train, SYN.—aim, direct, level, point; bid, command, instruct, order. ANT.—deceive, distract, misdirect, misguide.

training, SYN.—cultivation, development, education, instruction, knowledge, learning, schooling, study, tutoring.

trait, SYN.—attribute, characteristic, feature, mark, peculiarity, property, quality.

traitorous, SYN.—apostate, disloyal, faithless, false, perfidious, recreant, treacherous, treasonable. ANT.—constant, devoted, loyal, true.

tramp, SYN.—beggar, bum, hobo, rover, vagabond, vagrant, wanderer. ANT.—gentleman, laborer, worker.

tranquil, SYN.—calm, composed, dispassionate, imperturbable, pacific, peaceful, placid, quiet, serene, still, undisturbed, unruffled. ANT.—excited, frantic, stormy, turbulent, wild.

tranquility, SYN.—calm, calmness, hush, peace, quiescence, quiet, quietude, repose, rest, serenity, silence, stillness. ANT.—agitation, disturbance, excitement, noise, tumult.

transact, SYN.—carry on, conduct, execute, manage, negotiate, perform, treat.

transaction, SYN.—affair, business, deal, deed, negotiation, occurrence, proceeding.

transfer SYN.—convey, dispatch, send, transmit, transport; remove, transplant; assign, consign, relegate.

transform, SYN.—alter, change, convert, modify, shift, transfigure, vary, veer. ANT.—continue, establish, preserve, settle, stabilize.

transgression, SYN.—affront, atrocity, indignity, insult, offense, outrage; aggression, crime, injustice, misdeed, sin, trespass, vice, wrong. ANT.—gentleness, innocence, morality, right.

transient, SYN.—brief, ephemeral, evanescent, fleeting, momentary, short-lived, temporary. ANT.—abiding, immortal, lasting, permanent, timeless.

translate, SYN.—construe, decipher, decode, elucidate, explain, explicate, intepret, render, solve, unravel. ANT.—confuse, distort, falsify, misconstrue, misinterpret.

transmit, SYN.—communicate, confer, convey, disclose, divulge, impart, inform, notify, relate, reveal, tell. ANT.—conceal, hide, withhold.

transparent, SYN.—clear, crystalline, limpid, lucid, thin, translucent; evident, explicit, manifest, obvious, open. ANT.—muddy, opaque, thick, turbid; ambiguous, questionable.

transpire, SYN.—bechance, befall, betide, chance, happen, occur, take place.

transport SYN.—bear, carry, convey, move, remove, shift, transfer; enrapture, entrance, lift, ravish, stimulate.

trap, SYN.—ambush, artifice, bait, intrigue, lure, net, pitfall, ruse, snare, stratagem, trick, wile.

travel, SYN.—go, journey, ramble, roam, rove, tour. ANT.—stay, stop.

treachery, SYN.—cabal, collusion, combination, conspiracy, intrigue, machination, plot, treason.

treason, SYN.—cabal, collusion, combination, conspiracy, intrigue, machination, plot, treachery.

treasure, SYN.—appreciate, cherish, hold dear, prize, value; foster, nurture, sustain. ANT.—dislike, disregard, neglect; abandon, reject.

treat, SYN.—avail, employ, exploit, manipulate, operate, utilize; exercise, exert, practice; handle, manage, use. ANT.—ignore, neglect, overlook, waste.

treaty, SYN.—alliance, compact, covenant, marriage. ANT.—divorce, schism, separation.

tremble, SYN.—agitate, flutter, jar, jolt, quake, quaver, quiver, rock, shake, shiver, shudder, sway, totter, vibrate, waver.

trembling, SYN.—alarm, apprehension, dread, fear, fright, horror, panic, terror. ANT.—calmness, composure, serenity, tranquility.

trepidation, SYN.—alarm, apprehension, consternation, cowardice, dismay, dread, fear, fright, horror, panic, scare, terror, timidity. ANT.—assurance, boldness, bravery, courage, fearlessness.

trespass, SYN.—affront, atrocity, indignity, insult, offense, outrage; aggression, crime, injustice, misdeed, sin, vice, wrong. ANT.—gentleness, innocence, morality, right.

trespass, SYN.—attack, encroach, infringe, intrude, invade, penetrate, violate. ANT.—abandon, evacuate, relinquish, vacate.

trial, SYN.—examination,

experiment, ordeal, proof, test; attempt, effort, endeavor, essay; affliction, hardship, misery, misfortune, suffering, tribulation, trouble. ANT.—alleviation, consolation.

tribulation, SYN.—agony, anguish, distress, grief, misery, sorrow, suffering, torment, woe; calamity, disaster, evil, misfortune, trouble. ANT.—delight, elation, fun, joy, pleasure.

trick, SYN.—antic, artifice, cheat, deception, device, fraud, guile, hoax, imposture, ploy, ruse, stratagem, stunt, subterfuge, wile. ANT.—candor, exposure, honesty, openness, sincerity.

tricky, SYN.—artful, astute, clandestine, covert, crafty, cunning, foxy, furtive, guileful, insidious, shrewd, sly, stealthy, subtle, surreptitious, underhand, wily. ANT.—candid, frank, ingenuous, open, sincere.

trifling, SYN.—frivolous, insignificant, paltry, petty, small, trivial, unimportant. ANT.—important, momentous, serious, weighty.

trim, SYN.—clear, nice, orderly, precise, spruce, tidy, trim. ANT.—dirty, disheveled, sloppy, slovenly, unkempt.

trim, SYN.—adorn, beautify, bedeck, decorate, embellish, garnish, gild, ornament. ANT.—deface, deform, disfigure, mar, spoil.

trip, SYN.—cruise, expedition, jaunt, journey, passage, pilgrimage, tour, travel, voyage.

trite, SYN.—banal, common, hackneyed, ordinary, stale, stereotyped. ANT.—fresh, modern, momentous, novel, stimulating.

triumph, SYN.—achievement, conquest, jubilation, ovation, victory. ANT.—defeat, failure.

trivial, SYN.—frivolous, insignificant, paltry, petty, small, trifling, unimportant. ANT.—important, momentous, serious, weighty.

trouble, SYN.—affliction, anxiety, calamity, distress, grief, hardship, misery, pain, sorrow, woe; annoyance, bother, care, embarrassment, irritation, pains, torment, worry; disorder, disturbance, problem; care, effort, exertion, labor, toil.

trouble, SYN.—annoy, bother, chafe, disturb, inconvenience, irk, irritate, molest, pester, tease, vex. ANT.—accommodate, console, gratify, soothe.

troublesome, SYN.—annoying, bothersome, distressing, disturbing, irksome, trying, vexatious; arduous, burdensome, difficult, laborious, tedious. ANT.—accommodating, amusing, easy, gratifying, pleasant.

true, SYN.—accurate, actual, authentic, correct, exact, genuine, real, veracious, veritable; constant, faithful, honest, loyal, reliable, sincere, steadfast, trustworthy. ANT.—counterfeit, erroneous, false, fictitious, spurious; faithless, false, fickle, inconstant.

trust, SYN.—confidence, credence, dependence, faith, reliance, trust. ANT.—doubt, incredulity, mistrust, skepticism.

trust, SYN.—depend on, reckon on, rely on; believe, credit, hope; commit, confide, intrust. ANT.—doubt, impugn, question, suspect.

trustworthy, SYN.—certain, dependable, reliable, safe, secure, sure, tried, trust. ANT.—dubious, fallible, questionable, uncertain, unreliable.

truth, SYN.—accuracy, actuality, authenticity, correctness, exactness, fact, honesty, rightness, truthfulness, veracity, verisimilitude, verity. ANT.—falsehood, falsity, fiction, lie, untruth.

truthful, SYN.—candid, frank, honest, open, sincere, true, veracious; accurate, correct, exact, reliable. ANT.—deceitful, misleading, sly.

try, SYN.—attempt, endeavor, strive, struggle, undertake; afflict, prove, test, torment, trouble; aim, aspire, design, intend, mean. ANT.—abandon, decline, ignore, neglect, omit; comfort, console.

trying SYN.—annoying, bothersome, distressing, disturbing, irksome, troublesome, vexatious; arduous, burdensome, difficult, laborious, tedious. ANT.—accommodating, amusing, easy, gratifying, pleasant.

tumult, SYN.—agitation, chaos, commotion, confusion, disarrangement, disarray, disorder, ferment, jumble, stir, turmoil. ANT.—certainty, order, peace, tranquility.

tune, SYN.—air, concord, harmony, melody, strain.

turbulent, SYN.—blustery, gusty, inclement, roaring, rough, stormy, tempestuous, windy. ANT.—calm, clear, peaceful, quiet, tranquil.

turmoil, SYN.—agitation, chaos, commotion, confusion, disarrangement, disarray, disorder, ferment, jumble, stir, tumult. ANT.—certainty, order, peace, tranquility.

turn, SYN.—circle, circulate, invert, revolve, rotate, spin, twirl, twist, wheel, whirl; avert, deflect, deviate, divert, swerve; alter, change, transmute. ANT.—arrest, fix, stand, stop; continue, proceed; endure, perpetuate.

twist, SYN.—bend, bow, crook, curve, deflect, incline, lean, stoop, turn. ANT.—break, resist, stiffen, straighten.

type, SYN.—emblem, mark, sign, symbol; category, character, class, description, kind, nature, sort, stamp; examplar, model, pattern. ANT.—deviation, eccentricity, monstrosity, peculiarity.

typical, SYN.—accustomed, common, conventional, customary, familiar, habitual, normal, ordinary, plain, regular, usual, vulgar. ANT.—extraordinary, marvelous, remarkable, strange, uncommon.

tyrannous, SYN.—absolute, arbitrary, authoritative, despotic. ANT.—accountable, conditional, contingent, dependent, qualified.

tyrant, SYN.—autocrat, despot, dictator, oppressor, persecutor.

U

ugly, SYN.—deformed, hideous, homely, plain, repellant, repulsive, uncomely; disagreeable, ill-natured, spiteful, surly, vicious. ANT.—attractive, beautiful, fair, handsome, pretty.

ultimate, SYN.—concluding, extreme, final, hindmost, last, latest, terminal, utmost. ANT.—beginning, first, foremost, initial, opening.

unadulterated, SYN.—clean, clear, genuine, immaculate, pure, spotless, untainted; absolute, bare, sheer. ANT.—foul, polluted, sullied, tainted, tarnished; corrupt, defiled.

unannounced, SYN.—abrupt, hasty, precipitate, sudden, unexpected. ANT.—anticipated, expected; courteous.

unassuming, SYN.—compliant, humble, lowly, meek, modest, plain, simple, submissive, unostentatious, unpretentious. ANT.—arrogant, boastful, haughty, proud, vain.

unbeliever, SYN.—apostate, dissenter, heretic, nonconformist, schismatic, sectarian, sectary.

unbiased, SYN.—equitable, fair, honest, impartial, just, reasonable. ANT. — dishonorable, fraudulent, partial.

uncertain, SYN.—ambiguous, dim, hazy, indefinite, indistinct, obscure, unclear, undetermined, unsettled, vague. ANT.—clear, explicit, lucid, precise, specific.

uncertainty, SYN.—ambiguity, distrust, doubt, hesitation, incredulity, scruple, skepticism, suspense, suspicion, unbelief. ANT.—belief, certainty, conviction, determination, faith.

uncivilized, SYN.—barbarian, barbaric, barbarous, brutal, crude, cruel, inhuman, merciless, remorseless, rude, ruthless, savage, uncultured, unrelenting. ANT.—civilized, humane, kind, polite, refined.

unclad, SYN.—bare, exposed, naked, nude, stripped, uncovered; defenseless, open, unprotected. ANT.—clothed, covered, dressed; concealed; protected.

uncompromising, SYN.—contumacious, determined, dogged, firm, headstrong, immovable, inflexible, intractable, obdurate, obstinate, pertinacious, stubborn, unyielding. ANT.—amenable, compliant, docile, submissive, yielding.

unconcern, SYN.—apathy, disinterestedness, impartiality, indifference, insensibility, neutrality. ANT.—affection, ardor, fervor, passion.

unconditional, SYN.—absolute, unqualified, unrestricted; arbitrary, authoritative, despotic, tyrannous. ANT.—accountable, conditional, contingent, dependent, qualified.

uncouth, SYN.—coarse, crude, green, harsh, ill-prepared, raw, rough, unfinished, unpolished, unrefined; crass, unrefined. ANT.—finished, well-prepared; cultivated, refined.

uncover, SYN.—betray, disclose, discover, divulge, expose, impart, reveal, show. ANT.—cloak, conceal, cover, hide, obscure.

under, SYN.—below, beneath, underneath. ANT.—above, over.

undergo, SYN.—bear, endure, feel, stand, suffer, sustain, tolerate; feel. ANT.—banish, discard, exclude, overcome.

understand, SYN.—appreciate, apprehend, comprehend, conceive, discern, grasp, know, learn, perceive, realize, see. ANT.—ignore, misapprehend, mistake, misunderstand.

understanding, SYN.—accordance, agreement, coincidence, concord, concurrence, harmony, unison; bargain, compact, contract, covenant, pact, stipulation. ANT.—difference, disagreement, discord, dissension, variance.

understudy, SYN.—agent, alternate, deputy, proxy, representative, substitute. ANT.—head, master, principal, sovereign.

undertaking, SYN.—attempt, effort, endeavor, essay, experiment, trial. ANT.—inaction, laziness, neglect.

undesigned, SYN.—accidental, casual, chance, contingent, fortuitous, incidental, unintended. ANT.—calculated, decreed, intended, planned, willed.

undivided, SYN.—all, complete, entire, intact, integral, perfect, total, unimpaired, whole. ANT.—incomplete, partial.

undying, SYN.—ceaseless, deathless, endless, eternal, everlasting, immortal, infinite, perpetual, timeless. ANT.—ephemeral, finite, mortal, temporal, transient.

unearthly, SYN.—marvellous, metaphysical, miraculous, other-worldly, preternatural, spiritual, superhuman, supernatural. ANT.—common, human, natural, physical, plain.

uneducated, SYN.—ignorant, illiterate, uncultured, uninformed, unlearned, unlettered, untaught. ANT.—cultured, educated, erudite, informed, literate.

unemployed, SYN.—idle, inactive, inert, unoccupied. ANT.—active, employed, industrious, occupied, working.

uneven, SYN.—odd, remaining, single, unmatched. ANT.—even, matched.

unexpected, SYN.—abrupt, hasty, immediate, instaneous, rapid, sudden. ANT.—anticipated, gradual, slowly.

unfasten, SYN.—exhibit, expand, open, spread, unbar, unfold, unlock, unseal. ANT.—close, conceal, hide, shut.

unfavorable, SYN.—adverse, antagonistic, contrary, hostile, opposed, opposite; counteractive, disastrous, unlucky. ANT.—benign, favorable, fortunate, lucky, propitious.

unfeeling, SYN.—cruel, hard, harsh, rigorous, severe, stern, strict. ANT.—gentle, lenient, tender.

unfold, SYN.—amplify, create, develop, elaborate, enlarge, evolve, expand, mature. ANT.—compress, contract, restrict, stunt, wither.

unfurnished, SYN.—bare, exposed, naked, stripped; mere, plain, simple; open. ANT.—covered, concealed; protected.

uniform, SYN.—customary, methodical, natural, normal, orderly, ordinary, periodical, regular, steady, systematic, unvaried. ANT.—abnormal, erratic, exceptional, rare, unusual.

uninformed, SYN.—ignorant, illiterate, uncultured, uneducated, unlearned, unlettered, untaught. ANT.—cultured, educated, erudite, informed, literate.

unintelligible, SYN.—abstruse, ambiguous, cloudy, cryptic, dark, dim, dusky, enigmatic, indistinct, mysterious, obscure, unintelligible, vague. ANT.—bright, clear, distinct, lucid.

uninteresting, SYN.—boring, burdensome, dilatory, dreary, dull, humdrum, irksome, monotonous, slow, sluggish, tardy, tedious, tiresome, wearisome. ANT.—

amusing, entertaining, exciting, interesting, quick.

union, SYN.—combination, concurrence, fusion, incorporation, joining, solidarity, unification; agreement, concord, harmony, unanimity; alliance, amalgamation, coalition, concert, confederacy, league, marriage. ANT.—division, schism, separation; disagreement, discord.

unique, SYN.—choice, distinctive, exceptional, matchless, peculiar, rare, singular, sole, solitary, uncommon, unequaled. ANT.—common, common place, frequent, ordinary, typical.

unite, SYN.—amalgamate, associate, attach, blend, combine, conjoin, connect, consolidate, embody, fuse, join, link, merge, unify. ANT.—disconnect, disrupt, divide, separate, sever.

universal, SYN.—common, familiar, frequent, general, ordinary, popular, prevalent, usual. ANT.—exceptional, extraordinary, odd, scarce.

unlawful, SYN.—criminal, illegal, illegitimate, illicit, outlawed, prohibited. ANT.—honest, law, legal, permitted.

unlike, SYN.—contrary, different, dissimilar, distinct, divergent, diverse, incongruous, opposite, variant; divers, miscellaneous, sundry, var-

ious. ANT.—alike, congruous, identical, same, similar.

unlimited, SYN.—boundless, endless, eternal, illimitable, immeasurable, immense, infinite, interminable, unbounded, vast. ANT.—bounded, circumscribed, confined, finite, limited.

unlocked, SYN.—ajar, open, unclosed; clear, passable, unobstructed; disengaged, free, unoccupied; accessible, exposed, unrestricted.

unmatched, SYN.—odd, remaining, single, uneven. ANT.—even, matched.

unmistakable, SYN.—apparent, clear, distinct, evident, manifest, obvious, palpable, patent, plain, self-evident. ANT.—abstruse, concealed, hidden, obscure.

unobstructed, SYN.—clear, free, loose, open, unfastened. ANT.—restricted; blocked, clogged, impeded.

unoccupied, SYN.—dormant, idle, inactive, indolent, inert, lazy, slothful, unemployed. ANT.—active, employed, industrious, occupied, working.

unpretentious, SYN.—candid, frank, open, plain, simple, sincere. ANT.—adorned, embellished, feigned, insincere.

unqualified, SYN.—absolute, unconditional, unrestricted; arbitrary, authoritative, despotic, tyrannous. ANT.—accountable, conditional, contingent, dependent, qualified.

unreasonable, SYN.—absurd, foolish, inconsistent, irrational, nonsensical, preposterous, ridiculous, self-contradictory, silly. ANT.—consistent, rational, reasonable, sensible, sound.

unrestricted, SYN.—clear, passable, unobstructed; available, disengaged, free, unoccupied; accessible, exposed, open, public.

unsafe, SYN.—critical, dangerous, hazardous, insecure, menacing, perilous, precarious, risky, threatening. ANT.—firm, protected, safe, secure.

unselfish, SYN.—beneficent, bountiful, generous, giving, liberal, magnanimous, munificent, openhanded. ANT.—covetous, greedy, miserly, selfish, stingy.

unsophisticated, SYN.—artless, candid, frank, ingenuous, innocent, naive, natural, open, simple. ANT.—crafty, cunning, sophisticated, worldly.

unstable, SYN.—capricious, changeable, fickle, fitful, inconstant, restless, variable. ANT.—constant, reliable, stable, steady, trustworthy.

unswerving, SYN.—constant, fast, firm, inflexible, secure, solid, stable, steadfast, steady, unyielding. ANT.—slow, sluggish; insecure, loose, unstable, unsteady.

untainted, SYN.—clean, clear, genuine, immaculate, pure, spotless, unadulterated; chaste, guiltless, innocent, modest, sincere, undefiled, virgin. ANT.—foul, polluted, sullied, tainted; tarnished; corrupt, defiled.

untamed, SYN.—barbarous, fierce, outlandish, rude, savage, uncivilized, undomesticated; wild; desert, desolate, rough, uncultivated, waste; frantic, frenzied, impetuous, mad, turbulent, wanton, wayward; boisterous, stormy, tempestous; extravagant, foolish, giddy, rash, reckless. ANT.—civilized, gentle; calm, placid, quiet.

untoward, SYN.—contrary, disobedient, fractious, peevish, petulant; forward, intractable, obstinate, perverse, stubborn, ungovernable. ANT.—agreeable, obliging; docile, tractable.

unusual, SYN.—aberrant, abnormal, capricious, devious, eccentric, irregular, unnatural, variable. ANT.—fixed, methodical, ordinary, regular, usual.

unyielding, SYN.—constant, fast, firm, inflexible, secure, solid, stable, steadfast, steady, unswerving, unyielding. ANT.—slow, sluggish; insecure, loose, unstable, unsteady.

upbraid, SYN.—admonish, berate, blame, censure, lecture, rate, rebuke, reprehend, reprimand, scold, vituperate. ANT.—approve, commend, praise.

uphold, SYN.—assert, defend, espouse, justify, maintain, vindicate. ANT.—assault, attack, deny, oppose, submit.

upright, SYN.—direct, right, undeviating, unswerving; erect, straight, unbent, vertical; fair, honest, honorable, just, square. ANT.—circuitous, winding; bent, crooked; dishonest.

upset, SYN.—annoy, bother, disturb, harass, haunt, inconvenience, molest, perlex, pester, plague, tease, trouble, worry. ANT.—gratify, please, relieve, soothe.

urbane, SYN.—accomplished, civil, considerate, courteous, cultivated, genteel, polite, refined, well-bred, well-mannered. ANT.—boorish, impertinent, rude, uncivil, uncouth.

urge, SYN.—appetite, aspiration, craving, desire, hungering, longing, lust, wish, yearning. ANT.—abomination, aversion, distaste, hate, loathing.

urge, SYN.—coax, convince, exhort, incite, induce, influence, persuade, prevail upon, win over. ANT.—coerce,

compel, deter, dissuade, restrain.

urgency, SYN.—crisis, emergency, exigency, juncture, pass, pinch, strait.

urgent, SYN.—cogent, compelling, critical, crucial, exigent, impelling, imperative, important, importunate, insistent, instant, necessary, pressing, serious. ANT.—insignificant, petty, trifling, trivial, unimportant.

use, SYN.—custom, habit, manner, practice, training, usage, wont. ANT.—disuse, idleness, inexperience, speculation, theory.

use, SYN.—apply, avail, employ, exploit, manipulate, operate, utilize; exercise, exert, practice, consume, exhaust, expend; handle, manage, treat; accustom, familiarize, inure, train. ANT.—ignore, neglect, overlook, waste.

useful, SYN.—advantageous, beneficial, good, helpful, profitable, salutary, serviceable, wholesome. ANT.—deleterious, destructive, detrimental, harmful, injurious.

usefulness, SYN.—excellence, merit, price, utility, value, virtue, worth, worthiness. ANT.—cheapness, uselessness, valuelessness.

useless, SYN.—abortive, bootless, empty, fruitless, futile, idle, ineffectual, pointless, unavailing, vain, valueless, vapid, worthless. ANT.—effective, potent, profitable; meek, modest.

usual, SYN.—accustomed, common, customary, every-day, familiar, general, habitual, normal, ordinary. ANT.—abnormal, exceptional, extraordinary, irregular, rare.

utensil, SYN.—apparatus, device, instrument, medium, tool, vehicle. ANT.—hindrance, impediment, obstruction, preventive.

utilize SYN.—avail, employ, occupy. ANT.—discard, discharge, reject.

utopian, SYN.—exemplary, fancied, faultless, ideal, imaginary, perfect, supreme, unreal, visionary. ANT.—actual, faulty, imperfect, material, real.

utter, SYN.—complete, entire, finished, full, perfect, whole; complete, consummate, excellent, ideal, superlative, supreme; absolute, downright, unqualified. ANT.—deficient, incomplete, lacking; faulty, imperfect.

V

vacant, SYN.—bare, barren, blank, empty, unoccupied, vacuous, void.

ANT.—busy, employed, engaged, full, replete.

vacate, SYN.—abandon, abdicate, abjure, relinquish, resign, surrender, waive; desert, forsake, leave, quit. ANT.—maintain, uphold; stay, support.

vacillate, SYN.—change, fluctuate, hesitate, oscillate, undulate, vary, waver. ANT.—adhere, decide, persist, resolve, stick.

vacillating, SYN.—contradictory, contrary, discrepant, illogical, inconsistent, incompatible, incongruous, irreconcilable, paradoxical, unsteady, wavering. ANT.—compatible, congruous, consistent, correspondent.

vagabond, SYN.—beggar, mendicant, pauper, ragamuffin, scrub, starveling, tatterdemalion, wretch.

vagrant, SYN.—beggar, bum, hobo, rover, tramp, vagabond, wanderer. ANT.—gentleman, laborer, worker.

vague, SYN.—ambiguous, dim, hazy, indefinite, indistinct, obscure, uncertain, unclear, undetermined, unsettled. ANT.—clear, explicit, lucid, precise, specific.

vain, SYN.—abortive, bootless, empty, fruitless, futile, idle, ineffectual, pointless, unavailing, useless, valueless, vapid, worthless, conceited, proud, vainglorious.

ANT.—effective, potent, profitable, meek, modest.

vainglory, SYN.—arrogance, conceit, haughtiness, pride, self-esteem, superciliousness, vanity. ANT.—humility, lowliness, meekness, modesty, shame.

valiant, SYN.—adventurous, audacious, bold, brave, chivalrous, courageous, daring, dauntless, fearless, gallant, heroic, intrepid, magnanimous, valorous. ANT.—cowardly, cringing, fearful, timid, weak.

valid, SYN.—binding, cogent, conclusive, convincing, effective, efficacious, legal, logical, powerful, sound, strong, telling, weighty. ANT.—counterfeit, null, spurious, void, weak.

valuable, SYN.—costly, expensive, precious; dear, esteemed; profitable, useful. ANT.—cheap, mean, poor; trashy, worthless.

value, SYN.—excellence, merit, price, usefulness, utility, value, virtue, worth, worthiness. ANT.—cheapness, uselessness, valuelessness.

value, SYN.—appreciate, cherish, hold dear, prize, treasure; foster, nurture, sustain. ANT.—dislike, disregard; neglect; abandon, reject.

vanity, SYN.—complacency, conceit, egotism, pride, self-esteem; caprice, conception, fancy, idea, imagination, notion, whim. ANT.—diffidence, humility, meekness, modesty.

vanquish, SYN.—beat, conquer, crush, defeat, humble, master, overcome, quell, rout, subdue, subjugate, surmount. ANT.—capitulate, cede, lose, retreat, surrender.

vapid, SYN.—banal, commonplace, hackneyed, inane, insipid, trite. ANT.—fresh, novel, original, stimulating, striking.

variable, SYN.—changeable, fickle, fitful, inconstant, shifting, unstable, vacillating, wavering. ANT.—constant, stable, steady, unchanging, uniform.

variant, SYN.—contrary, different, dissimilar, distinct, divergent, diverse, incongruous, opposite, unlike; divers, miscellaneous, sundry, various. ANT.—alike, congruous, identical, same, similar.

variation, SYN.—alteration, alternation, change, modification, mutation, substitution, variety, vicissitude. ANT.—monotony, stability, uniformity.

variety, SYN.—assortment, change, difference, dissimilarity, diversity, heterogeneity, medly, miscellany, mixture, multifariousness, variousness; breed, kind, sort, stock, strain, subspecies.

ANT.— homogeneity, likeness, monotony, sameness, uniformity.

various, SYN.—different, divers, miscellaneous, sundry. ANT.—alike, congruous, identical, same, similar.

vary, SYN.—change, exchange, substitute; alter, convert, modify, shift, transfigure, transform, veer. ANT.—continue, establish, preserve, settle, stabilize.

vassalage, SYN.—bondage, captivity, confinement, imprisonment, serfdom, servitude, slavery, thralldom. ANT.—freedom, liberation.

vast, SYN.—ample, big, capacious, colossal, extensive, great, huge, immense, large, wide. ANT.—little, mean, short, small, tiny.

vault, SYN.—bound, caper, hop, jerk, jump, leap, skip, spring, start.

vaunt, SYN.—boast, brag, crow, flaunt, glory. ANT.—apologize, deprecate, humble, minimize.

vaunting, SYN.—boasting, display, flourish, ostentation, pagentry, parade, pomp, show. ANT.—humility, modesty, reserve, unobtrusiveness.

vehement, SYN.—ardent, burning, excitable, fervent, fervid, fiery, glowing, hot, impetuous, irascible, passionate. ANT.—apathetic, calm, cool, deliberate, quiet.

veil, SYN.—cloak, clothe, conceal, cover, curtain, disguise, envelop, guard, hide, mask, protect, screen, shield, shroud. ANT.—bare, divulge, expose, reveal, unveil.

venal, SYN.—avaricious, corrupt, greedy, mercenary, sordid. ANT.—generous, honorable, liberal.

venerable, SYN.—aged, ancient, antiquated, antique, archaic, elderly, old, old-fashioned, superannuated. ANT.—modern, new, young, youthful.

venerate, SYN.—admire, appreciate, approve, esteem, respect. ANT.—abhor, despise, dislike.

vengeance, SYN.—reparation, reprisal, requital, retaliation, retribution, revenge, vindictiveness. ANT.—mercy, pardon, reconciliation, remission; forgiveness.

vent, SYN.—belch, breathe, discharge, eject, emanate, emit, expel, shoot, spurt.

venture, SYN.—risk, speculate. ANT.—insure, protect, secure.

verbal, SYN.—literal, oral, spoken, vocal. ANT.—documentary, recorded, written.

verbose, SYN.—chattering, chatty, communicative, garrulous, glib, loquacious, talkative, voluble. ANT.—laconic, reticent, silent, taciturn, uncommunicative.

verbosity, SYN.—longwindedness, redundancy, talkativeness, verboseness, wordiness. ANT.—conciseness, laconism, terseness.

verification, SYN.—confirmation, corroboration, demonstration, evidence, experiment, proof, test, testimony, trial. ANT.—failure, fallacy, invalidity.

verify, SYN.—corroborate, confirm, determine, substantiate; acknowledge, assure, establish, settle; approve, fix, ratify, sanction; strengthen.

veritable, SYN.—accurate, actual, authentic, correct, exact, genuine, real, true, veracious. ANT.—counterfeit, erroneous, false, fictitious, spurious.

versed, SYN.—acquainted, aware, cognizant, conversant, familiar, intimate, knowing. ANT.—unfamiliar.

vertical, SYN.—erect, perpendicular, plumb, straight, upright. ANT.—horizontal, inclined, level, oblique, prone.

vestige, SYN.—brand, mark, scar, stain, stigma, trace; characteristic, feature, indication, symptoms, trait.

vex, SYN.—aggravate, annoy, chafe, embitter, exasperate, inflame, irritate, nettle, provoke. ANT.—appease, mitigate, palliate, soften, soothe.

vexation, SYN.—annoyance, chagrin, exasperation, irritation, mortification, pique. ANT.—appeasement, comfort, gratification, pleasure.

vibrate, SYN.—agitate, flutter, jar, jolt, quake, quaver, quiver, rock, shake, shiver, shudder, sway, totter, tremble, waver.

vice, SYN.—crime, evil, guilt, iniquity, offense, sin, transgression, ungodliness, wickedness, wrong. ANT.—goodness, innocence, purity, righteousness, virtue.

vicinity, SYN.—district, environs, locality, neighborhood; adjacency, nearness. ANT.—distance, remoteness.

victory, SYN.—achievement, conquest, jubilation, ovation, triumph. ANT.—defeat, failure.

view, SYN.—observation, regard, review, sight, survey; outlook, panorama, perspective, prospect, range, scene, vista; belief, conception, impression, judgment, opinion, sentiment.

view, SYN.—behold, discern, eye, gaze, glance, look, scan, see, stare, survey, watch, witness; examine, inspect, observe, regard. ANT.—avert, hide, miss, overlook.

viewpoint, SYN.—attitude, disposition, standpoint; aspect, pose, position, posture, stand.

vigilant, SYN.—alert, anxious, attentive, careful, cautious, circumspect, observant, wakeful, wary, watchful. ANT.—careless, inattentive, lax, neglectful, oblivious.

vigor, SYN.—fortitude, liveliness, spirit, verve, vitality, zeal. ANT.—languor, listlessness.

vigorous, SYN.—active, animated, blithe, brisk, energetic, frolicsome, lively, spirited, sprightly, supple, vivacious. ANT.—dull, insipid, listless, stale, vapid.

vile, SYN.—base, debased, depraved, foul, loathsome, obscene, odious, revolting, sordid, vicious, vulgar, wicked; abject, despicable, ignoble, low, mean, worthless, wretched. ANT.—attractive, decent, laudable; honorable, upright.

vilify, SYN.—abuse, asperse, defame, disparage, ill-use, malign, revile, scandalize, traduce. ANT.—cherish, honor, praise, protect, respect.

villainous, SYN.—bad, base, deleterious, evil, immoral, iniquitous, noxious, pernicious, sinful, unsound, unwholesome, wicked. ANT.—excellent, good, honorable, moral, reputable.

vindicate, SYN.—absolve, acquit, assert, clear, defend, excuse, exonerate, justify, support, uphold. ANT.—abandon, accuse, blame, convict.

violate, SYN.—break, disobey, infringe, invade, transgress, defile, desecrate, dishonor, pollute, profane, debauch, deflower, ravish.

violence, SYN.—coercion, compulsion, constraint, force. ANT.—feebleness, frailty, impotence, weakness; persuasion.

violent, SYN.—boisterous, fierce, forceful, furious, impetuous, passionate, powerful, raging, raving, turbulent, vehement, wild; acute, extreme, intense, severe. ANT.—calm, feeble, gentle, quiet, soft.

virgin, SYN.—clean, clear, genuine, immaculate, spotless, unadulterated, untainted, chaste, guiltless, innocent, modest, pure, sincere, undefiled. ANT.—foul, polluted, sullied, tainted, tarnished; corrupt, defiled.

virile, SYN.—bold, hardy, lusty, male, manly, mannish, masculine, robust, strong, vigorous. ANT.—effeminate, emasculated, feminine, unmanly, weak, womanish.

virtue, SYN.—chastity, goodness, integrity, morality, probity, purity, rectitude, virginity; effectiveness, efficacy, force, power, strength; excellence, merit, worth. ANT.—corruption, lewdness, sin, vice; fault.

virtuous, SYN.—chaste, decent, ethical, good, honorable, just, moral, pure, right, righteous, scrupulous. ANT.—amoral, libertine, licentious, sinful, unethical.

virulent, SYN.—bitter, evil-minded, hostile, malevolent, malicious, malignant, rancorous, spiteful, wicked. ANT.—affectionate, benevolent, benign, kind.

visible, SYN.—cloudless, fair; limpid; apparent, unclear, distinct, evident, intelligible, manifest, obvious, plain, unmistakable; open, unobstructed. ANT.—cloudy, foul, overcast; ambiguous, obscure, unclear, vague.

vision SYN.—apparation, daydream, dream, ghost, hallucination, mirage, phantasm, phantom, prophecy, revelation, specter. ANT.—reality, substance, verity.

visionary, SYN.—exemplary, fancied, faultless, ideal, imaginery, perfect, supreme, unreal, utopian. ANT.—actual, faulty, imperfect, material, real.

vital, SYN.—alive, animate, living; basic, cardinal, essential, indispensable, necessary, paramount, urgent. ANT.—inanimate, inert, lifeless; non-essential, unimportant.

vitality, SYN.—animation, being, buoyancy, existence, life, liveliness, spirit, vigor, vivacity. ANT.—death, demise, dullness, languor, lethargy.

vitiate, SYN.—abase, adulterate, alloy, corrupt, debase, defile, degrade, deprave, depress, humiliate, impair, lower, pervert, enhance, improve, raise, restore, vitalize.

vitiated, SYN.—contaminated, corrupt, corrupted, crooked, debased, depraved, dishonest, impure, profligate, putrid, spoiled, tainted, unsound, venal.

vivid, SYN.—bright, brilliant, intense, striking; animated, clear, expressive, fresh, graphic, lively, lucid. ANT.—dull, vague; dim, dreary, dusky.

vocation, SYN.—art, business, commerce, employment, engagement, enterprise, job, occupation, profession, trade, trading, work. ANT.—avocation, hobby, pastime.

void, SYN.—bare, barren, blank, empty, unoccupied, vacant, vacuous. ANT.—busy, employed, engaged, full, replete.

volatile, SYN.—buoyant, effervescent, light, resilient; animated, blithe, cheerful, elated, hopeful, jocund, lively, spirited, sprightly, vivacious. ANT.—dejected, depressed, despondent, hopeless, sullen.

volition, SYN.—choice, decision, desire, determination, intention, pleasure, preference, resolution, testament, will, wish. ANT.—coercion, compulsion, disinterest, indifference.

volume, SYN.—ability, capability, capacity, faculty, power, skill, talent; magnitude, size. ANT.—impotence, inability, incapacity, stupidity.

voluntary, SYN.—automatic, extemporaneous, impulsive, instinctive, offhand, spontaneous, willing. ANT.—compulsory, forced, planned, prepared, rehearsed.

volunteer, SYN.—advance, exhibit, extend, offer, present, proffer, propose, sacrifice, tender. ANT.—accept, receive, reject, retain, spurn.

voodoo, SYN.—black art, charm, conjuring, enchantment, legerdemain, magic, necromancy, sorcery, witchcraft, wizardry.

vulgar, SYN.—common, general, ordinary, plebian, popular; base, coarse, gross, low, obscene, ribald, rude, unrefined. ANT.—esoteric, select; aristocratic, polite, refined.

W

wager, SYN.—gamble, play, sport, stake.

wages, SYN.—allowance, compensation, earnings, fee, pay, payment, recompense, salary, stipend. ANT.—gift, gratuity, present.

wait, SYN.—abide, bide, delay, linger, remain, rest, stay, tarry; await, expect, watch; attend, minister, serve. ANT.—act, expedite, hasten, leave.

waive, SYN.—abandon, relinquish, renounce, surrender. ANT.—maintain, uphold.

wander, SYN.—deviate, digress, err, ramble, range, roam, rove, saunter, stray, stroll, traipse. ANT.—halt, linger, settle, stay, stop.

want, SYN.—destitution, indigence, necessity, need, penury, poverty, privation. ANT.—abundance, affluence, plenty, riches, wealth.

want, SYN.—covet, crave, desire, long for, wish; lack, need, require.

wariness, SYN.—care, caution, heed, prudence, vigilance, watchfulness. ANT.—abandon, carelessness, recklessness.

warlike, SYN.—antagonistic, hostile, inimical, opposed, unfriendly. ANT.—amicable, cordial, favorable.

warm, SYN.—ardent, cordial, earnest, gracious, hearty, sincere, sociable. ANT.—aloof, cool, reserved, taciturn.

warn, SYN.—admonish, advise, apprise, inform, notify.

warning, SYN.—admonition, advice, caution, indication, information, notice, portent, sign.

wary, SYN.—attentive, alert, alive, awake, aware, careful, heedful, mindful, observant, thoughtful, watchful. ANT.—apathetic, indifferent, oblivious, unaware.

wash, SYN.—bathe, clean, cleanse, launder, rinse, scrub, wet. ANT.—dirty, foul, soil, stain.

waspish, SYN.—fractious, fretful, ill-natured, ill-tempered, irritable, peevish, petulant, snappish, testy, touchy. ANT.—affable, genial, good-natured, good-tempered, pleasant.

waste, SYN.—abandoned, bare, bleak, deserted, desolate, forlorn, forsaken, lonely, solitary, uninhabited, wild. ANT.—attended, cultivated, fertile.

waste, SYN.—despoil, destroy, devastate, pillage, plunder, ravage, ruin, sack, strip; consume, corrode, dissipate, lavish, misuse, scatter, spend, squander, wear out; decay, diminish, dwindle, pine, wither. ANT.—accumulate, conserve, economize, preserve, save.

watch, SYN.—behold, contemplate, descry, discern, distinguish, espy, glimpse, inspect, look at, notice, observe, perceive, scan, scrutinize, see, view, witness.

waver, SYN.—doubt, hesitate, question; distrust, mistrust, suspect. ANT.—believe, confide, decide, rely on, trust.

wavering, SYN.—changeable, fickle, fitful, inconstant, shifting, unstable, vacillating, variable. ANT.—constant, stable, steady, unchanging, uniform.

wax, SYN.—accrue, amplify, augment, enhance, enlarge, expand, extend, grow, heighten, increase, intensify, magnify, multiply, raise. ANT.—atrophy, contract, decrease, diminish, reduce.

way, SYN.—avenue, channel, course, passage, path, road, route, street, thoroughfare, track, trail, walk; fashion, form, habit, manner, method, mode, plan, practice, procedure, process, style, system.

weak, SYN.—bending, fragile, frail, pliant, tender, yielding; debilitated, decrepit, delicate, feeble, impotent, infirm, illogical, inadequate, ineffective, lame, poor; vague; irresolute, pliable, vacillating, wavering; assailable, defenseless, exposed, vulnerable. ANT.—potent, powerful, robust, strong, sturdy.

weakness SYN.—disability, handicap, impotence, incapacity, incompetence. ANT.—ability, capability, power, strength.

wealth, SYN.—abundance, affluence, fortune, luxury, money, opulence, plenty, possessions, riches. ANT.—indigence, need, poverty, want.

wealthy, SYN.—affluent, costly, exorbitant, luxurious, opulent, prosperous, rich, sumptuous, well-to-do. ANT.—beggarly, destitute, indigent, needy, poor.

wearied, SYN.—faint, feeble, languid, irresolute, timid, weak. ANT.—vigorous, brave, forceful.

weary, SYN.—bored, exhausted, faint, fatigued, jaded, spent, tired, wearied, worn. ANT.—fresh, hearty, invigorated, rested.

wedlock, SYN.—espousal, marriage, matrimony, nuptials, union, wedding. ANT.—celibacy, divorce, virginity.

weigh, SYN.—consider, contemplate, deliberate, examine, heed, meditate, ponder, reflect, study. ANT.—ignore, neglect, overlook.

weight, SYN.—burden, gravity, heaviness, load, pressure; emphasis, import, importance, influence, significance, stress, value. ANT.—buoyancy, levity, lightness; insignificance, triviality.

welcome, SYN.—accept, gain, get, take; admit, shelter; entertain, receive. ANT.—bestow, give, impart, reject; discharge, turn away.

well, SYN.—hale, happy, healthy, hearty, sound; beneficial, convenient, expedient, good, profitable. ANT.—depressed, feeble, infirm, weak.

well-being, SYN.—contentment, delight, felicity, gladness, happiness, pleasure, satisfaction. ANT.—despair, grief, misery, sadness, sorrow.

well-bred, SYN.—courtly, cultivated, cultured, genteel, polished, polite, refined. ANT.—boorish, coarse, crude, rude, vulgar.

well-known, SYN.—celebrated, distinguished, eminent, famous, glorious, illustrious, noted, renowned. ANT.—hidden, ignominious, infamous, obscure, unknown.

whim, SYN.—caprice, fancy, humor, inclination, notion, quirk, vagary, whimsy.

whimsical, SYN.—curious, droll, eccentric, odd, peculiar, quaint, queer, singular, strange, unusual. ANT.—common, familiar, normal, ordinary, usual.

whole, SYN.—all, complete, entire, intact, integral, perfect, total, undivided, unimpaired; hale, healed, healthy, sound, well. ANT.—defective, deficient, imperfect, incomplete, partial.

wholesome, SYN.—hale, hearty, robust, sound, strong, well; healthy, hygienic, salubrious, salutary. ANT.—delicate, diseased, frail, infirm; injurious, noxious.

wicked, SYN.—bad, baleful, base, deleterious, evil, immoral, iniquitous, noxious, pernicious, sinful, unsound, unwholesome, villainous. ANT.—excellent, good, honorable, moral, reputable.

wide, SYN.—broad, expanded, extensive, large, sweeping, vast; liberal, tolerant. ANT.—confined, narrow, restricted.

wild, SYN.—barbarous, fierce, outlandish, rude, savage, uncivilized, undomesticated, untamed; desert, desolate, rough, uncultivated, waste; frantic, frenzied, impetuous, irregular, mad, turbulent, wanton, wayward; boisterous, stormy, tempestous; extravagant, foolish, giddy, rash, reckless. ANT.—civilized, gentle; calm, placid, quiet.

wilful, SYN.—contemplated, deliberate, designed, intended, intentional, premeditated, studied, voluntary. ANT.—accidental, fortuitous.

will, SYN.—choice, decision, desire, **determina**tion, intention, pleasure, preference, resolution, testament, volition, wish. ANT.—coercion, compulsion, disinterest, indifference.

win, SYN.—achieve, flourish, gain, prevail, prosper, succeed, thrive.

ANT.—fail, miscarry, miss.

wind, SYN.—blast, breeze, draft, gale, gust, hurricane, squall, storm, tempest, zephyr.

wisdom, SYN.—discretion, erudition, foresight, information, insight, intelligence, judgment, knowledge, learning, prudence, reason, sagacity, sageness, sense. ANT.—foolishness, ignorance, imprudence, nonsense, stupidity.

wise, SYN.—deep, discerning, enlightened, intelligent, penetrating, profound, sagacious, sound; erudite, informed, knowing, learned, scholarly; advisable, expedient, prudent. ANT.—foolish, shallow, simple.

wish, SYN.—appetite, aspiration, craving, desire, hungering, longing, lust, urge, yearning. ANT.—abomination, aversion, distaste, hate, loathing.

wish, SYN.—covet, crave, desire, hanker, hunger, long, thirst, want, yearn. ANT.—decline, despise, reject, repudiate, scorn.

wit, SYN.—comprehension, intellect, intelligence, mind, perspicacity, reason, sagacity, sense, understanding; banter, cleverness, fun, humor, irony, pleasantry, raillery, sarcasm, satire, witticism. ANT.—commonplace, platitude, sobriety, solemnity, stupidity.

witchcraft, SYN.—black

art, charm, conjuring, enchantment, legerdemain, magic, necromancy, sorcery, voodoo, wizardry.

withdraw, SYN.—abandon, depart, desert, forsake, give up, go, leave, quit, relinquish, renounce, retire. ANT.—abide, remain, stay, tarry.

wither, SYN.—droop, dry, sear, shrink, shrivel, waste, wilt, wizen; decline, fail, languish, sink, weaken. ANT.—refresh, rejuvenate, renew, revive.

withhold, SYN.—abstain, desist, forbear, refrain. ANT.—continue, indulge, persist.

withstand, SYN.—bar, combat, confront, contradict, counteract, defy, hinder, obstruct, resist, thwart. ANT.—agree, cooperate, submit, succumb, support.

witness, SYN.—attestation, confirmation, declaration, evidence, proof, testimony. ANT.—argument, contradiction, disproof, refutation.

witty, SYN.—adroit, apt, clever, funny, quick, quick-witted, talented; bright, ingenious, sharp, smart. ANT.—awkward, bungling, clumsy, slow, unskilled; dull, foolish.

wizardry, SYN.—black art, charm, conjuring, enchantment, legerdemain, magic, necromancy, sorcery, voodoo, witchcraft.

woe, SYN.—agony, anguish, distress, grief, misery, sorrow, suffering, torment, tribulation, calamity, disaster, evil, misfortune, trouble. ANT.—delight, elation, fun, joy, pleasure.

womanly, SYN.—female, feminine, girlish, ladylike, maidenly, womanish. ANT.—male, manly, mannish, masculine, virile.

wonder, SYN.—curiosity, marvel, miracle, phenomenon, prodigy, rarity, spectacle; admiration, amazement, astonishment, awe, bewilderment, curiosity, surprise, wonderment. ANT.—familiarity, triviality; apathy, expectation, indifference.

wont, SYN.—custom, habit, manner, practice, training, usage, use. ANT.—disuse, idleness, inexperience.

work, SYN.—achievement, business, drudgery, effort, employment, labor, occupation, opus, performance, production, task, toil, travail. ANT.—ease, leisure, play, recreation, vacation.

working, SYN.—active, operative; busy, industrious. ANT.—dormant, inactive, indolent, lazy, passive.

worldly, SYN.—animal, base, bodily, carnal, corporeal, fleshly, gross, lustful, sensual, voluptuous. ANT.—exalted, intellectual, refined, spiritual, temperate.

worn, SYN.—exhausted, faint, fatigued, jaded, spent, tired, wearied, weary. ANT.—fresh, hearty, invigorated, rested.

worry, SYN.—anxiety, apprehension, concern, disquiet, fear, trouble, uneasiness. ANT.—contentment, equanimity, peace, satisfaction.

worry, SYN.—annoy, bother, disturb, gall, harass, harry, haze, irritate, pain, persecute, tease, torment, trouble, vex; fret, fume, fuss. ANT.—comfort, console, solace.

worship, SYN.—adore, deify, honor, idolize, respect, revere, reverence, venerate. ANT.—blaspheme, curse, despise, loathe, scorn.

worth, SYN.—excellence, merit, price, usefulness, utility, value, virtue, worthiness. ANT.—cheapness, uselessness, valuelessness.

worthless, SYN.—abortive, bootless, empty, fruitless, futile, idle, ineffectual, pointless, unavailing, useless, vain, valueless, vapid. ANT.—effective, potent, profitable; meek, modest.

wound, SYN.—damage, disfigure, harm, hurt, impair, injure, mar, spoil; abuse, affront, dishonor, insult, wrong. ANT.—ameliorate, benefit, help, preserve; compliment, praise.

wrangle, SYN.—affray, altercation, argument, bickering, contention, disagreement, dispute, feud, quarrel, spat, squabble. ANT.—agreement, friendliness, harmony, peace, reconciliation.

wrap, SYN.—cloak, clothe, conceal, cover, curtain, disguise, envelop, guard, hide, mask, protect, screen, shield, shroud, veil. ANT.—bare, divulge, expose, reveal, unveil.

wrath, SYN.—anger, animosity, choler, exasperation, fury, indignation, ire, irritation, passion, petulance, rage, resentment, temper. ANT.—conciliation, forbearance, patience, peace, self-control.

wreck, SYN.—annihilate, demolish, destroy, devastate, eradicate, exterminate, extinguish, obliterate, ravage, raze, ruin. ANT.—construct, establish, make, preserve, save.

wretched, SYN.—comfortless, disconsolate, distressed, forlorn, heartbroken, miserable, pitiable; abject, contemptible, despicable, low, mean, paltry, worthless. ANT.—contented, fortunate, happy; noble, significant.

writer, SYN.—author, composer, creator, father, inventor, maker, originator.

wrong, SYN.—amiss, askew, awry, erroneous, fallacious, false, faulty, inaccurate, incorrect, mistaken, unprecise, untrue; improper, inappropriate, unsuitable; aberrant, bad, criminal, evil, immoral, iniquitous, reprehensible. ANT.—correct, right, true, suitable, proper.

Y

yearning, SYN.—appetite, aspiration, craving, desire, hungering, longing, lust, urge, wish. ANT.— abomination, aversion, distaste, hate, loathing.

yield, SYN.—crop, fruit, harvest, proceeds, produce, product, reaping, result, store.

yield, SYN.—afford, bear, bestow, breed, generate, impart, pay, produce, supply; accord, allow, concede, grant, permit; abdicate, accede, acquiesce, capitulate, cede, quit, relent, relinquish, resign, submit, succumb, surrender, waive. ANT.—deny, dissent, oppose, refuse; assert, resist, strive, struggle.

yielding, SYN.—compliant, deferential, dutiful, obedient, submissive, tractable. ANT.—insubordinate, intractable, obstinate, rebellious.

youthful, SYN.—boyish, callow, childish, childlike, girlish, immature, juvenile, puerile, young. ANT.—aged, elderly, mature, old, senile.

Z

zeal, SYN.—ardor, devotion, earnestness, enthusiasm, excitement, fanaticism, fervency, fervor, inspiration, intensity, vehemence, warmth. ANT.—apathy, detachment, ennui, indifference, unconcern.

zealous, SYN.—ardent, eager, enthusiastic, fervent, fervid, fiery, impassioned, intense, keen, passionate, vehement. ANT.—apathetic, cool, indifferent, nonchalant.

zenith, SYN.—acme, apex, climax, consummation, culmination, height, peak, summit. ANT.—anticlimax, base, depth, floor.

zone, SYN.—belt, climate, locality, region, sector, tract.